Spiritual Intelligence:

A Christian Perspective

DR. DOUGLAS A. LAWTON

Spiritual Intelligence: A Christian Perspective

Scripture quotations are from the following sources: the New American Standard Bible, © 1960, 1962, 1963, 1968, 1971, 1972, 1973, 1975, 1977 by the Lockman Foundation; the New International Version, © 1973, 1978, 1984 by the International Bible Society; and the Authorized King James Version, © 2003 by Thomas Nelson, Inc.

Efforts to locate sources and obtain permission, where necessary, for the quotations used in this book were made. In the event of any unintentional omission, modifications will gladly be incorporated in future editions.

ISBN 978-1-941632-28-4

Published by:

Livity Books LLC, West Palm Beach, Florida

ACKNOWLEDGEMENTS

I wish to express sincere gratitude to the people who in various ways have contributed to the writing and completion of this book. I am indeed grateful to Dr. Daniel Goleman, whose book on Emotional Intelligence awakened consciousness to the possible existence of Spiritual Intelligence. Special thanks to Dr. Richard Humphrey whose constructive criticisms and guidance have enhanced the quality of this work. Thanks to Dr. Marsha Harwell for proofreading the manuscript, to Drs. Hollis Green and Helen Morgan for their constructive criticisms. My colleague, Erica Gordon, reviewed the material in its early and latter stages, made useful suggestions and encouraged its completion. For this I am extremely grateful. Thanks also to Drs. Joan and Samuel Rawlins, Dr. Monica Dotson, Norman and Karen Christie, and to Letty Carrington for their support and encouragement along the journey. Most importantly, I give thanks to the Father of Lights, who enlightened my path and gave grace to complete this assignment.

DEDICATED

To the memory of my mother Maud, and my friends Christine and Reggie.
Your light shone brilliantly. Thank you.

Table of Contents

Table of Contents

Table of Contents

Table of Contents

Preface

Any discussion on spirituality is arguably controversial, regardless of the approach. There are religious and nonreligious spiritual models and conflicting views. Spirituality is not necessarily transformative and many are committing all kinds of atrocities in the name of God and religion. Moreover, despite years of religiosity, many who embrace religion are seemingly unaffected by the teachings of their religion. The problem, I propose, is spiritual underdevelopment or lack of spiritual intelligence.

Is there a spiritual intelligence? If so, what support may be found for it?

First, let us define the concept. There are many definitions of spiritual intelligence. However, defined by this writer, spiritual intelligence is: (a) the divine ability to receive knowledge supernaturally or by spiritual means; and (b) the ability to use spiritual means to identify and solve spiritual and other problems.

The concept of spiritual intelligence came to mind as a result of reading Goleman's (1995) book on emotional intelligence, in the summer of 2004. After reading Goleman's persuasive statements on emotional intelligence, spiritual intelligence emerged as a missing link supporting mental and emotional intelligence, and seemed critical to human development. In fact, spiritual intelligence appeared more critical than other intelligence paradigms, as spiritual intelligence potentially grounded the other intelligences and gave meaning and purpose to human existence. It was felt spiritual intelligence could contribute more to holistic development of the individual and society, there being a spiritual reality and a spiritual dimension to humanity.

The potential of an area of human cognitive capacity, such as spiritual intelligence, capable of providing insight in areas critical to human life and development gave impetus to the investigation. The possibility of acquiring knowledge other than by means of the physical senses, and of using this avenue to identify and solve problems was exhilarating. Exploring the subject as presented by writers such as Sisk and Torrance (2001) and Zohar and

Marshall (2000, 2001, 2004), intensified interest and encouraged research on the subject.

Motivation to pursue a study on spiritual intelligence was enhanced by religion's role in the socialization of people around the world and religion's potential impact on behavior and way of life globally. The proliferation of religion and abuses of religion by religious cults made a focus on spiritual intelligence compelling. Other sources of motivation included religious persecution (particularly against Christians), competing views on morality, moral confusion, attempts by some to create a godless and amoral society and increasing worldwide corruption at various levels.

Significance of the Study

Spiritual phenomena are experienced throughout the world and significantly impact the lives of people from various walks of life. People across the globe embrace the spiritual as being able to manifest in ways that are good and evil. There is general interest in religion and in other areas of the metaphysical, such as the occult. Both the religious and nonreligious aspects of spirituality are widely acclaimed. Spiritual relationships are common, and impact health and wellness. Many who have been skeptical or unduly critical of the spiritual in the past are now seeing value in spirituality and are seeing connections between spirituality and other aspects of personhood. For example, in the past, psychologists have devoted attention to links between religion and social change. Social scientists are now showing interest in spiritual transformation. Spirituality is attracting attention from scholars and scientists in psychology, sociology, anthropology, medicine and theology (Pargament, 2006).

Knowledge and understanding of the spiritual are therefore crucial. Spiritual intelligence holds out amazing and endless potential for both the religious and nonreligious. The significance of this study may be measured by the apparent interest in the spiritual, the present and potential impact of the spiritual on our way of life and the impact of spirituality on human development generally.

Questions of the Study

Questions to be addressed in this study include the following: Is there a case for spiritual intelligence? If so, what is the evidence? What does it mean to be spiritual? What does it mean to be intelligent? What does it mean to be spiritually intelligent? What are some of the benefits of spiritual intelligence?

In investigating the issues, I have taken an interdisciplinary approach. Insights from various disciplines have been included in the investigation. Perspectives from neuroscience, medical science, natural science, social science, philosophy, psychology, psychiatry, theology and other disciplines have been considered.

Many religious and nonreligious investigators have written on the subject of spiritual intelligence based on their own worldview. "And all of us have a worldview, whether we realize it or not. We act in accordance with our worldview, and our worldview rests on what to us is the ultimate truth" (Schaeffer & Koop, 1979, p. 121). This study is conducted from a Christian perspective.

CHAPTER 1
The Need for
Spiritual Intelligence

Several factors in society indicate the need for spiritual intelligence; chief among them are the many ways in which the spiritual and supernatural are experienced and the overwhelming interest in things spiritual. Interest in the spiritual and supernatural is apparent in areas such as law, literature, movies, theatre, medicine, psychology, psychiatry, sociology, the occult and religion, religion being the most apparent.

> In many indigenous traditions, there is no word for 'religion' in the language, because the concepts and practices that we call 'religious' were always understood to be an inherent part of the culture and day-to-day life of the group (Huff & Wetherilt, 2005, p. 13).

Religious mosques, temples, synagogues, churches and other religious meeting houses are found everywhere. Spiritual healers and diviners ply their trade publicly. Religious broadcasts and advertisements marketing the services of spiritual caregivers and consultants are featured regularly in the media. The electronic and print media abound with advertisements of the services offered by spiritual consultants and diviners. Law enforcement officers utilize the services of psychics and other paranormal people to help in troublesome investigations. Medical doctors consult alongside spiritual caregivers, especially when faced with extremely difficult cases; some invite the services of spiritual caregivers as a matter of course. Many engage the services of spiritual advisers or become part of a 'spiritual group' in order to obtain success in business or other ventures, protection from enemies, deliverance from curses or evil spirits, or to put a curse on others.

A significant number of people vicariously participate in supernatural activities through movies involving the supernatural. A plethora of movies – inclusive of television series – involving the supernatural, are available for public consumption, and have increased exponentially in recent years. Much of what we see in movies involving the supernatural was inspired by real events. The most popular and profitable movies for the decade are movies depicting the paranormal and supernatural. The list includes Harry Potter and the Half-Blood Prince; The Dark Knight; Harry Potter and the Goblet of Fire; The Lord of the Rings: The Return of the King; The Lord of the Rings: The Two Towers; and Harry Potter and the Sorcerer's Stone (Beck, 2011).

The supernatural is also experienced through literature. The Internet and bookstores supply the public with literature on virtually every aspect of the spiritual and supernatural. Spiritual interest and experience of the supernatural in various ways are evident globally, and thus underscore the need for spiritual intelligence.

Relationship Between Morality and Spirituality

Although association does not necessarily mean causation, there is no escaping the fact that people who embrace spiritual values generally operate at a higher moral level. In the Bible, morality and spirituality are connected and presented as the means by which wholeness and self-actualization are achieved.

> In the history of Christian spirituality moral and spiritual development has always been connected. . . Cultivation of virtues often was considered prerequisite for higher spiritual development. (Edwards, 1980, p. 137)

Moral and spiritual laws are intertwined, as breaches of spiritual laws are invariably manifested in immoral behavior, although motivations may differ. For example, breaches of the law to love one's neighbor as one's self are manifested in hate, violence and crime. Breaches of the law to honor God are manifested in various forms of idolatry and immorality. Breaches of the law of stewardship are manifested in the pollution and destruction of the natural environment and in modern slavery.

Breaches of God's created order are manifested everywhere, acutely propelling a vicious cycle of dysfunction morally, spiritually, socially, physically, mentally, environmentally and economically. Moral and spiritual contradictions are numerous. For example, whereas some people live in abundance and greed, others barely exist for want and need. Whereas some people are dying from obesity, others are dying from starvation. Whereas billions of dollars are spent to create weapons of mass destruction and to fight wars, not nearly enough is spent to develop the masses and fight illiteracy, starvation and diseases such as cancer and HIV/AIDS. While some people are experiencing the fulfillment of dreams of a better life, others are experiencing nightmares of hopelessness. Often, at the heart of this spiritual and moral dilemma is corruption.

Corruption figures prominently at many levels of societies worldwide. It is manifested in various forms, and mainly affects the poor. Many attribute the recession, more or less experienced globally between the period 2008-2012, to inappropriate ethical values in governments and businesses. Fueled by greed, individuals and corporations, through *ponsi* and other schemes, conned many out of their livelihoods, in various parts of the world. Scammers proliferated. Intellectually brilliant people, through sophisticated schemes, made off with vast sums of money belonging to governments, other institutions (both private and public) and individuals.

In America, banks and other financial institutions gave housing loans to people who were unqualified. These loans were later sold to unsuspecting institutions. It soon became apparent that many people were unable to service their loans. In some cases, real estate developers had overvalued properties. As property values fell, borrowers became reluctant to service mortgages as it seemed unwise to "throw good money after bad." Developers found it difficult to sell their remaining stock and therefore could not service their loans either. Supply of housing exceeded demand; so financial institutions were stuck with assets that seldom bore any correlation with the value of mortgages. This meant lending institutions were forced to sell at a loss. Eventually the housing market along with the financial sector collapsed.

The collapse of the housing and financial sectors spiraled downturn in other areas of the economy resulting in joblessness and hardships of massive proportions. The recession resulted in the destabilization of the world's economies, loss of fortunes, homes and livelihoods.

Corruption is not new. Many narratives point to corruption and the ability of corruption to destroy individuals, organizations, communities and nations. Rodney (1976) and Perkins (2004) have supplied solid evidence of corruption filtering down and deliberately orchestrated with a view of undermining the integrity of nations so as to gain economic and political advantage and control over them.

In many places of the world, the main issue affecting development, prosperity and peace is integrity, chiefly the integrity of leaders. If the head of the stream is bad, corruption spreads more violently. In politics, political expediency and greed trump morality. In the interest of survival, alignments are formed; disagreements become excuses for divisions and hate; divisions become a chasm, increasing insecurity and the likelihood of corruption becoming endemic.

Due to corruption, a vicious cycle of subhuman behavior is being perpetrated. Consciences are seared. Greed and unbridled passion have resulted in the selling of souls for temporary gain. On the other hand, conflicting moralities, including those based on religion, pose a real threat to world peace. The ideological war has moved from the classroom to the global village, spawning wars of terror.

Relationship Between Morality and Intelligence

The link between morality and intelligence, however, is not always apparent. Some people do not see a connection between morality and intelligence. Kemp (1964), for example, did not see any close parallel between morality

18

and intelligence, but did not rule out the possibility altogether:

> Certainly we cannot equate intelligence in general with knowing how to behave morally; it is an obvious empirical fact that general intelligence and morality do not always go together. It is obvious that stupid men often act morally (courageously or generously, for example) in the face of great temptation to the contrary, and that an intelligent man may also be a bad man. But these facts by themselves do not rule out the possibility that there is some close connection between morality and intelligence." (Kemp, 1964, pp. 157-158)

Kemp made the point that the fact that general intelligence and morality do not always go together could not possibly mean there is no association between intelligence and morality. Intelligence is essential for the attribution of any kind of moral and spiritual responsibility.

Others argue for a neutral logic; yet no one can truly lay claim to being neutral where morality is concerned (Cooper, 1981).

> The ideal of a neutral logic of morals is, it is argued, a sham and delusion. At the very best, it is almost an unattainable ideal, the approach to which is highly precarious and beset by logical pitfalls. Indeed, many a moral philosopher has begun his researches with high-minded neutralist ideals only in the end to furnish the world with yet another undercover morality. (Cooper, 1981, p. 10)

In the words of Cooper, the issue is not whether or not there is a close association between intelligence and morality. The real issue concerns the kind of intelligence informing morality and whose morality to follow.

Kemp (1964) stated that attempts to show a relationship between intelligence and morality require a special kind of moral theory. Since the Creator is a spiritual Being and human beings have a spiritual dimension, the moral theory most suitable to moral development needs to be supported by God, the Author of Spiritual Intelligence.

Spiritual Intelligence: A Christian Perspective

Defined by this writer, spiritual intelligence is: (a) the divine ability to receive knowledge supernaturally or by spiritual means; and (b) the ability to use spiritual means to identify and solve spiritual and other problems.

Gardner (1993) asserted that intelligence and morality do not belong in the same domain. However, if natural intelligence does not equate with knowing how to behave morally and does not belong in the same domain, how does one account for moral cognition? Although Gardner did not see a link between intelligence and morality, he recognized the need for intelligence and morality to work together to create a world in which a great variety of people would want to live. In this regard, Gardner has echoed an incontrovertible truth: the health, wellness and security of individuals and of the world at large, are contingent on moral character. Implicit in Gardner's statement is a universal and basic need – the need for safety and security. This need may not be met without an objective moral code, universally applicable, by which behavior may be appraised.

Moral and spiritual development is popularly deemed the domain of religion. Christians associate character development with spirituality, and the objective standard of character appraisal with spiritual laws found in the Bible. Based on the teachings of Christianity, a Common Creator, Divine Lawgiver and Final Judge make a common morality plausible and universal coherence of moral values possible and sustainable.

The making of appropriate moral and spiritual choices requires intelligence. Intelligence responsible for character development and an objective standard for the appraisal of character is critical to human life and development. Since natural intelligence does not inform moral and spiritual development, why not spiritual intelligence?

Hauerwas (1983) perceived a Christian ethic associated with Jesus' life, death and resurrection as the foundation for peace and character development, affecting both the individual and society. Delvin (1997) expressed the view that character is more important than intellectual ability. This is arguably so because when character development is left out of the picture, despite natural intelligence, human beings tend to live by their baser instincts and accordingly do the bizarre and unimaginable, both for selfish reasons and in order to meet security needs. Without character there is no foundation for security and no basis for peace; for in an insecure world, all that counts is survival, but only the fittest survive.

Sadly, the fittest invariably means the most unprincipled or ruthless. Accordingly, many in the human jungle live by the maxim "Do unto others before they do unto you." Such a rule, how-ever, serves to create and maintain axes of evil; in which case, everyone becomes a victim of insecurity. As behavior breeds behavior, unprincipled and ruthless behavior propels a vicious cycle of inappropriate behavior.

The need for a common morality, sustainable in something greater than natural intelligence is apparent. The failure of natural intelligence to successfully address issues relevant to moral and spiritual development makes a spiritual intelligence desirable and plausible.

Relationship Between Justice and Spirituality

The ability to make moral and spiritual judgments demands intelligence. Intelligence is necessary in order to exercise jurisprudence and to determine right from wrong. Whatever a person does or does not do is always the product of moral judgment (Kemp, 1964).

Morality and spirituality are inescapably linked. A moral wrong is a spiritual wrong, because it is an affront to the Creator and undermines God's creation. Moral judgments impact the social, spiritual, physical and emotional wellbeing of self and others. Affects spread phenomenally due to globalization and communication technology. In addition to the personal impact, people experience injustice, for example, vicariously through the media and other forms of communication. Upheavals caused by injustice could mean a strain on the resources of other countries as people flee to distant lands in order to find safe haven.

A common way in which injustice is being manifested is in the form of white collar violence. Whereas white collar crime undermines the economic fabric of society, white collar violence undermines the moral and spiritual fabric. White collar violence includes: violation of human rights through open denial or subtle repression, unjust discrimination, perversion of justice, treating minorities and people of a different caste or class as inferior and organizing to keep them "in their place" so as to obtain or maintain an unfair advantage, persecution, oppression, psychological abuse, and other forms of nonphysical violence against personhood, equating to injustice. Things such as these are acts of violence because they violate the soul of both the oppressed and oppressor.

White collar violence is an affront to God—it is subversion, an undermining of the law of love and of Divine order. Although white color violence might not constitute a crime in the strictest sense of the law, but is indeed a crime against humanity, and as such violates God's supreme laws. If goes unchecked, this form of violence not only results in anarchy from the Divine perspective, it results in social unrest—an unraveling of the social order. Both the individual and society are degraded and ultimately experience decay when moral and spiritual laws are flouted and justice denied.

Injustice violates personhood and contaminates the soul. Whether perpetrated in an overt or covert way, injustice fuels injustice and other forms of violence in return. Barring the grace of God, injustice usually breeds more injustice, as people affected by injustice may overreact and may not necessarily use legal channels to right the wrong. As justice through legal channels is often beyond the reach of the poor, justice invariably eludes the "weak." Furthermore, because justice is often determined by people having the most power to enforce their conceptions of truth and justice, laws are constantly changing to accommodate their views. Taking matters into one's own hands thus becomes a viable alternative for the disadvantaged. Absence of a constant and credible moral compass and of a just legal system results in moral judgment being impaired.

Attempts to stack the cards in favor of the powerful ultimately work against the best interest of everyone. Where the rights of others are frustrated or denied by legal systems, people are inclined to take matters in their own hands using inappropriate means such as crime and violence to level the playing field. "Loss of confidence in the law and the courts undermines civic morale and the cohesiveness of society in general" (Sowell, 1999, p. 160).

Exacerbating the problem is moral confusion. For example, in one breath, those in authority encourage individual freedom or permissiveness; and in another, attempts are made to regulate moral behavior through societal pressures and judicial systems. In some instances, the right of the individual to make moral choices is the accepted authority; in other instances, society or the state rules.

Clashing views on moral and spiritual issues are causing confusion, negatively impacting relationships and the social order locally and globally. In the meantime, extreme levels of permissiveness are being matched by extreme levels of intolerance in different parts of the world.

Intolerance has been a major cause of injustice globally, and the ripple of moral dysfunction due to permissiveness has resulted in a deluge of dysfunctional behavior, affecting the individual, society and society's institutions. Human rights continue to be violated and morality undermined. Many noncriminal behaviors abuse personhood and enslave human beings to a life of debauchery and abnormal behavior.

We know intuitively and from experience that a behavior does not have to be in the domain of criminality for it to be wrong or immoral. Unfortunately, noncriminal behavior is often defended and supported by claims of freedom of choice. Although human beings have freedom of choice, freedom of choice should not include the right to be immoral. Furthermore, if the choices we make are immoral, we ought to be prepared for criticism and the likely consequences. Ancient philosophers such as Socrates and Plato, believed objective universal concepts of justice and goodness were critical to ensuring a sure foundation for ascertaining true values (Tarnas, 1991).

Failure of Mental Intelligence and Academia

Unfortunately, while advancing intellectually and technologically, there is an apparent decline in the high standards of moral and spiritual behavior. Natural intelligence and its commonly-acknowledged outcome, academic success, have not led to successful navigation of moral and spiritual issues.

History has shown that although education may help people become better academically, and so increase their potential for upward social mobility, the educated are not necessarily helped morally and spiritually. People do not become morally and spiritually better by being educated any more than by being affluent or rich, do they? In fact, many have become more corrupt. This is so, because, in addition to the absence of moral and spiritual training in homes, moral and spiritual training are conspicuously absent from the curricula in educational institutions. Consequently, the well-educated may be sound naturally and intellectually but unsound spiritually and morally.

In two of our most basic institutions – home and school – moral and spiritual training are sadly lacking. In both institutions, greater value is placed on intellectual development. Moral and spiritual development are either downplayed or neglected altogether. The enormous disparity in the levels of rigor and resources applied to intellectual development when compared to resources that are applied to moral and spiritual development is manifest in current levels of indiscipline, inappropriate behavior and godlessness.

In some systems of education, a distorted view of spirituality prevails: God and the supernatural are perceived as myths. The current culture is spiritually ignorant, due in part to denial of the supernatural and spiritual, especially denial of the existence of God (Zohar & Marshall, 2000).

Zohar and Marshall averred a consequent crisis of meaning and chided modern-day culture for its folly in attempting to find meaning from meaninglessness. They noted that certain sicknesses and diseases, such as depression, fatigue, drug abuse, cancers and heart diseases, are rooted in a lack of meaning.

Diseases of meaning manifested as ill-health physically, psychologically, cognitively and spiritually, are evident in several aspects of culture; are responsible for negatively influencing culture; and for creating abhorrent subcultures. The authors further expressed the view that spiritual intelligence is not culture- or value-dependent; spiritual intelligence creates the possibility of having values in the first place, and is critical in recognizing existing values, discovering new ones, and in attaining wisdom.

Tragically, many do not see a connection between intelligence and spirituality. Spirituality is embraced for its relative value and its role in supporting culture. Culture therefore determines what is spiritual and moral, even when spiritual and moral practices fly in the face of reason or intelligence. Compounding the issues is the fact that moral and spiritual behaviors are often relegated to the personal domain, and, according to some, should not be the subject of criticism or evaluation. Yet this does not augur well for human development.

Human development takes place where there is opportunity to assess beliefs and behaviors at both the individual and societal levels. Since spirituality and morality are critical to human life and development, these areas need constant assessment. Despite the fact, the moral and spiritual are treated with a high degree of subjectivity and relativity. In some circles, all religions are deemed equally valid, and, therefore, are not subject to critical evaluation. For many, God is whomever one wants him to be. This is especially true among supporters of the New Age brand of spirituality.

> The first and cardinal rule in the New Age is simply this: "Believe in any god and in anything, but do not claim that your god, or your belief, is exclusive" . . . It does not matter whether you worship a Hindu guru, or your own Higher Self, the group, or a pagan deity from ancient Rome, Greece, or Babylon. (Marrs, 1996, p. 29)

To this line of reasoning, Harris (2010) offered a useful rejoinder. He questioned whether any educated person would really consider it a sign of bigotry if someone were to question another society's response, say for example, to a banking crisis. Harris stated it would be a terrifying thing if all views to avert a catastrophe were equally valid or equally nonsensical in principle. According to Harris, this is exactly what is being done where the most important questions of life are concerned.

Does what we believe matter? Ask President Bush, who started a war with Iraq, costing thousands of lives and billions of dollars, based on the belief that Iraq had been producing nuclear and other weapons of mass destruction. In 2003, in cahoots with Prime Minister Blair of the United Kingdom, Mr. Bush led an invasion of Iraq. It was felt Iraq posed a threat to the security of the United States and her allies. Nothing was further from the truth. Does what we believe matter? Ask the many people who languish in prison because of circumstantial evidence. Ask lawyers and judges, who mediate disputes for a living! The only way belief doesn't matter is if there is no right and wrong. And if that is the case, life has no purpose or meaning.

Everything cannot be equally true, can it? We know from experience and general knowledge that some things are right and that some things are wrong, and that what we believe matters. In the real world, it matters that we are right and not wrong, especially in areas that matter most to us and affect other people.

To be useful, there has to be accuracy in knowledge. Why the acquisition and usefulness of knowledge should be based on absolutism in some areas of life but on relativism in others defies reason. Truthfulness is not only relevant to the acquisition and usefulness of knowledge; it is also relevant to behavior. In fact, it is impractical (if not impossible) to separate knowledge from behavior. In general, people behave according to what they believe.

Belief is powerful and potentially life-changing. Belief determines behavior and how we operate in every area of life. Belief therefore needs to be grounded in facts.

Integrity in knowledge and integrity in behavior facilitate human growth and development in every area of life. Human growth and development are contingent on both intelligence and moral character. Unfortunately, in many institutions of learning, including religious institutions, there is an attempt to dissociate intelligence from moral and spiritual behavior. "The machinery of reason is being increasingly neglected in the pulpit, the religious press, and even in religious educational circles" (Blamires, 1980, p. 144).

Attempts to circumnavigate spirituality because of links to morality have resulted in secularization becoming the main religion. In turn, secularization has created a moral and spiritual vacuum, which is being filled in unhealthy and bizarre behaviors such as ritual murders, witchcraft and other occult practices (White, 1987; Zohar & Marshall, 2000).

Where moral centering is lacking, people are apparently more susceptible to moral and spiritual distortions, involvement in the occult, and other forms of bizarre and inhumane behavior.

> History had shown that those who would not listen to the voice of virtue – whether that of Christ or of the best men of Rome's past – would turn to self-indulgence, and that of the most scurrilous and violent kind. (Moore, 2007, p. 31)

Another consequence of the moral and spiritual vacuum created by secularization is the inappropriate use of knowledge. For instance, while facilitating development in some areas of life, advances in science and technology have facilitated destruction at unprecedented levels of sophistication in other areas.

> What promises the best forebodes the worst. Modern media of global communication disseminate lies as well as truth. The airplane is a machine of destruction as well as an instrument of neighborly goodwill. The conquests of outer space are opening up secrets of the universe, but it is also extending the scope of the deadliest forms of warfare. Even advances in medicine and psychiatry for assuaging the ills of men and women are iniquitously perverted to the invention of ever more diabolical methods for tormenting persons with inconvenient views and destroying their minds. (Hughes, 1989, p. 142)

While accelerating the pace of human development via access to information, the Internet has also facilitated cybercrimes such as identity theft and other forms of immoral and criminal behavior. The Internet is being used to spread information as well as misinformation. Instead of using advances in science and technology for good, scientific and technological advances are being used inappropriately to perpetuate evil in the world. Nuclear technology and biological science are being used to develop weapons of mass destruction, for instance.

The world has virtually turned upside down. In today's world, the right to privacy is displaced by freedom of information, the sin of gossip by sharing, and slander by oversharing. To complicate things, bad news make good news, evil spreads like wildfire, and good news are suppressed. Freedom of speech is constrained by alignment to interest groups, including political and religious affiliations, and free speech is under attack by people offended by divergent views or inconvenient truths. Fake news is confused with real news, and the line between right and wrong is blurred by expediency and liberalism. Scapegoating has developed into an art displayed at every level. Instead of taking responsibility we blame others for moral turpitude and our own ineptitude, and attribute responsibility to them for righting wrongs or for fixing the problems in society.

Attempts are made to create an amoral society; and where present morality has become so commercialized that everyone has a price. The commercialization of morality has become so endemic that the success of churches are no longer measured by the number of lives changed or by their impact on society, but by the number in attendance, their income and by the size of the budget.

In our inverted world, in addition to being displaced by money, God is displaced by nature. Few ever stop to think that nature could not exist by itself: in order for nature to exist, there has to be a Source – a Super Nature – a Supreme Being capable of knowing all things, of creating all things, and who is the beginning and end of all things. When we show disregard for the supernatural or remove the "super" from the natural, we not only show disregard for the Spirit that enables us, we limit ourselves to the natural domain, are diminished and thus spiritually unintelligent.

Failure of mental intelligence and academia to successfully address moral and spiritual issues is apparent. Despite obtaining what may be perceived a good education, the highly educated in western society appear just as ignorant spiritually and morally as many who have not had the good fortune of educational opportunities or of succeeding at academics.

Evil overtakes both the ignorant and educated alike. Although education plays a key role in human development, in the hands of the morally and spiritually depraved, education may do more harm than good. A more holistic approach to education is needed. "To educate a man in mind and not in morals is to educate a menace to society" (Theodore Roosevelt). Since current moral theories based on natural intelligence have not succeeded in solving moral and spiritual problems – there being a connection between morality and spirituality – a moral theory based on spiritual ability is needed.

Limitations of Natural Intelligence

Is natural intelligence sufficiently capable of comprehending and navigating the spiritual? In terms of scope, natural intelligence is limited to the five senses and does not go beyond the natural and physical. One cannot therefore use physical lens to discern the spiritual; spiritual lens are needed.

Moreover, it is possible for problems manifested at the physical level, such as heart attack, cancer and insanity to have moral and spiritual roots, as in guilt and being unforgiving, for example. Since it is possible for physical problems to have spiritual roots, spiritual lens are needed.

It is also possible for a set of facts to have more than one meaning or interpretation. The same set of facts may have a physical, social, spiritual and psychological interpretation. There is therefore need for intelligence in every area of life, in order to facilitate a fuller understanding and encourage development holistically.

Sometimes it is not what we know that poses challenges for us; it is our interpretive framework and the assumptions we make. One's interpretive framework is influenced by a number of factors, such as social conditioning, peer pressure, training, motive/agenda, prejudice and experience. These and other factors profoundly affect how facts are interpreted. Moreover, facts may be insufficient and misrepresented, and may be interpreted differently. And since the spiritual and supernatural do not fall in the perceptual framework of the physical and natural, spiritual lens are needed. The spiritual and supernatural are best perceived and interpreted through spiritual lens.

Perceptual lens need to be consistent with the *lenscape*. Appropriate instruments to ensure the validity of conclusions are necessary across disciplines. For example, a scientist is not adjudged qualified to appraise art on the merit of intellectual brilliance alone, is he? One must be art smart. In order to be a valid appraiser of art, knowledge of art is imperative. This is why, for instance, the work of scholars of a given field is best judged or reviewed by their own peers. It is difficult to make appraisals outside one's field of competence. The difficulty is magnified by the fact that each discipline has its own theoretical framework and perceptual lens; plus, invariably operatives in each discipline are affected by myopia, prejudice or bigotry.

Based on differences in scope between the natural and physical, perspectives which may be complementary are often seen as contradictory, without any serious attempt to make connections. Spiritual connections are often the most difficult to make, as much of life is experienced at the physical level.

The interpretive framework of physicality (the flesh) has inherent weaknesses and, as a consequence, leads to inaccuracies where the natural and physical are concerned, and even more so in areas of the spiritual and supernatural. Where the spiritual and supernatural are concerned, spiritual lens are needed.

Since natural intelligence has been found inadequate for perceiving the spiritual and for solving moral and spiritual problems, it is critical that moral theories informed by natural intelligence are reexamined. "Just as the unexamined life is a life poorly lived, no life is complete without some effort to connect with the deeper meaning of our existence" (Das, 2001, p. 10).

Moral theories impact moral and spiritual values, as well as perceptions of the meaning and purpose of life. Ultimately, human development is affected. Understanding the deeper meaning of our existence is contingent on levels of spiritual intelligence. Spiritual intelligence is needed in order to interpret facts correctly and to find meaning and purpose, and is indeed required in the areas of spirituality and morality. In fact, in every area of human life, spiritual intelligence is needed. Spiritual intelligence is indeed required in order to appreciate, understand and discern the spiritual, to apply spiritual truths, and to identify and solve spiritual and other problems.

Summary

Several factors in religion and society indicate a need for spiritual intelligence. Factors indicating a need for spiritual intelligence include: the preponderance of religions and religious cults, increasing interest in the supernatural and paranormal, competing *spiritualities*, competing moralities, moral and spiritual contradictions, the failure of natural intelligence-based moral theories to meet the needs of moral and spiritual development, moral and spiritual ignorance, corruption, diseases of meaning, injustice and other forms of immorality, religion's popularity, and the general acknowledgment of religion as being responsible for moral and spiritual development.

Moral and spiritual development restrain the forces of evil, ensure the appropriate use of resources (including spiritual gifts and natural talents) and give a sense of meaning and purpose. Yet the moral and spiritual are being neglected. Other competencies are given higher priority and are deemed more needful. At the same time moral and spiritual dysfunction continue to undermine the survival and ability of human beings to live peacefully and successfully.

In order to deal with the complex issues of morality, spirituality and intelligence, divine help is needed. Natural instruments are insufficient to identify, apprehend and solve problems of a spiritual nature; spiritual intelligence is needed. Spiritual intelligence is also needed in order to facilitate meaning and to avoid diseases that may be the result of a lack of meaning.

Challenges to spiritual intelligence will be the highlight of the next chapter.

CHAPTER 2
Challenges to
Spiritual Intelligence

The development of spiritual capacity has not kept pace with the development of natural capacity. Spiritual intelligence is sadly lacking, and where present is underdeveloped. This is due in part to the fact that most of life seemingly involves the physical and that physicality is more apparent.

Because the physical and visible is more apparent than the spiritual and invisible, much of life revolves around physicality. A disproportionate amount of resources are therefore deployed toward the development of physical capacity in comparison to resources deployed in the development of spiritual capacity. Moreover, since interpretation of experiences invariably involves physical lens only, there is myopia resulting in impaired spiritual vision, and as a consequence partial or inappropriate solutions to problems.

To compound matters, although the spiritual is universally experienced, matters of spiritual concern evoke controversy due to a multiplicity of spiritual models and the high levels of subjectivity involved in some religious models. Furthermore, the concept of intelligence is the subject of contention. There is disagreement as to whether or not intelligence is unitary and static or multiple and fluid.

Both spirituality and intelligence are controversial subjects. When combined to create a new concept, the controversies become more intense and pose additional challenges. Overcoming these and other challenges mean

33

expanding the scope of the investigation, hence increased complexity. This study of spiritual intelligence is controversial and complex, because of diverse views on spirituality, intelligence and spiritual intelligence, and the interdisciplinary nature of the study.

There are challenges emanating from a selective and incomplete interpretive framework. The fact of not knowing everything about anything serves to intensify moral and mental challenges. Ignorance of the unknown causes knowledge to be in a state of flux, and faulty assumptions lead to error.

Complexity of the Study

In order to increase the depth of understanding, the investigation necessarily incorporates several disciplines. Anthropologically, a study of spiritual intelligence involves the study of human origins, customs, traditions and beliefs. Sociologically, it involves the study of human behaviors and their effects on society. Psychologically, it involves the study of the human cognitive, intuitive, spiritual and emotional capacity to make moral and spiritual decisions, and the development of human personality. Theologically, it involves the study of righteousness, religion and God. Philosophically, it involves the study of epistemology and ontology – the acquisition of knowledge and the nature of truth and reality.

The nature of truth and reality poses a major challenge to the concept of spiritual intelligence. Major epistemological and ontological differences exist between science and religion. The perceptual framework of science from which knowledge is determined conflicts with that of religion. Science insists that knowledge may only be obtained via the five senses or empiricism; religion insists there are other ways of knowing. Epistemologically, the perceptual framework of natural intelligence is limited to the five senses of seeing, hearing, feeling, tasting and smelling; the perceptual framework of spiritual intelligence is unlimited and includes divine revelation, illumination, prophesy, spiritual guidance and faith.

Because of the apparent contradiction between science and religion, there is disagreement concerning what may be regarded as truth and what may be regarded as reality. In the main, scientists believe in a physical and material world only; religious scholars believe there is a spiritual world interacting with the physical.

Conceptual Challenges

Because of the relative newness of the concept of spiritual intelligence, there are conceivable perceptual blocks and prejudices to overcome. Since concepts are still being constructed, there is also the challenge of presenting clear constructs. Presentation of clear constructs is needed in order to: (a) encourage and maintain new thought and (b) prevent misunderstanding or reversion to a mindset influenced by incomplete knowledge and ignorance. The need for clarity in the face of ignorance and conflicting theories is daunting, especially since this study seeks to disclose a paradigm unfamiliar to the majority.

Existing knowledge of certain aspects of spirituality, increases the possibility of confusing the old with the new or of "pouring new wine into old wineskins" (Matt. 9:17). Some may assume that spiritual intelligence is received and developed in the same way as natural intelligence. Because religious or church-related activities are associated with high moral and spiritual standards, both the religious and nonreligious may confuse religion with spiritual intelligence. Healing rooted in psychology and the occult may be confused with spiritual intelligence as well.

There is also the possibility of confusing emotional intelligence with spiritual intelligence because of overlapping features. The ethos of emotional intelligence is self-control or the mastery of one's emotions, enabling appropriate behavior, particularly affecting interpersonal and intrapersonal relationships. Where spiritual intelligence is concerned, these values are similarly stressed, although motivation is different. Emphasis is on developing a positive mindset, getting rid of negative emotions through the enabling power of the Spirit and allowing the Spirit to produce virtues such as self-control and love. Whereas the motivation behind the development of emotional intelligence is humanistic and naturalistic, the motivation behind the development of spiritual intelligence is spiritual and supernatural.

Spiritual Intelligence: A Christian Perspective

Worldview Challenges

Appreciating and understanding spiritual intelligence may be affected by a person's worldview. Worldviews not only influence perceptions of truth and reality but also have implications for virtually every area of life, including the meaning of life. "If a person believes that everything is only matter or energy and carries this through consistently, meaning dies, morality dies, love dies, hope dies" (Schaeffer & Koop, 1979, p. 138).

Distinct differences exist between the worldview of scientists postulating materialistic evolutionism and the worldview of religion advancing creationism as explanation for the existence of the world as we experience it. The existence of God and an immaterial spirit world have been the pivot of the theory of creation, and consequently, the source of a long-standing controversy between science and religion.

Materialistic evolutionists, for example, do not believe in the existence of God and a spirit world. Evolutionists of this ilk theorize that the world began with cataclysmic activity and evolved over billions of years, that there have been gradual transformations in the structure of the physical world and its inhabitants over time, that natural laws observable in the physical world are self-created and self-directed, and that despite its complexity and variety, nature alone explains the origin of life. However, since science is limited and only deals with approximations of the truth, science cannot produce definitive and complete understanding of reality (Capra, 1991; Collins, 1999).

From the perspective of an observer-participant: life is comprised of a series of relationships impacting each other in a vicious cycle of cause-and-effect; and there is interconnectedness in all of nature.

Interconnectedness implies an Original Source. There has to be an Original Source possessed of infinite intelligence to have set everything in motion in an ordered and intelligent way, or capable of creating order out of chaos. If nature is the Source, then nature is responsible for creating the world and everything in it. It seems impossible, however, for the impersonal in nature to have created personal beings?

The theory that impersonal forces in nature created personal, intelligent, spiritual and physical beings is difficult to accept. The view that order observable in the world emanated from disorder and chaos, as claimed by some scientists, is also a hard one to swallow. There had to be a First Cause – an original being, self-existent and self-sufficient in nature, capable of infinite intelligence and power ordering everything in its place, every creature and everyone into being.

> We look out upon our world and we judge that it expresses the conscious purpose of a divine maker, in that it seems too coherent, too ordered, too dramatic, too packed with hidden and discoverable meanings to be the product of accidental growth. (Blamires, 1980, pp. 149)

Creationism advances the view that a Supreme Being, called God is such a person. By faith Christians understand that the universe was formed at God's command and that what is seen was not made from what is visible (Gen. 1, 2; John 1:1-3; Heb. 11:3). God created the world and set natural and spiritual laws in motion to regulate how the world should function. Based on biblical data, creation reveals the glory of God (Ps. 19). "Since the creation of the world, His invisible attributes, His eternal power and divine nature, have been clearly seen, being understood through what has been made" (Rom. 1:20, NASB).

This view resonated with Blamires (1980), who stated:

> As for the question whether God exists or not, it resolves itself basically into acceptance of purpose or chance as a first cause. It is not easy for any man to look out upon our universe and say "It must have made itself – by accident" (p. 148)

Based on observable orderliness in the universe and the cosmic fine-tuning for life, Leslie (2001) concluded that had properties of the universe been slightly different in any way or any number of ways, conscious and intelligent life would not be possible. Leslie claimed that the cosmos exists because of an ethical need for it; humanity and all the intricate structures of the universe are the result of the structured thoughts of a Divine Mind, knowing everything worth knowing.

Spiritual Intelligence: A Christian Perspective

> Long ago, Issac Newton, regarded as one of the founders of the scientific age, yet also a deeply religious man, acknowledged that the more he understood the nature of things, the more he was convinced of a greater power and purpose that lay behind it. Similar viewpoints can be found in the writings of many other great scientists, from Einstein to Hawking. Perhaps then we do not have to think in terms of science or spirituality, but of science and spirituality. (Wright & Sayre-Adams, 2000, p. 34).

Religion and science do not always disagree. In fact, scientists from the Christian, Jewish, Muslim and other religious communities have made notable contributions to science and technology, many of whom have attributed discoveries and inventions to their religious beliefs, claiming their work was supernaturally inspired.

Moreover, religion and science do share a number of things in common. For example, some things previously regarded fiction, are now proven facts of science. The same may be said of religion. In both fields, it takes time for the imagined to be translated to reality and for doubt to be translated to faith. In both fields, knowledge is revealed in part or over time, and there have been misunderstandings and corrections along the way. Although different faculties and methodologies may be employed, everything begins with faith or belief and is given flesh by a creative spirit, facts and interpretation of facts supporting or not supporting theories.

Since all facts gain their meaning in the context of our view of the world, conflicting truth claims may not be adjudicated on the basis of facts alone. There are two distinct lenses at work influencing perception: the lens of sight and the lens of belief (John10:29). Insight garnered through the five senses is generally how knowledge is gained. But belief also plays a crucial role in the investigative process via intuition, assumptions and theories, and is part of the perceptual framework and interpretative base.

Notwithstanding, the fact that we believe something doesn't make it factual or true, does it? In addition, things are not always what they seem. Furthermore, because of prejudice or bias, we sometimes need to see in order to believe; other times we needs to believe in order to see, for despite the claim that "seeing is believing," many will not see because they will not believe.

Since we can see and still not believe, we must at least be open to the possibility or be willing to believe in order to see. In many cases, believing is seeing, as ultimately our belief system determines how facts are interpreted or seen. Accordingly, even the greatest scholar may be hindered or helped by their belief system.

Controversies surrounding spiritual intelligence are due, in part, to differences in worldviews, ignorance, and prejudice regarding a spiritual reality. "We need the courage to move beyond the prejudice of our age and affirm with our best scientists that there exists more than the material world" (Foster, 1978, p. 3).

Moral Challenges

In the main, spiritual intelligence speaks to morality. Morality has to do with issues of right and wrong and, therefore, to issues of righteousness and justice. In order for morality to make sense and for human strivings to have any real currency, there must be moral absolutes. Moral absolutes presupposes a Creator, Law Giver and Final Judge, and One necessarily possessed of infinite wisdom and immortality.

Of necessity, matters of morality must be the purview of God, who alone qualifies as Final Judge, being Creator. Belief in God, a Final Judge and an afterlife of immortality not only impacts values and morality; purpose and meaning are impacted as well. Without God, a Final Judge and an afterlife of immortality, life has no ultimate meaning and purpose (Craig, 2000); human beings are nothing more than a higher form of animal looking forward to the only certain thing in life, death. Under such a circumstance, it would not matter how life was lived.

If we believe there is a purpose or end to life and that we are created beings, it matters how life is lived. Since creation appears supported by natural and spiritual laws, it follows the same might be true of human beings.

Everything in creation is intelligently designed and reflects intelligence, and there is apparent order in creation. The survival of the planet, the survival of humanity, and the fulfillment and purpose of life is based on the ability of laws to create and facilitate order. Most people understand the importance of natural laws in enabling order in all of nature. However, where moral and spiritual laws are concerned, misunderstanding and confusion prevail; maybe because, unlike nature, human beings have the power to decide what laws we want to embrace and abide by and what laws we want to reject or ignore.

Despite a Common Creator, human beings struggle with natural and spiritual laws and universal codes of ethics, which not only have the potential to enable harmony within and among fellow human beings, but also have the potential to preserve the environment and enable each of us to flourish.

Weaknesses of the physical and attempts to exclude the spiritual impair decision-making capacity, resulting in inappropriate choices where morality is concerned. The effects of inappropriate choices are felt at many levels, including ways in which knowledge is used. "Today both science and technology are used predominantly for purposes that are dangerous, harmful and anti-ecological" (Capra, 1991, p. 335).

The inappropriate use of knowledge is being felt not only in the negative impact on the physical environment but also on the moral and spiritual landscape of human endeavor. In addition to overt barbarism, which prevailed in centuries past, increase in knowledge has enabled more sophisticated and subtle ways of expressing dehumanized behavior. Unfortunately, while propelling the pace of development in some areas, advances in science and technology have enabled a vicious cycle of violence and dehumanized behavior in others. Advances in communication, transportation, medicine, psychiatry, and conquests in space, for example, have been perverted to uses that are diabolic and destructive (Hughes, 1989).

How to stem the tide of humanity's inhumane behavior and encourage a greater sense of stewardship are some of the problems spiritual intelligence is capable of solving. If spiritual misstep or ignorance is at the root of underdevelopment morally and spiritually, then in order for human beings to flourish in the moral and spiritual domain spiritual intelligence is necessary.

Unfortunately, in many areas of life, spiritual intelligence has not kept pace with natural intelligence. Discourse is not as fluid in the moral and spiritual domain as it is in other areas of life. Contrary views are not as readily tolerated and not as freely expressed. In the areas of morality and spirituality, there is an attempt to enforce political correctness: disagreement is equated with hate and bigotry. If disagreement does not mean hate and bigotry in academia and in other areas of life, why do we equate disagreement with hate and bigotry in areas of spirituality and morality? Could this account for the reason we are so bright intellectually and so dumb spiritually?

Religious Challenges

Nothing more powerfully informs and transforms human behavior than religion. In fact, religion has been the most vocal and visible proponent of moral and spiritual issues. Since religion has been the main advocate where moral and spiritual issues are concerned, spirituality is mainly associated with religion.

However, religion is a complicated subject. There are many religions and divergent views on the spiritual. Considering the diverse and contrasting views on spirituality, is it reasonable to accept that all paths lead to the same God, as some proclaim? If all roads lead to the same God, it really doesn't matter what we believe, and there is no special moral code by which all may be held accountable. Yet how do we explain moral codes universally held by nations despite geography?

Adding to the dilemma is the perception that God may be equated with nature or is an impersonal force of nature, and there are many gods. If that were the case, it seems implausible that an impersonal force of nature should be able to create beings that are personal, doesn't it? Furthermore, if there is no God or many gods, how do we account for orderliness in the universe and purpose in the design of the created?

Indeed, the confusion in religion and society at large bears testimony to the need for spiritual intelligence. Each religion has its own brand of spirituality, and there are many faces to religion. Disagreement among the religious regarding the meaning of spirituality, spiritual ignorance and low levels of spirituality, complicate the issue. Since there are several spiritual models, the choice to build a theory of spiritual intelligence based on one religious model and not on others is another possible source of contention.

It is important to make a distinction between religion and spiritual intelligence. Although there is an apparent relationship between religion and spirituality, not everyone who claims to be religious is spiritually intelligent. Whereas some people are spiritually alive, others are spiritually dead (Luke 9:59-60). Based on the Bible, it is also possible to be healthy spiritually and unhealthy physically (3 John 2).

A distinction needs to be made also between religious knowledge and spiritual intelligence. Religious knowledge is not coterminous with spiritual intelligence. It is possible to have religious knowledge or be well-versed in religion and remain spiritually obtuse. Jesus encountered many such cases involving religious scholars, to whom he often referred as "blind leaders of the blind" (Matt. 15:14).

Morality is not coterminous with religion either. Accordingly, there are persons living morally good lives who claim neither God nor religion. Some live as if there is a God and a transcendent moral code, while remaining unwilling to acknowledge openly that there is a God (Bertrand, 2007). "Christians would argue that this is because man, whatever he might think of himself and his origins, is made in God's image and is, in some sense, instilled with a moral sense" (p. 46).

It is possible to be "good" and conform to the letter of the Law and not be righteous. Being good morally and legally is admirable and ought to be commended, but self-righteousness or righteousness imposed by society or the legal system does not make anyone righteous from the divine standpoint. Conformity to the letter of the Law without conformity to the character of the Law Giver is legalism. Even the religious gets it wrong at times.

In addition, since perceptions of God may be both negative and positive, religion may be transformative for some and not for others. For example, some religions see God as a malevolent being in need of constant appeasement. As a result, adherents develop an unhealthy fear of God and engage in unwholesome rituals designed to appease God. Other religions view

God as benevolent, as never angry and in need of no appeasement. This view assumes that since God is love, God will not punish people for doing wrong. Believers, therefore, accommodate or excuse wrong, see no need for repentance and do not strive to be godly.

Throughout history, people have created their own gods and their own religions: God is viewed as whomever or whatever a person desires God to be. Accordingly, some people see God as an impersonal force of nature. In some places, the expressed power of God in nature results in the worshipping of nature as God. Perceptions of God may even include the diabolic. Among the religious, there are people who overtly and covertly worship the devil, hence churches dedicated to the worshipping of Satan: and since people generally behave based on what they believe, perceptions of God are reflected in their character.

The need for spiritual intelligence in religion is underscored by many case studies, for example, the People's Temple. The People's Temple, led by James (Jim) Jones, an American, was founded in the United States in the 1970s. Based on Jones' teaching, members would die together and translate to a better place at the appointed time. Suspicions of illegal activities caused Jones to move his congregation to Jonestown, Guyana. In 1978, further investigations into the People's Temple resulted in over nine hundred people – including more than two hundred children – losing their lives. The majority is believed to have committed suicide by drinking a grape drink laced with cyanide and a number of sedatives; others were murdered by fellow cult members (http://www.religious tolerance.org/dc_jones.htm).

The practices of certain religions and religious cults reveal injustices (especially against women), bondage, mental and physical slavery, the promotion of hate and the death of nonconformists. In America, subsets of Christianity include the White Church and the Black Church. White evangelicals are accused of racism and of aligning with White supremacists; division is most noticeable on Sundays, when churches generally convene for worship. There are glaring contradictions among the religious. Moreover, some religions are oppressive and inimical to the physical, psychological, social, moral and spiritual wellbeing of followers.

Spiritual Intelligence: A Christian Perspective

Evidence of a shallow form of spirituality and of *spiritualities* based on ignorance are apparent. Spiritual ignorance has spawned religious wars and crimes against humanity, including slavery. Arterburn and Felton (1991) referenced toxic faith, unbalanced faith and misguided religiosity. According to the authors, religion may be toxic when it becomes a means to avoid control of life: when it becomes an addiction and used to avoid commitments, pain and reality, and when used to avoid growth. In making the case, Arterburn and Felton asked the following:

- Where is the balance between an ungodly independence that leaves the person overwhelmed from the need to be self-sufficient and an ungodly passivity that leaves them doing nothing unless "God has spoken" with personal direction?

- Where is the line between conviction to help people out of a love of God and addiction to compulsive work and striving to please God?

- What is the difference in giving money to honor God and in giving to buy God's favor?

- When does growing in faith become a futile attempt to be perfect?

- When does dependence on God become a cop-out, a way to avoid dealing with tough life situations?

- At what point does faith turn into something ugly, void of a loving God, toxic to the believer, and toxic to those who are near?

- How can a person determine when it is right to follow a leader and when it is dangerous?

- Having developed a toxic faith, how does one recover and grow in the grace and knowledge of God? (Page xvi)

Spiritual ignorance and misunderstanding pose a major threat to human functioning and to civilization on the whole. Spiritual ignorance is responsible for many atrocities, making some people suspicious of anything connected with God or religion; others are turned off from God and religion for the said reasons. Although not every religion is transformational, religion is the soul of civilization; is endemic in most cultures, and significantly impacts people's way of life.

The ability of religion to transform lives is relative to perceptions of God, which vary according to religion. Unfortunately, while validation is sought and deemed desirable in other disciplines, in some circles all religions are deemed equally valid; religion is regarded a personal matter and therefore not subject to criticism.

The view that religion is personal, that all religions are equally valid and therefore neither subject to criticism nor validation, is inconsistent with how other matters are judged in the real world. One would not say all views on economics are equally valid, would one? Why should it be acceptable for all religious claims to be regarded as equally valid when the same is not true of other disciplines or in other areas of life? Apparently, in our postmodern world, political correctness and tolerance trump the need for due process and proper judgment.

While freedom of religion should be supported and promoted, freedom of religion should not mean freedom from constructive criticism or evaluation, should it? Freedom form constructive criticism has the potential to restrict personal growth, the growth of others in society, and may encourage the proliferation of religions that are destructive.

As in other disciplines, growth takes place where there is free flow of information and where there is open discussion and evaluation. Moreover, religious truth involves the same sort of truth by which people operate in their daily lives. If something is true, then its opposite cannot be true (Schaeffer & Koop, 1979). Notwithstanding paradoxes, this is generally the case. In addition, since there is order and intelligence in the natural and physical world – believed to be the effect of an ordered and Intelligent Mind – it is reasonable to expect order in the spiritual world also.

Be that as it may, the reality is that we live in a broken and disordered world. There is constant battle for the minds of human beings between forces good and evil. It is guerilla warfare, which must be won on two fronts – the natural and the spiritual. The battle is especially challenging since we are up against ignorance masquerading as knowledge and darkness masquerading as light.

45

Spiritual Intelligence: A Christian Perspective

Acceptance of the natural, plus years of training and experience in the physical realm have made it easier for victory at the natural and physical level, at least intellectually. The final and most important frontier is spiritual. This is an extremely difficult fight as the subtlety and perniciousness of spiritual darkness can be overwhelming; plus spiritual reality is not readily accepted.

The spiritual is not as well-acknowledged as the physical, hence a lag in the development of spiritual intelligence. To compound the issue:

> Christians have acted as if Christ did not save the mind, and in the past several hundred years Christianity has gradually moved from the intellect to the heart. In the modern world, science and reason . . . based on humanistic and not a theistic view have taken over the minds of Christians" (Webber, 1999, pp. 123-124).

In addition, the gatekeepers of education seldom include spiritual reality as part of their worldview. Consequently, the brightest minds are being encouraged to exclude spiritual and non-physical reality from consciousness, thereby depriving the spiritual world of much-needed talent.

The spiritual and invisible realm cannot be successfully navigated by natural means. The spiritual eyes of the understanding must be opened before spiritual darkness may be successfully dispelled, and spiritual gifts developed and deployed.

Differences between natural intelligence and spiritual intelligence are reconcilable where there is recognition of human beings as possessing both a physical and a spiritual capacity, and where purpose is embraced as an inherent feature of human design. The notion of purpose implies a Creator, intelligent design and order in creation, and has implications for every area of human functioning, including perceptions of autonomy.

Autonomy is constrained by purpose. Intelligence presumes the autonomy to make choices in keeping with the nature of capacity, relative to one's purpose or design. A spiritual capacity implies the possibility for spiritual intelligence. Universal spiritual consciousness and religion's impact on the wellbeing of people everywhere makes a case for spiritual intelligence.

Summary

The concept of spiritual intelligence is birthed in controversies. There is disagreement regarding the existence of a spiritual reality, the meaning of spirituality, the nature of intelligence and the nature of truth and reality. People who believe solely in a materialistic and biological explanation of reality may resist a concept of intelligence associated with spirituality; people who believe solely in a single intelligence may reject spiritual intelligence. The conceptual framework of science, from which knowledge is largely determined, conflicts with that of religion.

There are many challenges to spiritual intelligence. Challenges to understanding spiritual intelligence exist because of the newness and complexity of the subject, because development of spiritual capacity has not kept pace with the development of natural capacity and because of various spiritual models. Associating only one religious model with spiritual intelligence potentially creates perceptual blocks.

Ignorance in religion compounds the problem. Contrary views on God, religion and spirituality have led to misperceptions and confusions. Some people confuse religion or church-related activities with spiritual intelligence. Although spirituality promotes morality, moral behavior is not coterminous with spirituality. It is possible to confuse emotional intelligence with spiritual intelligence, because of overlapping features. It is possible to attribute works rooted in the occult or psychology to spiritual or divine intelligence. Discourse in morality and spirituality is not as fluid as in other areas of life. Attempts to enforce political correctness perpetuate ignorance and stymie spiritual growth.

This examination of challenges to spiritual intelligence provides the background and foundation to explore the related literature in the next chapter.

CHAPTER 3

Support for
Spiritual Intelligence

Investigation into whether a case may be made for spiritual intelligence reveals excellent and insightful support. This chapter includes a review of literature concerning views on intelligence and various intelligence paradigms, views on spiritual intelligence and spiritual consciousness, discovery of a God-spot, and views on the soul and/or spirit and the immaterial in nature. It also reviews the literature on spirituality, and the spiritual in various disciplines, in various aspects of culture, in religion, in the occult and in healing.

The spiritual and supernatural are universally experienced and loom large in various aspects of culture. There are multiple views on spirituality, intelligence, spiritual intelligence and other related aspects of the study. Spirituality means different things to different people and describes subjective experiences as well as the personality and the character of a person. There are nonreligious and religious views on spirituality and on spiritual intelligence.

Views on Intelligence

Intelligence is a term generally used in reference to the ability or abilities involved in learning and adaptive behavior (Morris & Maisto, 2005). Intelligence includes the capacity to think, plan, create, translate ideas into reality, adapt to changing circumstances, find and solve problems, reflect on problems and communicate well with self and others, and to grow from mistakes (Gardner, 1993).

Prior to the 1980s, mental intelligence was regarded as the only intelligence, as a factor of inherited genes only, as static and measurable by IQ tests, proven by success at academics. Since the 1980s, scholars from various disciplines have taken issue with earlier views on intelligence; chief among them is Howard Gardner.

Gardner (1983, 1993) challenged the notion of a single or general intelligence and postulated a theory of multiple intelligences, involving eight intelligences: linguistic, logical-mathematical, spatial, bodily-kinesthetic, musical, interpersonal, intrapersonal and naturalist. Gardner, however, did not believe the list to be final or complete and left the door open for other intelligence paradigms. He believed it was impossible to arrive at an irrefutable and universally accepted list of intelligences. A theory of intelligence, according to Gardner, should account for a wide range of skills, including the skills of a shaman, psychoanalyst, yogi and saint.

Gardner (1999) alluded to the role of culture in making meaningful distinctions in knowledge. The point is important since intelligence is not developed in isolation. Skill sets are understood in social context and are relative to the value placed on them by one's culture.

Gardner listed eight signs of an intelligence: (a) potential isolation by brain damage, (b) existence of idiots and wise persons, (c) prodigies and other exceptional individuals, (d) an identifiable core operation or set of operations, (e) a distinctive development history along with a definable set of end-state performances, (f) evolutionary history and plausibility, (g) support from experimental psychological tasks, (h) support from psychometric findings, and (i) susceptibility to encoding in a symbol system. The criteria for acknowledging the existence of intelligence are delimited by two prerequisites: (a) a set of problem-solving skills and (b) the potential for finding or creating problems. Gardner caveated, however, that the selection of intelligences is based more on artistic judgment than science. Integral to the dialogue is the notion that intelligence is manifested according to the nature of the individual or being and at several levels. Based on Gardner's propositions, does a spiritual intelligence qualify?

Various Intelligence Paradigms

Many academics have supported Gardner's (1983) theory of multiple intelligences and have proposed similar and other theories. The theory of multiple intelligences resonated with Armstrong (2009), Lazear (2004) and Nardi (2001). Bradberry, Greaves and Lencioni (2009), and Goleman (1995) postulated theories of emotional intelligence. Albrecht (2009), Emery, Clayton and Frith (2008), and Goleman (2007) postulated theories of social intelligence. Livermore (2009), Peterson (2004), and Thomas and Inkson (2004) postulated theories of cultural intelligence. Brighton (2007), Minsky (2006), and Russel and Norvig (2002) postulated theories of artificial intelligence. Sinetar (2002), Tipping (2005), and Zohar and Marshall (2000, 2001, 2004) postulated theories of spiritual intelligence.

Views on Spiritual Intelligence

"Spiritual intelligence is the soul's intelligence. It is the intelligence with which we heal ourselves and with which we make ourselves whole" (Zohar & Marshall, 2001, p. 9). Zohar and Marshall asserted that spiritual intelligence is the compass of the soul, used to solve the problem of meaning, value and creative vision. It has the power to transform lives and enable the development of spiritual thinking. A highly developed spiritual intelligence is manifested through flexibility, self-awareness, the capacity to face and transcend suffering, inspiration, a refusal to cause harm, a holistic outlook, a search for answers to fundamental questions, and a capacity to work against convention.

In a more recent work, Zohar and Marshall (2004) explored the concept of spiritual intelligence as spiritual capital, defined as our shared meaning, purpose and vision, and their impact on behavior. It is "taken to mean meaning, values, and fundamental purposes" (p. 27). The authors believed that by building spiritual capital, a critical mass of people acting from higher motivations could change the world.

Spiritual Intelligence: A Christian Perspective

Zohar and Marshall (2004) advanced the following principles, believed necessary for building the spiritual capital capable of bringing about world change:

1. *Self-awareness.* Knowing what one believes in and values and what deeply motivates one. Being aware of one's deepest life's purpose.

2. *Spontaneity.* Living in and being responsive to the moment and all that it contains.

3. *Vision- and value-led.* Acting from principles and deep beliefs, and living life accordingly.

4. *Holism.* A sense of the system or of connectivity. Having the ability to see larger patterns, relationships, connections. A strong sense of belonging.

5. *Compassion.* Being able to show empathy. Groundwork for universal sympathy.

6. *Celebration of diversity.* Valuing other people and unfamiliar situations for their differences, not despite them.

7. *Field independence.* Being able to stand apart from the crowd and maintain one's own convictions.

8. *Tendency to ask fundamental 'why' questions.* Needing to understand things; to get to the bottom of them. Basis for criticizing the given.

9. *Ability to reframe.* Standing back from the problem or situation and looking for the bigger picture, the wider context.

10. *Positive use of adversity.* Being able to own and learn from mistakes and to see problems as opportunities. Resilience.

11. *Humility.* Having the sense of being a player in a larger drama, and the sense of one's true place in the world. Basis for self-criticism and critical judgment.

12. *Sense of vocation.* Being 'called' to serve something larger than

oneself. Gratitude towards those who have helped one, and a wish to give something back. Basis for "servant leader." (Zohar & Marshall, 2004, pp. 79-80)

Notions of spirituality did not have anything to do with religion or theological beliefs systems, but with reframing our minds to embrace fundamentally better ways of doing things and making a difference. To attain such a grandiose goal, however, would involve not just reframing, but remaking, as human nature tends toward selfishness. Instead of cooperation and mutual development, there is competition and exploitation, the emphasis being on independence instead of interdependence.

Bowell (2005) perceived spiritual intelligence as the ability to understand the world and self through God-centered living and as the ability responsible for shaping and directing other abilities. He saw spiritual intelligence in terms of an evolving self and believed spiritual intelligence varies from person-to-person, although the reason for living might be the same. Manifestations of spiritual intelligence include faith, humility, gratitude and self-control.

Sha (2008) did not mention a spiritual intelligence directly. However, a spiritual intelligence may be inferred from Sha's discourse on Wisdom of the Soul. Sha postulated a language of the soul, believed to be a universal language with the capacity for healing, enlightening, and energizing the body, soul and spirit. He expressed the view that the soul has the ability to receive "Divine Downloads," thereby enabling communication between the individual and the Divine, including angels. Through this medium people may receive healing powers and the ability to transmit the power of healing to others. By Divine, Sha did not necessarily mean God; Sha meant the supernatural. The Divine may transform the soul using several means, namely the application of various eastern disciplines. According to Sha, if the soul was transformed, the mind would follow.

Woolman (2001) perceived spiritual intelligence as an innate ability. Believed to be a specific human function for perceiving spiritual knowledge and events, spiritual intelligence is defined as the ability to ask ultimate questions about the meaning of life, and as the ability to experience a connection with others and with the world in which one lives. Woolman developed a PsychoMatrix Spirituality Inventory Test (PSI) to reveal patterns of spirituality and spiritual development. The assumption is that a high score on the spiritual inventory test reflects virtuous or moral character.

Sisk and Torrance (2001) defined spiritual intelligence as a multisensory approach to answering life's most fundamental questions, such as the meaning of life and how one can make a difference. The authors emphasized human interconnectedness, finding a purpose and creating a vision. According to Buzan (2001), spiritual intelligence involves the ability to see beneath the surface, to get a better or deeper understanding and to have an enlarged and global vision. Spiritual intelligence is perceived to be a way of learning to know self and others, in order to relate more compassionately and deeply. Manifestations include truth, honesty, cheerfulness, enthusiasm and helpfulness.

Tipping (2005) believed spiritual intelligence to be part of the mind connected to Universal Intelligence, capable of producing instantaneous results, such as forgiveness and healing. Morris (2005) viewed spiritual intelligence as the ability to discover gradually the deeper significance of familiar elements of everyday life, including the spiritual. Spiritual intelligence is the illuminating interplay of one's unique experience, reflection and practice.

According to Sinetar (2002), spiritual intelligence is an innate spiritual ability; when activated it inspires one to achieve self-actualization. Activation takes place when a person gets in touch with the inner self. Spiritual intelligence is not necessarily associated with religion. Khavari (2000) defined spiritual intelligence as the ability to assert self-control over how a person thinks, feels and behaves, and as such spiritual intelligence enables personal happiness. Noble (2001) believed that, like any other talent or gift, spiritual intelligence is an innate human potential expressed in various ways and in various degrees.

Painton (2007) believed spiritual intelligence to be a special gift involving the ability to be receptive to pain and the emotions of others, and the ability to experience paranormal phenomena, such as the ability to communicate with deceased relatives. Hart (1998) viewed spiritual intelligence in terms of inspiration. Schwartz (2011) discerned spiritual intelligence as attunement to the Spirit and spiritual direction: it is possible to attune oneself to the Spirit and receive guidance from the Spirit.

Zukav (1989) saw spiritual intelligence in terms of an evolving self via the evolution of consciousness into abilities beyond the five senses. He believed there are essentially two types of people in the world – those who are five-sensory and those who are multisensory. The five-sensory person has external power, derived from the ability of the five senses to perceive and manipulate the physical. The multisensory person has authentic power, derived from abilities beyond the five senses to interpret and manipulate events. The multisensory person is not limited to the physical, and therefore does not need to rely solely on his or her own perceptions and interpretations for guidance. Zukav asserted that one's deepest values originate from an invisible realm and that, because of the limitations of the five senses, a five-sensory individual finds evil more attractive than one whose awareness is expanded. Zukav defined evil as the absence of light. Light is equated with Divine Intelligence, the absence of which causes people to stumble in darkness.

Peck (1978, 1983, 1993) expressed similar sentiments, but saw spirituality in terms of an evolving intelligence involving four stages. Peck listed the stages as:

1. The chaotic – a period of lawlessness or absence of spirituality.

2. The formal or institutional – religious attachment or adherence to religion

3. The skeptic or individual – principled behavior characterized by doubt and inquisitiveness.

4. The mystical or communal – maturity characterized by adherence to the spirit of the law.

Peck believed the stages are sequential, there are people between stages, and that there are gradations within the stages. He did not confine these stages to any particular religion.

Ruth (1999) perceived spiritual intelligence in terms of spiritual and psychological growth. He argued that the human spirit is restored to wholeness whenever the shadow of the hidden, repressed, and guilt-laden aspects of a person's personality is confronted.

Blamires (1963) suggested there are two distinct ways of thinking: one way associated with the sacred, the other with the secular. A Christian mind and a secular mind rival each other. Blamires identified the Christian mind by the following characteristics: its supernatural orientation, its awareness of evil, its conception of truth, its acceptance of authority, its concern for the person, and its sacramental cast. "The Christian mind synthesizes in terms of God's demand and man's response" (Blamires, 1963, p. 182).

Boa (2001), Collins (2000), Nee (1968) and Sager (1990) supported the concept of a spiritual intelligence, but did not use the same terminology. Spiritual intelligence was expressed from a biblical and evangelical perspective and couched in language such as spiritual and psychological growth.

Pinker (2002) averred the views of Locke (as cited in Pinker, 2002), who believed humankind came into the world with a "blank slate," filled over time by experience. Pinker discerned a connection between experience and differences of opinion. According to Pinker, differences of opinion do not suggest a defective mind or that one mind is equipped to grasp truth and the other is not; differences arise simply because of different histories or experiences. Pinker therefore concluded that truth is relative: there is no right and wrong.

Tarnas (1991) postulated the views of ancient philosophers (as cited in Tarnas, 1991) on Transcendent Intelligence. Plato believed Transcendent Intelligence ruled and ordered all things; Heraclitus posited a divine intelligence, conveyed in the concept of Logos. According to Tarnas, Logos originally meant word, speech, or thought and was a divine revelatory principle, operative within the human mind and the natural world.

Views on Consciousness

Noble (2001) claimed physical reality is embedded in a larger, multidimensional reality in which people interact consciously and unconsciously. Wilber (2000) opined that consciousness is hierarchical in structure and that there are four levels of consciousness: the body, mind, soul and spirit. Wilber associated the higher states of consciousness with psychic powers and the metaphysical.

Jung (1969) believed perception of reality could be impacted by consciousness and attitude. Conscious activity is perceived from the lens of either the introvert or the extrovert, processing information subjectively or objectively. Jung postulated that a person functions at four levels:

- The feeling level – the value a person associates with conscious activity.
- The thinking level – the meaning a person associates with conscious activity.
- The sensing level – the method a person associates with knowing something exists.
- The intuiting level – the act of knowing without conscious awareness.

Damasio (1999) expressed the view that the brain knows more than what is revealed by the conscious mind, and that intuition has a basis in biology. Although consciousness is recorded as a mental state, this does not mean consciousness is explainable by biology alone. Since consciousness is not dependent on the physical, consciousness is not reductively explainable (Rowlands, 2001).

Bruce Greyson, Professor of Psychiatry and Neurobehavioral Sciences, and a founding member of the International Association of Near-Death Studies, studied hundreds of near-death experiences and the works of others on consciousness, and found that:

1. People whose brain had been damaged or in an advanced degenerative state functioned at an exceptionally high or normal intellectual

level with virtually no brain at all.

2. People with near death experiences (clinically dead for a brief period of time), after they were resuscitated, reported with accuracy events that took place while they were clinically dead. Among those accurately reporting were people born blind.

3. Patients who had suffered from the inability to think, including patients suffering from Alzheimer's disease, experienced death-bed recovery of lost consciousness. In these patients, there were a sudden return of mental clarity and memory.

These findings led Greyson to conclude that it is impossible to reduce consciousness to brain processes alone, and that consciousness may function independently of the brain. (https://www.youtube.com/watch?v=en3Bz1-RMig).

The foregoing suggests there is an immaterial aspect to consciousness, the reality of which increases the possibility of the invisible and spiritual as inherent features of human design, and as such makes spiritual intelligence plausible.

Rosenblum (2011) and others proposed a field theory of consciousness, in which they advanced the view that consciousness operates similarly to other aspects of nature, like a particle field, for instance. It is believed consciousness spreads beyond the brain, is unbounded and nonmaterial, and operates at various frequencies, sending and receiving signals in all of nature. According to them consciousness can penetrate any barrier and can travel faster than the speed of light through objects without affecting the quality of the communication.

Other scientists expressed the view that space, time, and matter are malleable, and that there is a unified source that governs the laws of the universe at every level. The most fundamental level is strung together by vibrations of different amount of energy and frequency (Greene, 2010).

Vibrations of energy permeate the entire universe and connect us all. We are so interconnected that even our intentions can affect the world (McTaggart, 2007). There is interconnectedness in all of nature. According to McTaggart, all living organisms, inclusive of plants, have auras that transmit and receive information, irrespective of distance. The ability to send and receive messages is possible due to a unique identifying frequency associated with the living. We can therefore talk to nature if we know its harmonizing language. Even biological cells can communicate with each other at a distance due to this unique frequency. McTaggart is convinced that "we can improve our health, enhance our performance in every area of our lives, and possibly even affect the future by consciously using intention" (p. 143).

This view resonated with others such as Losier (2010), who expressed the possibility of similar manifestations based on the law of attraction. Losier believed that by tapping into one's internal energy and increasing its vibrational pitch a person can attract to one's self whatever is desired. Renowned author Peale (2003)expressed similar sentiments in his famous work, *The Power of Positive Thinking.*

In the natural realm, communication by use of energy derived psychologically is astounding. In the meantime communication technology is so advanced that we can communicate with people millions of miles apart audibly and visually, in the comfort of our homes. If this is possible at the natural level, communication at the supernatural level holds out endless possibilities.

Haisch (2006) averred a Universal Consciousness from which all consciousness devolves. This Universal Consciousness possesses infinite intelligence and omnipotence and is the origin of matter and the laws that operate in the universe. According to Haisch, reality does not consist of matter and energy alone. Haisch referred to a natural cognitive faculty, the *sensus divinatus*, which, when functioning properly, gives human beings a basic awareness of God in various circumstances. Other theologians and philosophers, such as Teilhard de Chardin (1959, 2001), referred to a spark of divinity.

"There are certain properties of consciousness, the phenomenal properties, which are transcendental relative to our experience of consciousness" (Rowlands, 2001, p. 216). As reality is comprised of both the physical and spiritual, there is physical consciousness and spiritual consciousness. The spiritual, however, is not embraced by everyone, even when consciousness is aroused.

Due to apparent contradictions between the physical and the spiritual, whenever consciousness and awareness of the spiritual are manifested, spiritual consciousness and awareness are suppressed, denied, treated as superstition, or explained away as something else. Challenges to long-held assumptions evoke fear as a typical response.

The way to overcome the apparent contradiction between the physical and non-physical, however, is not the way of fear. Fear hinders understanding and inhibits discovery and development. One needs to seek understanding. In the quest for understanding, a good place to begin is to determine the function or functions of the phenomena and the intended purpose as per design of the subject in question.

Neuroscientists, Beauregard and O'Leary (2007), claimed:

1. There is more to the brain than matter

2. Physical explanations for religious experiences are insufficient

3. There is such a thing as a spiritual nature

4. The existence of God is highly probable

5. There is a universal higher consciousness

Beauregard and O'Leary attributed causation of spiritual experience to an immaterial soul or spirit residing in human beings. Hamer (2004) proffered an explanation in biology, based on claims of having found a God gene responsible for producing mystical and spiritual sensations. Hamer believed human beings inherited a set of genes which predisposes us to spiritual and mystical experiences; although predisposition does not cause belief in God, spirituality is partly genetic; and that the God gene is a sign of the Creator's ingenuity.

Discovery of a God-spot

Schmeling (2009) found evidence of distinct neural networks in the temporal lobes of the brain associated with religious experiences. Schmeling called these networks "God-spots." This resonated with Zohar and Marshall, who found similar evidence.

> The "God-spot" is an isolated module of neural networks in the temporal lobes. Like other isolated modules in the brain – our speech center, our rhythm center and so on – it confers a special ability, but it has to be integrated. We may "see" God, but that doesn't bring Him into our lives. . . . From this it must be concluded that the "God-spot" may be a necessary condition for [spiritual intelligence], but it cannot be a sufficient condition. (Zohar & Marshall, 2000, p. 112)

Zohar and Marshall believed that spiritual consciousness is an intrinsic state of the brain, not a by-product of sensory stimuli. Although a God-spot is a necessary condition for spiritual intelligence, it is not a sufficient condition. Neural mechanisms alone cannot account for spiritual intelligence.

Brown (2004) believed neurological networks in the brain associated with religious beliefs and experiences cannot be explained in terms of neurology. Neurological explanation for religious beliefs and experiences was dismissed as speculation. Even though links in the brain to religious beliefs may allow an explanation in neurology, this does not necessarily mean that neurology is the cause of those beliefs. Association does not necessarily mean causation, hence other possibilities. Zukav (1989) and Beauregard and O'Leary (2007) provided an explanation in both biology and spirituality. They attributed spiritual beliefs and experiences to both abnormal temporal lobe activity in the brain and to an immaterial soul or spirit.

Sitze and Sylwester (2005) believed there is knowledge-based and belief-based reactivity in the brain: the brain reacts to truth in both belief and knowledge. According to Albright, "Changes in personality organization and changes in brain organization probably mirror one another" (Albright, 2006, p. 169). These insights do not rule out the possibility of supernatural revelation, or awareness of the Divine linked to an immaterial soul or spirit. Biology alone cannot be responsible for spiritual experiences. As far as interpretation goes, Brown asked a poignant question: "Do we interpret our spiritual experiences as a way the brain can function, normally or abnormally, or as manifestations of an immaterial soul?" (Brown, 2004, p. 61). For the religious, the question does not arise. Christians do not see a conflict between the physical and the spiritual. There is recognition that both can work together to produce spiritual experiences. Belief in the existence of the soul or spirit has wide appeal.

Whatever the cause of spiritual experience, a "God-spot" in the brain coheres with the theory of multiple intelligences and by extension with the theory of spiritual intelligence. Human beings are hardwired for spiritual intelligence. Areas of the temporal lobe of the brain lights up due to spiritual experience.

Different Ways of Knowing

There are other ways of knowing besides use of the five senses, such as: visions, dreams, interpretation of dreams, revelation, illumination, inspiration, clairvoyance, telepathy, intuition, precognition, kinesiology, use of pendulums, radionics, dousing rods, experienced globally. These sources of knowledge are outside the scope of natural and scientific explanations.

> Some people claim to have an extra power of perception, one beyond those of the normal senses. This unusual power . . . refers to a variety of phenomena, including clairvoyance – awareness of an unknown object or event; telepathy – knowledge of someone else's thoughts or feelings; and precognition – knowledge of future events. (Morris & Maistro, 2005, p. 98)

Both Old and New Testament Scriptures predicted a unique spiritual ability, universally experienced via the Spirit enabling knowledge through dreams, visions and prophesies (Joel 2:28-29; Acts 2:17-18). Other Scriptures indicated the existence of divine revelations and spiritual discernment (Matt. 16:13-17; Eph. 3:1-6; Philip. 1:9). In addition, the Bible warns of over reliance on natural understanding and avers the need for spiritual direction (Prov. 3:5, 6).

Views on the Soul and Spirit

What happens to the soul or spirit at death, and whether there is life after death has been a long-standing controversy. Is life after death a real possibility? Besides the inability to disprove an afterlife or the experience of people who have actually encountered the deceased in the form of spirits, scientists are now able to prove the presence of spirits via scientific inventions, thus supporting notions of an afterlife.

An immortal soul and/or spirit appears part of the explanation for spiritual consciousness, conscious awareness and desire. Concepts of an immaterial soul and/or spirit have found support among medical doctors and researchers such as Moody (2001). Investigation of over 150 case studies involving people who have experienced death or have had near-death experiences revealed an overwhelming majority who expressed belief in life after death. Based on the experiences narrated by those who have been to the other side and back and those who have had near-death experiences, Moody concluded that human beings are both physical and spiritual and that the spiritual survives the physical at death.

A study conducted by Gallup and Proctor (1982) revealed findings from which similar conclusions may be inferred. The study involving Americans, ages 18 years and older, was conducted in 1980 and 1981. Of the number polled, about 100 million people (two-thirds of the population) expressed belief in life after death. Forty-seven million (one-third of the population) had a mystical or religious experience, 15 million of whom reported a feeling of connection with a divine being. Two million reported an out-of-body experience, and about 23 million reported a near-death or temporary death experience, many of whom reported having had a mystical experience associated with the event.

Reports of mystical experiences varied but the experiences were not influenced by age, gender, or ethnicity. Some people reported out-of-body experiences during which their spirits travelled to heaven or hell. Some people reported out-of-body experiences during which their spirits left their physical bodies and hovered in the environment (e.g., near the ceiling of an emergency or operating room, from where they observed happenings as doctors worked on their bodies in an attempt to bring them back to life). Upon returning to life and to the amazement of doctors, patients reported with extreme accuracy events which transpired in the operating theatre or hospital. Others reported that while their bodies were in a state of coma their spirits left their bodies and visited friends and relatives. Some people reported having had a glimpse of heaven or hell through dreams or visions. Some people described heaven as a place of extraordinary pure light where people communicated via telepathy. (Gallup & Proctor, 1982).

Alexander (2012), a neurosurgeon of over 25 years in practice and an unbeliever in spiritual phenomena, became utterly convinced when he had a near-death experience of his own. In his book "Proof of Heaven," Alexander recalled the experience of his spirit leaving his body, visiting heaven and talking to an angel. Based on additional research and recall of a number of dreams he had from childhood which became reality, Dr. Alexander is now convinced of the validity of spiritual reality: of heaven, angels, dreams, near-death experiences, and of life after death. These views resonated with Neal (2011), who narrated her visit to heaven and conversations with angels. Bennett (1997) and Malarkey (2012) recorded similar events. Schwartz and Simon (2002) averred scientific evidence of life after death. The International Association for Near-Death Studies and the Near-Death Research Foundation have archived a number of cases involving people who have had near-death experiences.

Most religions are of the view that there is both a physical and spiritual dimension to humanity. Christians believe humans are comprised of a body, soul and spirit. According to biblical literature, although united, the soul and spirit survive the body at death, and are of greater value than the body (Matt. 10:28; Mark 8:35-36; 1 Thess. 5:23).

Attribution of greater value to the soul and spirit, and their survival at death indicate preeminence or superiority of the soul and spirit over the body. Nee (1968) expressed the view that "Man's spirit is originally the highest part of his being to which soul and body are to be subject" (p. 43). Nee's view gains currency in light of the following:

1. The physical and visible are temporal.

2. The spiritual and invisible are eternal (2 Cor. 4:16-18).

3. The spirit is responsible for giving physical life to the body (James 2:26; Jhn 19:30).

4. The Spirit is responsible for giving spiritual life to the spirit (1 Cor. 2:6-16).

5. The Spirit is responsible for connecting human beings with Divinity (Jhn. 3:1-8; Rom. 8:9).

Views on the Immaterial in Nature

Evidence of the nonmaterial may also be found in other areas of creation, including nature. Scientists such as Capra (1991) expressed the view that quantum physics has proven there is an invisible foundation to physical reality. This evidence has rendered the materialist paradigm scientifically untenable, and as such has caused a shift in the study of science from thinking in terms of structure to thinking in terms of process:

> The recognition that mass is a form of energy eliminated the concept of a material substance from science and with it also that of a fundamental structure. Subatomic particles are not made of any material stuff; they are patterns of energy. Energy, however, is associated with activity, with process, and this implies that the nature of subatomic particles is intrinsically dynamic. When we observe them, we never see any substance or fundamental structure. What we observe are dynamic patterns continually changing into one another – a continuous dance of energy. (Capra, 1991, p. 329)

Capra did not state where this dance of energy comes from or why it has produced intelligently designed galaxies, plants, animals, buildings, and so on, or why there is interconnectedness in all of nature. He stated, however, that the material and immaterial should not be viewed as contradictory but as complementary, and proffered the phenomenon of light as an example of complementarity between the material and immaterial. In science, at the subatomic level light, describes both a particle and a wave.

It appears light was not only intended to govern day and night, as stated in the Bible, but was intended to play an integral role in all of creation. Light is the very foundation of human existence and does indeed underlie the foundation of the world.

Scientists are of the view that light and sound are opposite ends of the wave spectrum, and that there are waves of light or vibrations of energy (photons) in the physical universe, including the plant and animal kingdoms. This fundamental aspect of nature supports belief in the interconnectedness of all of nature.

In the universe, every entity is supported by a source of energy based on the nature of life, through a network of energy fields. Energy may manifest in various ways, are distributed naturally based on the laws of nature, and may be manipulated by external forces. Despite the source or kind of energy, energy may be used for good or ill. Only God is self-existent and self-sufficient, and thus remains consistently constant where divine attributes are concerned. It is no wonder He is described as Light of the world.

Although differences between religion and science exist, there is common belief in a Universal Light. Notwithstanding, a common belief does not mean a common interpretation. There are a variety of views, even in religion. Pantheists are of the view that Universal Light is another name for nature, that human beings are part of nature, and that nature is divine (Marrs, 1996). Panentheists believe God is in every part of nature and is the animating force behind nature, but is greater than nature (Fox, 1991, 2000).

Christianity holds that Universal Light is the reflection of a personal God, who, although may be seen in nature (Psa. 19:1-3), is not the same as nature. Christians believe God existed before nature, God is above and beyond nature, and that God should not be confused with nature.

In addition to light, energy may manifest as sound waves or breath, transmitted audibly or inaudibly. In fact, philosophers, mystics and others are of the view that everything begins with a thought or an idea, that the intangible is the foundation for the tangible, and that life itself is supported by breath: breath permeates the entire universe and is ultimately the channel through which everything is communicated and created.

Breath may manifest in a number of ways; and as a source of power and creativity affects the structure and life of that which it possesses. Breath in each sphere of existence has its own language, laws or principles encoded, operating at different frequencies, which may be decoded and manipulated naturally and supernaturally. Despite its self-regulatory capacity, breath may be guided toward constructive or destructive ends.

Energy may also manifest as spirit, and has a life of its own. The aura associated with people, places and things is a reflection of the character of the spirit/s attached or assigned thereto. As Spiritual Intelligence is associated with God, who is Spirit, spiritual intelligence is associated with people connected to God or indwelt by Spirit.

Views on Spirituality

Brown (2004) noted that there are many views on the meaning of spiritual and spirituality. These views can be organized into two categories: (a) subjective experiences and (b) personality or character description. "When used to designate certain subjective experiences, a person may describe as 'spiritual' an experience of ecstasy, awe, or transcendence" (p. 75). Another meaning refers to a worldview that includes God and a nonmaterial world to the extent of shaping one's personality and behavior.

Cavanagh et al (2003) stated that even though spirituality is generally identified with a religious tradition, some views of spirituality are secular or nonreligious. Cavanagh et al also claimed there are several *spiritualities*, everyone has spirituality, and spirituality is not generic: there are multiple meanings of the root word, spirit, from which spirituality is derived. One meaning of spirit is God: spirituality refers to a relationship with God, the Great Spirit.

A second meaning of spirit refers to the ability to transcend immediate circumstances and search for meaning in life, whether it includes belief in a transcendent reality or not. Spirituality is a fruit of the spirit: "our capacity to stand above our immediate circumstances and ask questions about the meaning of life and what will eventually become of us" (Cavanagh et al, 2003, p. 121). Cavanagh et al believed spirituality is the deliberate pursuit of a life of meaning. The pursuit involves a set of practices consistent with a worldview and is developed in a nurturing relationship.

McGrath (1999) grounded spirituality in the creation, Trinity, incarnation, redemption, resurrection and consummation, and thus explains Christian spirituality within the context of evangelical theology:

> To talk about the spirit is to discuss what gives life and animation to someone. Spirituality is thus about the life of faith – what drives and motivates it. It is about that which animates the life of believers and urges them on to deepen and perfect what has at present only begun. (McGrath, 1999, p. 2)

Fox (1991, 2000) perceived spirituality as a consequence of a common Creator. He saw God in everything and as indistinguishable from nature. Based on perceptions of the presence of Christ in all of creation and interconnectedness in all of nature, Fox saw a connection between personal salvation and salvation of the rest of creation. According to Fox, spirituality was lost at the Fall but is reclaimable.

Fox's sentiments resonated with Teilhard de Chardin (2001), who averred human beings are workers together with God and that the world is partly saved through human activities. Spirituality is perceived in terms of an evolving consciousness toward an Omega point, described as Christ.

Sin brought disorder and disturbed the harmony of creation. Adam's sin did not affect human beings alone. The whole of creation was affected (Romans 8:19-24), because there is interconnectedness in all of nature. The redemption of humanity therefore involves the redemption of the rest of creation. Thus the goal of spirituality is the reconciliation of all things to God (Col. 1:9-23).

Immortality of the human soul and our capacity for good and evil makes redemption viable; our ability to respond to the grace of God makes redemption possible. In order for redemption to take place the will of human beings must cohere with the Divine Will. Although the process of becoming spiritually intelligent is first initiated by the Father (John 6:44), it is by the exercise of volition that darkness is overcome.

Once the grace of God is accepted, the Spirit imparts spiritual life (John 6:63; 2 Cor. 3:6; Rom. 8:9-11). Having been born by the Spirit (Titus 3:5; 2 Cor. 5:17), we are able to see more clearly and live more fully. We become people of light as opposed to people of darkness.

According to Amman (1979), "the spiritual life is a supernatural life. . . . The word *spiritus* or *pneuma* refers to a divine power and therefore to the supernatural" (p. 17). Amman believed that the only authentic spirituality is one that is centered in Jesus. Webber (1999) saw Jesus as the basis for Christian spirituality and viewed Christians as having the mind of Christ.

Does this means everything a Christian does or says is right? Of course not! The mind of Christ needs to be developed in us. We need to develop our spiritual intelligence. Accordingly, Peter exhorted believers to grow in grace and knowledge (2 Peter 3:18). Timothy advocated study and observance of the truth (2 Timothy 2:15). Paul admonished submission to the influence of the Spirit (Gal. 5:22, 23). Elsewhere in Scripture a correlation is made between being blessed with godliness or being hungry and thirsty for righteousness (Psalm 1; Matt. 5:6).

Peck (1993) perceived a universal spirituality, responsible for moral goodness, not necessarily associated with organized religion. According to Peck, there is an unseen order to which people commit, some consciously, others unconsciously. This is demonstrated in the passion with which some people – whether atheists or not – pursue things such as truth and social justice, believed to be part of an unseen order.

Rollins (2004) stated that since God is responsible for making human beings, the conduct of human beings is governed by the Law of God's nature. The operating principles and guidelines of God's Law were included in the creation of human beings. Rollins, however, intimated dysfunction but did not mention how dysfunction came about.

Dysfunction implies the need for recovery or salvation. Rollins believed salvation takes place "when the life of God becomes an inner resident in man joining together with him in Spirit" (p. 19). Spirituality therefore meant a relationship with God.

Wakefield (1983) expressed the view that "Spirituality comprises those attitudes, values, beliefs and practices that animates people's lives and helps them to reach out toward supersensible realities" (p. 549). Thurston (2005) believed spirituality was a life of spiritual power based on a relationship initiated by a source outside human beings:

> Something, indeed, someone from outside the finite and human initiates a relationship with individuals by means of a manifestation of power. The response is a life turned toward that power; how that response is lived out is spirituality. (p. 58)

Thurston noted early Christians had a multidimensional world-view. Christians recorded spiritual experiences as real, as influencing the will, emotions and ethics of people, and as affecting the community in general:

> Insofar as it has an "affective" quality, spirituality encompasses not only the will that decides to respond, but also the emotions. Insofar as it seeks to integrate faith and action, spirituality has an ethical component. Insofar as it is done in the company of others, it is communal. (Thurston, 2005, p. 58)

Thurston averred early Christians lived in a world of matter and spirit, and believed that the spirit world exerted influence on the material world. This view resonated with Blamires (1963).

Blamires posited: the universe is sustained by God's power and love; there is a spiritual and natural order; the physical order is dependent on the spiritual.

According to Butler (1966), the claim of the great mystics regarding spirituality was consistently expressed in the following ways: conscious direct contact of the soul with transcendental reality, direct and objective intellectual intuition of transcendental reality, conscious relation with the absolute, and the soul's possible union in this life with absolute reality.

Lampe (1977) attributed spirituality to the Spirit of God: "The Spirit of God is God disclosing himself as Spirit, that is to say, God creating and giving life to the spirit of man, inspiring man, renewing him, and making him whole (p. 61).

Oden (2001) asserted that the presence and power of the Holy Spirit in the lives of individuals and communities is integral to spiritual life.

Pargament (2006) saw spirituality as a search for the sacred involving discovery, conservation and transformation. Discovery begins in childhood and is the result of several factors. Conservational functions are the means for sustaining the relationship with God over time; transformation refers "to a fundamental change in the place of the sacred . . . the individual experiences a shift from self-centered strivings to God-centered strivings" (p.18). He saw transformation as having taken place at two levels: the primary and secondary. Primary spiritual transformation speaks of fundamental changes in character or goals that motivate the individual; secondary spiritual transformation has to do with the paths people take to attain goals.

Fowler (1981) explained spirituality in terms of an evolving faith, developed in six stages. He did caveat, however, that development may be stopped at any time. He listed these stages as:

1. Intuitive – projective (2-7 years of age): awareness of God.

2. Mythic – literal (7-12 years of age): internalization of family's perspective on God and morality.

3. Synthetic – conventional (adolescence onward): uncritical acceptance of faith.

4. Individuative – reflective: one's beliefs are critically examined and reconstructed.

5. Conjunctive (midlife and beyond): disillusionment with belief system and openness to other religious perspectives

6. Universalizing (late life): sense of oneness with God; desire to pro-

mote justice and fellowship with others regardless of religious beliefs or affiliations.

According to Fowler, there are many faith-identity relationships wherein claims are made in an infinite source and center of value and power, the main groups being polytheistic, henotheistic and radical monotheistic. Polytheistic faith is a diffused pattern of faith and identity, a type of faith-identity relationship in which there are many minor centers of value and power. Henotheistic faith is loyalty to a god which turns out to be something/someone inappropriate or not of ultimate concern.

> Radical monotheism is a type of faith-identity relation in which a person or group focuses its supreme trust and loyalty in a transcendent center of value and power, that is neither a conscious extension of personal or group ego nor a finite cause or institution. Rather, this type of monotheism implies loyalty to the principle of being and to the source and center of all value and power. (Fowler, 1981, p. 23)

Fowler noted a pull toward polytheism and henotheism, and that faith can be misplaced leading to idolatry. He expressed the view that real idolatry is the committing of ourselves to finite sources of value and power for confirmation of worth and meaning, and as guarantors of quality survival. Fowler's view on spirituality implies commitment to only one God.

Cary (2006) defined spirituality as matters pertaining to the spirit or outside the experience of one's limited five senses; spirituality is a path or goal in achieving understanding or improving relationship with the sacred. He expressed the view that spirituality may be associated with religion or may be self-directed.

Brown (2004) perceived spirituality as God's presence mediated in man's spiritual capacity, namely the soul and spirit. Brown stated there are at least two meanings of soul:

> (1) the concept of the spiritual part of the person that, though it is not material, is nevertheless credited with faculties such as think-

ing, willing, and feeling, and is the source of moral responsibility; and (2) the property of having deep interpersonal feelings and subjective experiences. (Brown 2004, p. 59)

In addition to a physical capacity, human beings have a spiritual capacity, comprised of a soul and spirit. The spiritual was designed to exert influence over the physical. According to Brown, although corrupted by sin, the soul and spirit are the focus of human religiousness and spirituality, the source of moral agency and the target of human redemption. Brown believed a unique relationship with God and an immaterial soul give dignity, value, meaning and purpose, and elevate human beings above all other earthly forms of creation.

The Spiritual in Various Disciplines

Spirituality as a concept is recognized in various professions and academic disciplines. Spirituality is recognized in disciplines such as leadership (Blackaby & Blackaby 2001; Houston & Sokolow, 2006; Sanders, 1986), counseling (Fukuyama & Sevig, 1999; Moodley & West, 2005), psychotherapy (Miller, 2002; Peck, 1978, 1993; Schreurs, 2002; Sperry, 2001), education (Houston, Blankstein, & Cole, 2007; Miller, Karsten, & Denton, 2005; Shields, Edwards, & Sayani, 2005; Wright, 2001), social work (Derezotes, 2006), medicine (Hamilton, 2008; Lloyd-Jones, 1971), and politics (Hodges, 1992; McLaughlin, 1994; Silk, 1989; Spretnak, 1986).

What accounts for this recognition and interest? Such wide-ranging recognition and interest not only validate spirituality as an important aspect of human life, but also underscore the need for spiritual intelligence.

The Spiritual in Various Aspects of Culture

From the dawn of human history, supernatural phenomena have been evident in the world and have found expression in practically every aspect of human life and culture. Data in support of the supernatural are abundant. Supernatural phenomena have found expression in art (Bazin, 1962; Fraser, 1962; Hay, 2007; Promey, 2003; Visona, 2005; Whitmore, 1971), science

(Clark, 1966; Gasparin, 1857; Hood, 2008), philosophy (Hugel, 1974; Kainz, 2006), movies (Badley, 1995; Clark, 2003; Gilmore, 1998), music (Busoni, 1957; Jones, 1963; Yung, Watson, & Rawski, 1996), sex (Cohen, 1999; Walker, 1970), plays (Dreiser, 2009; Kaye, 1990; Lucy, 1972), poetry (Backman, 2001; Dutt, 1977), literature (Buxton, 1980; Canning, 1988; Cosette, 1987; George, 2001), psychology and psychiatry (Korem, 1988; Werning, 1975), medicine (Hamilton, 2008; Lloyd-Jones, 1971), paranormal people (Bright, 1986; Chambers, 1998; Ginsberg, 1979; Holroyd, 1976), religion (Jacobs, 2005; Johnson, 2005; McIntosh, 2006; Wentroble, 2009), the occult (de Lisser, 2007; Gay, 1989; Maxwell-Stuart, 1998; Myers, 2008), sickness and tragedy (Klotsche, 2003; Maupassant, 1997), healing and health (Ghezzi, 1996; Pfeiffer, 2002), healing (Bentley, 2008; Lewis, 2001), personal experiences (Dickinson, 1920; Jennings, 2005), experiences of people in the city as well as in the country (Baker, 1983; Cunniff, 1985; de Los Santos, 2004; McKissack, 1992; Stevens, 2002; Wilson, 1975), nations (Booker, 2009; Cohen, 1979; Hardin, 1995; Sinner, 2003), and is the subject of on-going investigation (Baddiel & Blezard 1999; Kan, 1996; Lehman & Myers, 1997; Phillips, 1972; Whale, 2008). Scientist, researcher and member of the well-respected Society for Psychical Research in Britain, Deane (2003) narrated a number of reported cases of people claiming to have had sexual encounters with demons.

The Spiritual in Religion

One of the chief ways in which belief in the spiritual and supernatural is supported is through religion. "Man is incurably religious. The only difference is what they are religious about" (Collins, 2000, p. 76). According to Leslie (1965), "The persistent biblical image of man responding to God's call is more than an introjected parental admonition; it is also man reaching out to realize the full potential for which he was created" (p. 13).

> We are incomplete without God. If we leave Him out of our lives, we have an empty place in our souls, a yearning deep inside us that only God can satisfy. No matter how hard we try, if we ignore God

that hollow place stays with us, and our search for lasting peace and happiness will be futile. (Graham, 2006, p. 24)

Wherever human beings may be found, regardless of social status, there are serious attempts at worship by people seeking to fill an apparent spiritual need. Since volition is an integral part of the human framework and people are informed differently, this need may be acted out appropriately or inappropriately: "Choices either express a false worldview and thus contribute to a disordered broken world or express God's truth and help build a world that reflects God's created order" (Colson & Pearcey, 1999).

In most cultures, freedom of choice in the matter of religion is recognized as a human right and has been a long-standing tradition from time immemorial. "In every culture, since the beginning of recorded time, human beings have communicated directly with their God or gods, and with spirits evil and benign" (Zohar & Marshall, 2000, p. 92).

Because of its significant and generally positive role in impacting human behavior and way of life, religion is widely endorsed. Even atheists see value in religion (Sheiman, 2009). In an article published by Times, January 2012, award-winning writer and self-proclaimed atheist, Matthew Parris, based on research in Africa, concluded that God and missionaries are the solution to Africa's biggest problem. (See full article in appendix).

The Spiritual in the Occult

Religion is not the only means through which the supernatural is recognized and promoted. Occult phenomena are significant aspects of the supernatural, and flourishes throughout the world. "The Black Mass is said today in Paris and in London, and Satanism has its faithful followers" (Miller, 1933, p. 25).

The art of witchcraft is practiced in every part of the globe. Although names and systems differ, the practice is the same. In Africa, there is the witch doctor; in Tibet, the red-hooded monks; in Malaysia, the Pawang and Poyang; in China, idol priests and geomancers with their system of Fungshui; in East Siberia, the Shamans; in Alaska, the Angekok; in America, tribal or magic priests; and in Europe, practitioners of divination (Koch, 1972). In the Caribbean, witchcraft is practiced under names such as Santeria, obeah and voodoo.

> Occultic groups range from those who advocate and practice the black magic arts to those who profess the value of occultic astrology and esoteric occultism, finally to the more bizarre and aberrant groups involved in devil worship and Satanism (Marrs, 1996, p. 4).

There is recognition of spiritual power and 'intelligence' associated with the occult or with the devil. Based on personal interviews with care-seekers, Koch has supplied the following narratives as cases in point:

Refugee Couple

> A refugee couple came to a pastor to apply for marriage. On departing the girl suddenly grasped the clergyman's hand and said, "Oh, pastor, how interesting!" She proceeded, unsolicited, to read his palm. As the pastor assured me later, all her comments about his past were accurate, and all her predictions were fulfilled within the course of subsequent years. (Koch, 1972, p. 90)

Farmer

> A robbed farmer sought help from a shepherd who had a flourishing "trade" as conjurer, clairvoyant and diviner. He was not disappointed: the shepherd was able to give valid information about the thief. (Koch, 1972, pp. 90, 91)

Young woman

> A young woman came during an evangelistic campaign to have an interview. She complained of spiritual troubles and of ennui. She also had fits, which were not, according to the doctor, of an epileptic nature. He called them attacks of anxiety. Since medical treatment brought no relief from her suffering, she desired pastoral advice. An anamnesis of occult relations revealed an unusual background. Her great grandfather had been a conjurer. . . . Worthy of

special note from the pastoral angle is the fact that this young woman turned to Christ and was thereupon freed from attacks for several months. (Koch, 1972, pp. 134-135)

Young man

A young man of Christian disposition lost his wife. After one and a half years he married again. With the second wife he enjoyed a successful and happy marriage, except that from the time of this second wedding he was plagued at night by spook apparitions. His first wife, now dead, would appear to him in the night in a waking state and try to approach him sexually. He found this apparition a great burden, and came for pastoral help. (Koch, 1972, p. 163)

In the book, *The World's Greatest Psychics and Mystics*, Nicholas (1986) supplied the following narratives as evidence in support for the existence of paranormal phenomena:

Jeane Dixon

The violence which cut down three brothers of the Kennedy family was foreseen by Jeane Dixon, America's famous modern seer. The beautiful dark-haired prophetess predicted the assassination of two of them and the accident that nearly killed the third. (Nicholas, 1986, p. 68)

John Dee

John Dee was a scholar, highly revered for his work on mathematics and navigation, but besides being a man of science he also accepted the existence of a sixth sense which could emerge spontaneously in dreams, visions, or intuitions. (Nicholas, 1986, p. 79)

The Fox Sisters

Both girls began to give séances and to produce new phenomena. People felt themselves being touched by spirit hands, objects moved of their own volition, musical instruments played though no one went near them. (Nicholas, 1986, p. 83)

Pearl Curran

Pearl Curran was regarded as nothing more exciting than a quiet, plain-living housewife by her friends and neighbors in St. Louis, Missouri. . . Then, one fateful evening in July 1913, she somewhat reluctantly went to a séance. What happened there turned her into a literary phenomenon, a prolific writer of novels, poetry and plays, a creator of stories told in perfect Elizabethan English and of manuscripts rich in detail of places entirely foreign to her experience. (Nicholas, 1986, p. 107)

Uri Geller

A fork lying on a table bent without him even touching it, another contorted till it broke in half. Broken watches scattered in front of him began to tick but the hands inside a perfectly good watch suddenly curled up against the glass face. (Nicholas, 1986, p. 107)

Belief in the supernatural is not new. "Both European colonists and native Americans believed in the reality and authority of the supernatural, and their stories reflect these beliefs" (George, 2001, p. 21). This view resonated with Fuller. According to Fuller (2001):

Divination, fortune-telling, astrology, witchcraft, and even folk medicine competed with then Christian churches as sources of the colonists' understanding of the supernatural powers that affected their destiny. (p. 14).

Fuller noted that interest in magic and the occult was not the purview of any particular class but was equally prevalent among all classes of people. Motivation for involvement in the occult varied:

Different individuals and groups involved in the occult have widely differing impulses behind them. Some people from a jaded experience of life, are in it for kicks; some are seriously pursuing higher psychic ends; some have an almost antiquarian interest in the revival of pagan nature worship; some are openly selling their souls to the devil; and others demonstrate a weird amalgam of semi-beliefs and practices, involving themselves in the esoteric world in a totally eccentric way. (Guinness, 1973, pp. 279-280)

Belief in the supernatural include the religious as well as the nonreligious, reflected in dogmas and the various practices through which adherents seek to harness supernatural powers on their own behalf or on behalf of others. Spiritual powers may be harnessed to produce good or evil. It is indeed possible for afflictions, sicknesses and diseases and healing to have spiritual roots. Examples of spiritual-related illnesses and healing are recorded in a variety of sources, including Scripture. See Table 1.

Spiritual Intelligence: A Christian Perspective

SPIRITUAL-RELATED ILLNESSES AND HEALING	SCRIPTURE
A demon-possessed man who was blind and mute was brought to Jesus, and he healed him, so that the mute man spoke and saw.	Matt. 12:22 NASB
And he was casting out a demon, and it was mute; when the demon had gone out, the mute man spoke; and the crowds were amazed.	Luke 11:14 NASB
And there was a woman who for eighteen years had had a sickness caused by a spirit; and she was bent double, and could not straighten up at all...And he laid His hands on her; and immediately she was made erect again and began glorifying God.	Luke 13:11-13 NASB
When they came to the crowd, a man approached Jesus and knelt before him. 'Lord, have mercy on my son,' he said. 'He has seizures and is suffering greatly. He often falls into the fire or into the water. I brought him to your disciples, but they could not heal him.'... Jesus rebuked the demon, and it came out of the boy, and he was healed from that moment.	Matt. 17:14-18 (NIV)
Some men brought to him a paralytic, lying on a mat. When Jesus saw their faith, he said to the paralytic, 'Take heart, son; your sins are forgiven.' . . . Then he said to the paralytic, 'Get up take your mat and go home.' And the man got up and went home.	Matt. 9:2-7 NIV-UK
When he arrived at the other side in the region of the Gadarenes, two demon-possessed men coming from the tombs met him. They were so violent that no one could pass that way. . . . The demons begged Jesus, 'If you drive us out, send us into the herd of pigs.' He said to them, 'Go!' So they came out and went into the pigs, and the whole herd rushed down the steep bank into the lake and died in the water.	Matt. 8:28-31 NIV-UK

Table 1: *Spiritual-Related Illnesses & Healing in Scripture*

In her profession as medical doctor, Brown (1992) encountered a number of cases of occult phenomena manifesting in the physical and mental states of patients. These discoveries resonated with Koch (1972). Koch, a psychiatrist and theologian, noted that demonic influences may be the cause of conditions such as depressions, schizophrenia, psychopathology and other mental illnesses. He discerned the breaking up of the personality structure of patients due to their involvement with the occult, and made a distinction between psychiatric disease-patterns and psychological disturbances due to demonic influences. Peck (1993) expressed the view that "Conditions like schizophrenia are not just somatic disorders: they are also psycho-spiritual-socio-somatic disorders" (p. 58).

The Spiritual in Healing

Numerous case studies involving people, who have experienced healing via spiritual intervention, attest to the veracity of the spiritual in healing. Sherman (1972), Jorgensen (1994), Prather (1996), Lewis (2001), Harline (2003), Stone and Marszalek (2003), Baker and Baker (2007), Bentley (2008), and Roth and Joseph (2009) reported several cases of spiritual interventions resulting in physical, spiritual, emotional and moral healing.

> When certain physical and mental conditions are established, through prayer, meditation, or rituals, employed by the healer and patient acting in concert or by the healer alone, miraculous healings frequently take place. Often an ill person suddenly will become conscious of a convulsive reaction in the affected part of his body, of a hot sensation, an electric, tingling vibration, or a shriveling-up feeling, and notice that a change has occurred. A growth may disappear; a crippled arm or leg may straighten out; or a heart, lung, stomach, or other organic condition may heal. (Sherman, 1972, p. 123)

Although unexplainable by medical science, because of the overwhelming number of indisputable cases, medical science is forced to accept healing miracles (Sherman, 1972).

Prayer is the chief means of healing, and is supported in Scripture (James 5:13-18). The use of prayer as an instrument of healing is also supported by secular research. In 1988, the San Francisco General Hospital, for instance, published its findings of a study on the effect of prayer on sickness, namely on heart diseased patients. The study involved 393 patients, admitted to the coronary care unit. Over several months, a group of evangelical Christians prayed for persons randomly chosen from the list. Neither the doctors, nor the nurses, nor the patients knew who would be prayed for.

The study revealed that patients prayed for were significantly less likely to require antibiotics, to develop pulmonary edema and to require insertion of a tube in the throat to assist breathing. The men and women whose medical care were supplemented with prayer needed fewer drugs, spent less time on the ventilator and fared better overall than those who were not prayed for. Experiments conducted in other institutions showed that prayer positively affects high blood pressure, wounds, attacks, headaches and anxiety. (www. 1stholistic.com/prayer/holisticprayer_proof. htm).

Based on biblical literature, illness and dysfunction are not part of God's design. Dysfunction in creation became part of human experience as a result of the Fall, and, subsequently, healing became part of the redemptive work of God. Biblical literature indicates the following:

- Health was natural and eternal before the Fall (Gen.1:26-31; 2:17).

- Both death and sickness originated with sin (Rom. 5:12-21; Job 2:6-7; Luke 13:16; John 10:10; Acts 10:38; 1 John. 3:8).

- The first recorded bodily affliction came through wrong-doing (Gen. 20:1-18).

- Prophecy and the promise of redemption included healing (Gen. 3:15; Isa. 53:5; Matt. 8:16-17; 1 Pet. 2:24).

- The first recorded healing came through the prayer of a prophet (Gen. 20:7, 17).

- Spiritual means to heal were used in the wilderness by Israel (Exod.

15:26; Num. 11:1-3; 12:13-26; 21:1-9; John 3:14)

- Spiritual means to heal were promised and commanded (Exod. 15:26; Ps. 91; Isa. 58; Matt. 8:17; 13:15; James 5:14-16; 1 Pet. 2:24).

Philosophers and epistemologists are in agreement that concrete experience is a basis for knowledge. Healing miracles and other spiritual experiences, therefore, support the concept of spiritual intelligence.

Summary

Many views on spirituality, intelligence and spiritual intelligence support a theory of spiritual intelligence. There are religious and nonreligious views. Maslow (1976) and others have found that there are various levels of consciousness; the highest level is associated with religious awareness, leading to greater self-actualization and peak experiences. Theological and other sources attribute consciousness to the various dimensions of personhood, namely our body, soul and spirit. Scientists have discovered a God-spot or God-spots in the brain, responsive to spiritual experience. Some neuroscientists attribute spiritual experience to an immaterial soul or spirit triggering neurological activity. Other scientists proffer an explanation in neurology alone. Research by Gallup and Proctor (1982) and other researchers, who studied death and near-death experiences, support the existence of an immaterial soul or spirit and of life after death. Research supporting the existence of an immortal soul and spirit and of life after death, discovery of various levels of consciousness, the highest level associated with peak experiences and discovery of "God spots" in the brain make spiritual intelligence plausible.

Several intelligence paradigms including cultural, social, and emotional intelligence support theories of multiple intelligences, thereby opening the door for spiritual intelligence to be included in the mix. Spiritual experiences, noted in cultures everywhere, make spiritual intelligence a necessary and plausible intelligence paradigm. A growing recognition of spirituality in various disciplines, such as health, business and education, supports the concept of spiritual intelligence. In science, there is evidence of the existence of a nonmaterial reality; for example, quantum physics and the theory of relativity. Existence of a nonmaterial reality makes the concept of spiritual intelligence plausible. The spiritual in all of nature is universally accepted as an inherent feature of nature's design and is supported by a dualistic worldview, deeply imbedded in philosophy and theology. Evidence of spiritual phenomena such as spiritual-related sicknesses and spiritual healing also support the concept of spiritual intelligence. Supernatural phenomena in practically every aspect of human life and culture, including occult phenomena, experienced across age groups and professions, make the theory of spiritual intelligence plausible. Besides use of the five senses, there are other ways of knowing, such as intuition, telepathy, clairvoyance, precognition, prophesy and revelation. Other ways of knowing, besides the five senses, also make the concept of spiritual intelligence plausible. Various views on spirituality support the concept of spiritual intelligence. In fact, religion on the whole supports the concept of spiritual intelligence, religion being a spiritual affair.

In this chapter, several sources of authority support the concept of spiritual intelligence. In addition to traits of spiritual intelligence, the next chapter will present and discuss theories of spiritual intelligence, developed by this writer.

CHAPTER 4
THEORIES OF
SPIRITUAL INTELLIGENCE

The emphasis of this chapter will be on theories of spiritual intelligence. Intelligence needs to be viewed in proper context and in light of purpose. Theories to be postulated are based on the notion that there is an external spiritual reality corresponding to an internal spiritual capacity, and on the assumption that human beings possess an immaterial soul or spirit capable of spiritual life and intelligence. Others have made the case that the brain is hardwired for spiritual experiences.

It is apparent that human beings are equipped to function effectively at the outer level via physical abilities and at the inner level via psychological and spiritual abilities, corresponding to these realities.

The proposition is that human beings are comprised of both a physical and spiritual dimension. Each dimension is designed with purpose. Whatever the purpose, fulfillment is contingent on the presence of life in each area of capacity or dimension; and where life is present, there must be intelligence capable of sustaining and developing that life.

There must be life in a capacity area for intelligence to manifest; and where intelligence is present, intelligence must be developed. Development in a given capacity is not obtained in the abstract or in a vacuum. Development takes place through interaction with the real world, is mediated by purpose and is contingent on a number of factors, namely the nurturing environment.

Spiritual Intelligence: A Christian Perspective

Spiritual intelligence implies a worthy spiritual goal or purpose, the ability to achieve it, and objective means of knowing whether the goal or purpose is being realized, hence the importance of spiritual traits.

Spiritual Traits

Spiritual traits identified by Vaughn (2002) include: self-awareness, awareness of transcendence, emotional maturity, moral maturity, spiritual maturity and mental clarity. Hart (1998) included feelings of connection, openness and energy. Zohar and Marshall (2004) listed humility, holism, a sense of vocation, the ability to ask ultimate questions about the meaning of life, and the positive use of adversity.

The biblical perspective may be summarized as follows:

♦ *Spiritual attitude.* A godly mindset; a predisposition or tendency to reflect theologically, and to worship.

♦ *Spiritual receptivity.* Openness to spiritual truths; receptive to revelation, inspiration and illumination.

♦ *Spiritual perceptivity.* The ability to discern the presence of the spiritual, such as demons, angels, God, spiritual truths, and being able to find answers to difficult or perplexing spiritual problems.

♦ *Spiritual striving.* Striving toward holiness; pursuit of moral excellence.

♦ *Spiritual knowledge.* Knowledge of spiritual light and of sacred writings, such as the Holy Scriptures.

♦ *Spiritual discernment.* The ability to discern right from wrong and truth from error; the ability to discern hidden meanings and to interpret facts.

♦ *Spiritual wisdom.* The ability to apply knowledge or find practical solutions to problems; strong decision-making skills.

♦ *Spiritual insight.* The ability to grasp spiritual truths, see connections and make applications.

♦ *Spiritual kinship.* The ability and desire to forge and maintain spiritual relationships such as a relationship with God and other members of God's spiritual family. A sense of interconnectedness and commitment to others.

♦ *Spiritual purpose.* A sense of being called to a higher or divine purpose.

♦ *Spiritual stewardship.* A sense of accountability to God and a desire to please God.

♦ *Spiritual gifts.* Supernatural or spiritual abilities divinely imparted. Spiritual faith. Trusting God; confidence in the will, way and Word of God.

♦ *Spiritual love.* A special inclination or desire to love God and others; a divine love for others, including love for one's enemies.

♦ *Spiritual humility.* An attitude of gratitude reflecting acknowledgement that all we are and have are due to the grace of God and are to be used in service to God. It is the surrendering of self to a higher cause.

♦ *Spiritual help.* A supernatural ability enabling one to serve God and others in various ways, such as exercising leadership and performing healing miracles. Spiritual help includes a special enablement to experience divine grace, guidance, deliverance, empowerment and miracles.

Theories of spiritual intelligence are informed by, among other things, spiritual traits and the ways in which these traits are understood or defined. Spiritual traits and their definitions are especially useful in light of the fact that concepts described by others do not necessarily carry the same meaning as biblical concepts and are not necessarily supported by the same assumptions.

Based on study and reflection on the related literature, three theories of spiritual intelligence have evolved – a theological model, a relational model and a psychological model.

Theological Model Theory of Spiritual Intelligence

The Theological Model Theory of Spiritual Intelligence is based on the view that there are multiple levels of consciousness. (See Figure 1).

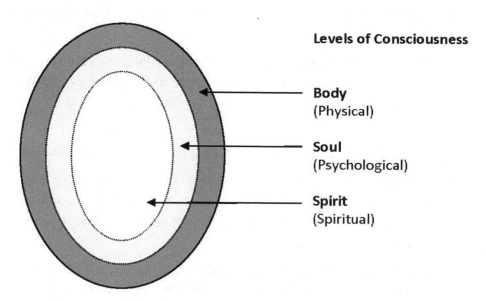

Figure 1: *Theological Model Theory of Spiritual Intelligence*

According to biblical literature, physicality is just one dimension of personhood: human beings possess a body, soul and spirit (1 Thess. 5:23; Luke 1:47; 2 Cor. 7:1), and as such are capable of functioning at three fundamental levels of consciousness. Albeit, consciousness in a given capacity implies the potential for intelligence, not the presence of intelligence:

> Consciousness of a mental state includes an awareness of it, but a special kind of awareness seems required if the awareness is to count as an instance of conscious awareness. (Kim, 1998, p. 167).

The theory of multiple levels of consciousness is supported by neuroscientists, such as Haisch (2006), and by transpersonal psychologists, such as Maslow (1964, 1976), Jung (1969), and Wilber (2000). Wilber averred there are four levels of consciousness (the consciousness of the body, mind, soul and spirit), and that they are hierarchical in structure: the higher states are associated with psychic and metaphysical powers.

Assuming there is purpose to human design, consciousness needs to be accompanied by intelligence, as consciousness alone is not sufficient to enable the fulfillment of purpose. Spiritual consciousness implies the potential for spiritual intelligence but does not imply the presence of spiritual intelligence.

The Theological Model Theory of Spiritual Intelligence resonates with the theory of multiple levels of consciousness associated with human beings, with a number of organisms, and with man-made systems.

> Various organisms and man-made systems have sensory receptors or scanners through which they acquire information about their environment, process and store the information in various ways, and use it to guide their behavior. (Kim, 1998, p. 167)

Besides the five senses associated with physicality, human beings have sensor receptors associated with spirituality. At the core, humans are spirit beings. The spirit animates both body and soul. The soul is the essence of self – the intrinsic self, affected by the will, emotions and intellect.

According to Jacobi (1973), Jung referred to the soul as an inner personality, capable of behavior reflective of inner psychic processes, and as having the same autonomy as that which characterizes the outer personality. Nee (1968) believed the spirit is originally the highest part of humanity, to which the body and soul are to be subjected.

There is general agreement that human beings have the capacity to function effectively at the physical, emotional and intellectual levels. The ability to function effectively at these levels may be labeled natural intelligence. Natural intelligence is supported by physical, emotional and cognitive sensory receptors imbedded in the physical framework of the flesh, enabling competencies relative to development at the natural level. The ability to function effectively at the spiritual level is spiritual intelligence, supported by spiritual senses (Heb. 5:14), associated with the Spirit, enabling competencies relative to spiritual development.

> As power of some kind belongs to every substance, the power which belongs to spirit, to the substance self is that of thought, feeling, and volition. . . . We know ourselves only as thus thinking, feeling and willing, and we therefore are sure that these powers or faculties are the essential attributes of a spirit, and must belong to every spirit. (Hodge, 1982, p. 378)

Since there is intelligence associated with one's natural capacity, there must be intelligence associated with one's spiritual capacity also, for intelligence corresponds with the nature of being and with the nature of reality. "The assessment of each ability depends on an assumption of a certain reality; the intelligence in question corresponds to that reality" (Langer, 1997, p.101). Natural intelligence corresponds to natural reality. Spiritual intelligence corresponds to spiritual reality. Spiritual intelligence is to the soul and spirit what natural intelligence is to the mind and body (Matt. 6:22-23; Luke 11:34-36).

Since God is the source of spiritual life and intelligence, spiritual competencies may be realized only when human spirits are connected to the Divine Spirit. In other words, spiritual life and intelligence stem from a personal relationship with God: The greater or deeper the relationship, the greater the manifestation of spiritual life and intelligence.

Relational Model Theory of Spiritual Intelligence
The Relational Model Theory of Spiritual Intelligence is based on the view that human beings are multidimensional and relational creatures. Human beings have a physical dimension that needs to process things physically, an intellectual dimension that needs to process things cognitively, a psychological dimension that needs to process things emotionally and intuitively, and a spiritual dimension that needs to process things spiritually.

Dimension assumes the capacity for intelligence but not the actual possession of intelligence. Capacity does not imply health or actual possession of intelligence. The possession of a brain, for example, does not mean a person is intellectually able or intelligent, nor does the possession of emotions necessarily make anyone emotionally intelligent. For a number of reasons, including brain damage, it is possible for a person to experience health and function effectively in one or more areas while experiencing ill health and dysfunction in others.

Intelligence in one area does not imply intelligence in all areas. Despite a symbiotic relationship, intelligence in each capacity or dimension needs to be acquired and developed.

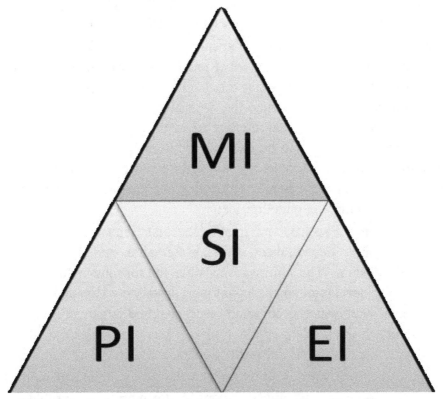

Figure 2: *Relational Model Theory of Spiritual Intelligence*

Spiritual Intelligence: A Christian Perspective

Based on the way the human system is designed, human beings have the capacity to function and relate at several levels: at the physical, emotional, mental, and spiritual levels. Each level requires intelligence or special skills relevant to a basic developmental need, and is interconnected. The relationship network is not only external but also internal.

The most obvious is physical. Physical relationships are contingent on the ability of human beings to interact with different aspects of their physical selves, with other selves and with their physical environment. There is intelligence associated with physicality enabling physical movement and skills, as demonstrated in athletes, for example. Relating appropriately with one's body and with the physical environment necessitates physical skills, hence the need for physical intelligence (PI).

Support for physical intelligence is found in Gardner's (1983, 1993) schema of intelligences, which includes bodily-kinesthetic intelligence.

Relating appropriately to one's emotions and developing emotional skills, speak to the need for emotional intelligence (EI). Emotional intelligence is the ability responsible for intrapersonal and interpersonal relationships (Goleman, 1995). Goleman, the originator of the theory of emotional intelligence, defined emotional intelligence as the ability to understand self, to relate well with others, to be in touch with one's emotions and those of others, to feel for other people, and to exercise self-control. Being an integral part of consciousness, human processing and interactions, emotions imply the need for emotional intelligence.

Human beings also have a mental/intellectual faculty. This answers the need for cognitive development, and the formation and development of mental relationships. The ability responsible for forming mental relationships and for developing one's cognitive capacity is Mental Intelligence (MI). Mental intelligence is commonly accepted and is generally described as the ability to think, plan, create, translate ideas into reality, and to find and solve problems (Morris & Maisto, 2005; Gardner, 1993).

There is also a spiritual dimension to humanity linked to moral and spiritual development. The ability responsible for moral and spiritual development is Spiritual Intelligence (SI). Spirituality is at the core of personhood and is critical to overall development of human beings: "Their internal faculty of knowing was made by God to correspond to the world and its form which He made and which surrounds them" (Schaeffer & Koop, 1979, p. 135).

The Theory of Spiritual Intelligence was originated by Zohar (1997). Other writers, such as Woolman (2001), Bowell (2005) and Sha (2008), proffered similar theories with various shades of meaning.

Spiritual intelligence is a divine or supernatural ability to appreciate, receive, discern, understand and apply spiritual knowledge; and the ability to use spiritual means to identify and solve spiritual and other problems. The main purpose of spiritual intelligence is moral and spiritual development. Like mental intelligence and emotional intelligence, spiritual intelligence implies the capacity to choose between alternatives aimed at accomplishing a particular end or purpose.

Developmental psychologist and author, Howard Gardner, has been the chief advocate for multiple intelligences. Although Gardner (1983, 1993, 1999) did not support a spiritual intelligence per say, he conceded an existential intelligence: the ability to address the big questions about existence.

Biblical literature does not use the words "spiritual intelligence" but spiritual intelligence is implied throughout. The Scriptures, however, do speak of spiritual wisdom, direction, knowledge, discernment, illumination and power, and of the possession of human beings of a spiritual capacity.

Human beings may be likened to a computer, whose central processing unit (the brain of the computer) is designed to function with multiple programs. Irrespective of how well-built the central processing unit, it cannot function without computer programs. Computer programs are the software that runs the computer. The central processing unit is the hardware. This allows for smooth interface with the software. A fully functional computer allows for interaction between hardware and software.

There must be compatibility between the hardware and the software for the computer to function effectively or at all. In the human system, intelligence may be likened to software corresponding to various aspects of the hardware (the brain). For example, natural intelligence is the software corresponding to the natural or physical dimension of the hardware; spiritual intelligence is the software corresponding to the spiritual dimension of the hardware. Functionality is dependent on external stimulus and a source of energy. In the case of the spiritual, in order for spiritual life and intelligence to manifest, the human spirit needs to connect with the Divine Spirit.

> Whereas the ordinary man is ruled and governed by the exigencies of his superficial ego, at the deep root of the mystics being, at his center, there is a conscious direct contact with Transcendental Reality. This center or ground of being is the fount and unifying source of all the lower psychological functions, not another self, but the essential ego – the fundamental transcendent self – where man is not himself and most open to God. (Tart, 1976, pp. 399, 400)

Intelligence in each area of human capacity is crucial. Because spiritual intelligence grounds and gives meaning and value to the other intelligences, spiritual intelligence is extremely important. "Spiritual intelligence is the central and most fundamental of all the intelligences, because it becomes the source of guidance for the others." (Covey, 2004, p. 53)

Spiritual intelligence is a supernatural ability. It is the work of God activating and influencing human spiritual capacity to receive knowledge via divine revelation and perception, enabling application and faithful stewardship.

The concept of stewardship is consistent with the need for meaning and purpose, and with the theory of intelligent design. Being the Designer and Creator of the world and all that it contains, God uniquely placed human beings in a position of stewardship.

Based on the teachings of Christianity, love for God is the strongest motivation for faithful stewardship, and the greatest expression of spiritual intelligence (Matt. 6:33). "The essence of the spiritual life is charity. When his love of God is perfect man is perfect" (Tart, 1976, p. 401). Accordingly, God should be loved:

- with all one's heart – emotional dimension (EI)

- with all one's soul – spiritual dimension (SI)

- with all one's mind – cognitive dimension (MI)

- with all one's strength – physical dimension (PI)

Human beings were not only designed to relate to God in love, but were also designed to relate in love toward fellow human beings. Love is the best motivation for faithful stewardship. Consequently, human development is most assured in an environment of love, for love assures the proper use of intelligences. According to biblical literature, love is the "most excellent way."

> If I speak in the tongues of men and of angels, but have not love, I am only a resounding gong or a clanging cymbal. If I have the gift of prophecy and can fathom all mysteries and all knowledge, and if I have a faith that can move mountains, but have not love, I am nothing. If I give all I possess to the poor and surrender my body to the flames, but have not love, I gain nothing. Love is patient, love is kind. It does not envy, it does not boast, it is not proud. It is not rude, it is not self-seeking, it is not easily angered, it keeps no record of wrongs. Love does not delight in evil but rejoices with the truth. It always protects, always trusts, always hopes, always perseveres. Love never fails. (1 Cor. 13:1-8, NIV-UK)

Love for God is proven in obedience (Luke 6:46-49; John 8:3; Rom. 6:17-18). "The obedience we owe to God includes benevolence and love toward other people and careful stewardship of the world around us" (Bertrand, 2007, p. 82).

Stewardship involves appropriate use of our faculties, inclusive of spiritual, emotional, mental and physical intelligences. Although these intelligences bear a symbiotic relationship, intelligence in each capacity area is developed separately. Where development is delayed in a given capacity, growth is restricted in that area and may lead to underdevelopment in other areas as well, but not necessarily. Ways in which other capacity areas are

95

affected by delayed development in a given capacity are not easily predictable, as people react differently to various situations.

Unintelligence in a given capacity does not necessarily mean unintelligence in every area of human capacity. Although overall effectiveness may be compromised, it is possible to excel in one or more areas and not in others. People generally compensate for weakness in a given capacity by over-emphasis in areas of strength. Areas of weakness are usually denied or ignored.

In keeping with the Creator's design, the goal should be holistic development. Holistic development is achievable where there is balance – where every area of human capacity relates intelligently to its inner and outer worlds. Intelligent relationships are critical to achieving one's full potential, and to success generally.

Maslow's Motivational Theory

The Relational Model Theory of Spiritual Intelligence resonates with Maslow's Motivational Theory of a hierarchy of needs responsible for motivating human behavior. In a study of motivation and human personality, Maslow (1954) postulated that there are several levels of awareness and corresponding need. Accordingly, Maslow presented a hierarchical sequencing of needs based on perceptions of what humans are expected to need at given moments in time. Motivation is determined by the fulfillment of lower level (primary) needs, which must be met before higher level (secondary) needs are met; the meeting of needs at one level determines the next level of need to be met.

According to Maslow, human beings have five basic needs: the need for safety, the need for belonging, the need for self-esteem, and the need for self-actualization. Later, Maslow (1964, 1976) added self-transcendence as the last need to be fulfilled. (See Figure 3).

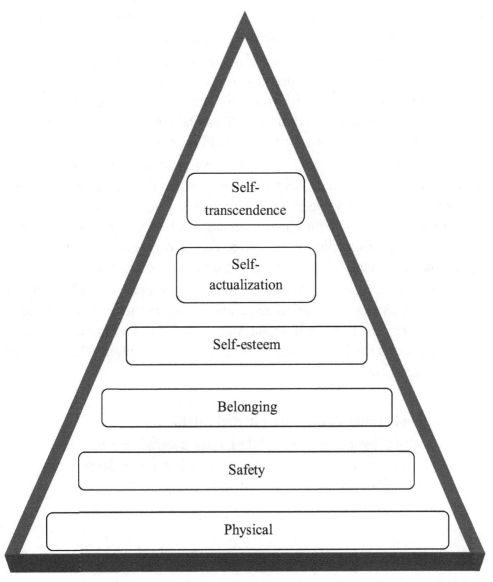

Figure 3: *Maslow's Motivational Theory*

Maslow described self-transcendence as an intense religious awareness, and saw a connection between self-transcendence and peak experiences. This led him to conclude that religious awareness leads to greater self-actualization.

Maslow's theory, however, does not hold true for everyone. There are differences in perception of primary needs and the sequencing of those needs. For example, many religious people see self-transcendence as the primary and most important need to be fulfilled and not the last as advanced by Maslow. Others see the need for love and affection as foundational.

There are also differences in perception regarding motivation and self-actualization. Motivation in Maslow's theory is based on fulfilling one's full potential for one's own sense of satisfaction and personal reward. From the perspective of persons living for the greater good, motivation is based on a sense of calling or on spiritual concerns. For such persons, it is impossible to become self-actualized without reference to God or some higher purpose.

Nonetheless, Maslow's Motivational Theory proposing a hierarchy of needs, his observation of the contribution of religion to peak experiences and to higher levels of self-actualization, and his recognition of self-transcendence as the highest human need to be met, supports the theory of spiritual intelligence.

Psychological Model Theory of Spiritual Intelligence

Neuroscientists, biologists and psychologists averred specific neural networks in the brain are responsible for various aspects of human cognitive processing, abilities and gifts. (See Figure 4).

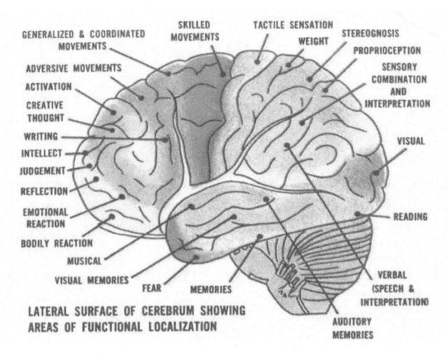

Figure 4: Psychological Model Theory of Spiritual Intelligence

Source: http://www.becindonesia.com/smg/wp-content/uploads/2009/07/
Brain-Functions.jpg

Belief that there is a correlation between neural networks in the brain and areas of special ability, led Gardner (1983) to theorize that there are multiple intelligences. Gardner's Theory of Multiple Intelligences resonated with others such as Kosslyn and Rosenberg (2004), who listed the intelligences as:

1. Linguistic intelligence – sensitivity to sounds, structure, meanings and functions of words and language; the ability to use language well, as relied on by writers, orators and lawyers.

2. Logical-mathematical intelligence – the capacity to discern logical or numerical patterns; the ability to handle long chains of reasoning and

99

to manipulate abstract symbols, as relied on by scientists, mathematicians and computer programmers.

3. Spatial intelligence – the ability to perceive the visual-spatial world accurately and to perform transformations on one's initial perceptions, as relied on by artists, architects and surgeons.

4. Bodily-kinesthetic intelligence – the ability to control one's body movements and to handle objects skillfully, as relied on by athletes, dancers, sculptors and surgeons.

5. Musical intelligence – the ability to compose and understand music; to produce and appreciate rhythm, pitch, and timbre; appreciation of the forms of musical expressiveness, as relied on by composers, performers, and audio engineers.

6. Interpersonal intelligence – the ability to discern and respond appropriately to the moods, temperaments, motivations, and desires of other people, as relied on by counselors, political leaders and teachers.

7. Intrapersonal intelligence – the ability to access one's own feelings and the ability to discriminate among one's emotions; knowledge of one's own strengths and weaknesses, as relied on by psychotherapists and religious leaders.

8. Naturalist intelligence – the ability to observe carefully, as used by forest rangers. (pp. 355, 356)

A theory of intelligence, according to Gardner (1999), should account for a wide range of skills, including the skills of a shaman, psychoanalyst, yogi and saint. Gardner's criteria for acknowledging the existence of intelligence are delimited by two prerequisites: (a) a set of problem-solving skills, and (b) the potential for finding or creating problems.

Assuming the existence of spiritual abilities and gifts, capable of meeting the above criteria, spiritual intelligence is supported. The Psychological Model Theory of Spiritual Intelligence is also supported by scientists and psychologists, such as Zohar and Marshall (2000), and Beauregard and O'Leary (2007), who discovered a God-spot in the brain associated with spiritual experiences. A God-spot in the brain associated with spiritual experiences has made a spiritual intelligence plausible.

Emmons (2000) expressed the view that spirituality may cohere with the theory of multiple intelligences in the following ways: (a) the capacity to transcend the physical and material, (b) the ability to experience heightened states of consciousness, (c) the ability to sanctify everyday experience, (d) the ability to use spiritual resources to solve problems, and (e) the capacity to be virtuous. Problem-solving ability is believed to be consistent with traditional conceptions of intelligence.

It is apparent that human beings are wired for multiple intelligences, spiritual intelligence included. However, being wired for multiple intelligences does not mean that all intelligences are activated at the same time in everyone, are operational in everyone and to the same degree of competency. We do not develop at the same pace, and we all do not have the same gifts. Furthermore, there may not be life in a given capacity responsible for a particular intelligence.

Based on the teachings of Scripture, on account of the Fall, human beings are born spiritually disabled. When God is personally embraced, the Spirit regenerates our spirit man or spiritual dimension, and thereby imparts spiritual life and intelligence. Our connection or relationship with God makes spiritual life and intelligence possible.

To be noted is the fact that some people are more receptive to the spiritual, more understanding, more discerning, and more capable of using spiritual means to identify and solve spiritual and other problems. As stated above, everyone does not operate at the same level of spiritual competence. "In general religious terms, it is obvious that certain individuals have a greater sensitivity to the spiritual or mystical due sometimes to their temperament, heredity or cultural background" (Guinness, 1973, p. 298).

Summary

Based on the way the human system is designed, human beings have the capacity to relate to their inner and outer environment, and function at several levels. Each level requires intelligence or special skills relevant to a basic developmental need and is interconnected. The relationship network is not only external but also internal. Spiritual capacity is activated when the spiritual is personally embraced via volition and by the Spirit who enables spiritual life and intelligence. Initially this was not the case. Spiritual intelligence was an innate ability. Due to the Fall, human beings are born spiritually disabled. Theories of spiritual intelligence presented in this chapter include: (a) a theological model, (b) a relational model and (c) a psychological model. Each theory presents human beings as being multidimensional, inclusive of a spiritual capacity. A spiritual capacity provides the basis for spiritual intelligence. Association of natural intelligence with a physical capacity and the physical world, makes spiritual intelligence associated with a spiritual capacity and the spiritual world plausible.

In the next chapter, support from biblical sources will be examined.

CHAPTER 5

Biblical Foundation
for Spiritual Intelligence

In this chapter, a biblical foundation will be laid for spiritual intelligence. It is important that the biblical literature be reviewed separately, for besides being the number-one bestseller of all literature since compilation, the Bible is regarded as the most sacred document in the western world and the primary source of authority on things spiritual. In addition, because of the voluminous nature of the text, special consideration of the biblical data is needed. The Bible is a compendium of 66 books divided into two major categories – the Old and New Testaments. The Old Testament comprises 39 books, and the New Testament, 27. Based on the teachings of Christianity, the Bible was written to enable spiritual intelligent living; it is the blueprint for the development of a spiritual kingdom ruled by God.

In chapter three, a variety of views on spiritual intelligence were presented. Spirituality had a variety of meanings and included nonreligious perspectives. There was disagreement in respect to the source and scope of spiritual intelligence, the motivation or reason behind it, how it is operationalized, and as to whether spiritual intelligence was an innate ability possessed by everyone.

Perspectives on spiritual intelligence were chiefly non-religious and humanistic. From the nonreligious and humanistic perspective, spiritual intelligence did not necessarily have anything to do with God or religion. Notions of transcendence included the natural ability of human beings to transcend self, to be inspired, to experience the surreal, to experience oneness with nature, and to experience oneness with God (based on whomever or whatever God was perceived to be). Believed to be an innate ability, needing to be developed for its perceived value to the individual, the organization and society, spiritual intelligence was perceived integral to human development.

Although moral virtues were recognized as important spiritual traits, moral virtues were not necessarily based on any sense of acknowledgment that God exists or on any notion of accountability to a Supreme Being. Notions of forgiveness from sin and reconciliation to God as bases for spiritual life and intelligence did not factor in humanistic definitions and explanations for spiritual life and intelligence. So why were moral virtues important?

Humanistic sentiments are summarized and explained as follows:

> Charity is a virtue, partly because it stretches what is prudent. A proper risk that will help a cooperative enterprise is more likely to be taken by somebody who knows that he will be cared for if things go wrong, and a willingness to help others to whom one is not (already) co-operatively related is a quality of character which will at least help to get cooperative enterprises off the ground. Loyalty is a virtue, because it is much easier to cooperate with somebody who will stick with it once he has joined in rather than abandon the enterprise and the others involved in it as soon as a better offer comes along for him. Courage is a virtue, because it helps to keep an enterprise running properly in the face of danger, protecting against invasion of our rights in the life we share with others. (Ewin, 1981, p. 171)

Moral virtues offered personal and corporate benefits. They advanced the interests of individuals and corporations in the following ways:

- ◆ Increased productivity
- ◆ Increased motivation
- ◆ Increased profitability

♦ Increased reciprocity

♦ Increased accountability

♦ Actualization of employees

♦ Actualization of the corporation

Zohar and Marshall (2004) believed that by acting on spiritual intelligence a critical mass of spiritual capital may be created to change the face of capitalism so that it becomes a more sustainable economic model of development.

The bases for espousing moral virtues in the secular literature are distinctly different from those advanced in the sacred literature. Morality in biblical literature is rooted in God, a Spirit Being, deemed the Creator and Sustainer of life. Based on the Bible, God created human beings in His image, defined our boundaries and established moral and spiritual laws.

Clearly defined standards of moral and spiritual laws are crucial to the validation and promotion of authenticity. In all of human strivings there is need for authenticity. Authentic personhood presumes connection to the Creator and knowledge of God's moral code. Moral and spiritual behavior necessarily originate in Divine Intelligence, reflecting the nature and character of God.

In order for human beings to reflect the character of God, knowledge of God's moral and spiritual code and the will to follow through on the same are needed. There being a spiritual capacity to humanity, a personal relationship with God is possible. Connecting with God at the spiritual level enables spiritual life and intelligence, and accordingly increases the likelihood of purpose being fulfilled.

In order for purpose to be fulfilled, something in the inner physical world of human nature must resonate with the outer physical world, and something in the inner spiritual world must resonate with the outer spiritual world. When the inner worlds cohere with the outer worlds, there is health, peace and contentment, and purpose is fulfilled.

Motivation for pursuing purpose has to be both intrinsic and extrinsic. There has to be something intrinsically self-motivating, encouraging the voluntary pursuit of purpose. And there has to be something or someone extrinsic, establishing and validating the worth or worthiness of the pursuit. Motivation therefore involves both God and man working in tandem to reflect the divine image, will and purpose.

Authenticity is necessarily contingent on a type of intelligence capable of actualizing self and fulfilling purpose, consistent with the nature and purpose of life. If the nature of life is natural and spiritual, then both natural and spiritual intelligences are required. An authentic, integrated human being implies a standard of authenticity and the intelligence to maintain or achieve it. A common God, a common Creator, a common moral standard, and a common purpose make spiritual intelligence plausible and universal coherence possible.

Notion of God

In Scripture, there is no explanation for the existence of God. Indications are that God existed from beginning and that God is self-existent, self-sufficient and infinitely intelligent. Another of God's amazing attributes is the ability to manifest in a number of ways. In both the Old and New Testament Scriptures, God is presented as a plurality or as a triune Being: one God manifested as three persons – Father, Son, and Holy Spirit (Gen. 1:26; 3:22; 11:7; Matt. 28:19; John 17:20-23). In Genesis 1:26, God is reported as saying: "Let **us** [emphasis added] make man in **our** [emphasis added] image and in **our** [emphasis added] likeness," and, in the following verse, "God created man in **his own** [emphasis added] image." Throughout the Bible God is represented as a Spirit Being possessing attributes consistent with personality. God is cast not just as superior to all beings but as Supreme and Infinite in all His attributes. As the Creator of us, God is above us; we are subjected to him because we are His subjects.

Notion of Creation

The sacred writings of Scripture begin with narratives of how the world came into existence and of human origin. Biblical literature attributes the existence of the world and its contents to the creative powers of God, a Spirit Being who, by acts of the will, literally spoke the world into existence and named its several aspects (Gen. 1, 2; Col. 1:16-17; Acts 4:24; John 1:1-5).

In the creation story, God repeatedly said, "Let there be," and whatever God declared came into being. In the New Testament, the Word is described as the incarnate Christ and Son of God, declared to have played an active role in creation also (John 1:1-3; Col. 1:15-17). The Spirit of God was active in creation as well (Gen. 1:1-3). Based on biblical literature, God the Father, God the Son, and God the Spirit were involved in the creation process.

In the Bible, God is portrayed as Creator through the spoken Word, and creation as revealing the greatness and glory of God (Genesis 1 & 2; Ps. 19; 90:1-4; 104). Although not fully understood, everything in creation speaks of intelligent design, and a First and Final cause capable of Infinite Intelligence. Based on biblical literature, an active Spiritual Intelligence created the world and is responsible for sustaining it. If God is the Spirit who created the world by intelligent design, Spiritual Intelligence associated with God may be inferred.

Creation of Humanity

According to the Bible, God is also responsible for creating human beings. God created humans in His image:

> Then God said, "Let us make man in our image, in our likeness, and let them rule over the fish of the sea and the birds of the air, over the livestock, over all the earth, and over all the creatures that move along the ground." So God created man in His own image, in the image of God he created him; male and female he created them. (Gen. 1:26-27, NIV)

Like God, human beings are multidimensional: we have a body, soul and spirit (1 Thess. 5:23; Luke 1:47). It seems the tripartite nature of humanity has something to do with the triune nature of God and may speak, in part, to what it means to be created in God's image. It could be that the human body is representative of Jesus, the Word made flesh; the human spirit is representative of the Holy Spirit; and the human soul is representative of God the Father. Based on the creation story, it seems mankind was originally created a triune being in likeness of our Creator, but due to sin (the Fall) a splitting of human personality occurred.

Whether there is a correlation between the composition of God and the composition of humanity or not, every human being needs to come to terms with four fundamental questions: What or who is the cause of my existence? What is the purpose of my existence? Am I accountable? If so, to whom?

The first question resolves itself in the fact that however we came into existence is connected to a Personal Being and not an impersonal force of nature. Although it is possible for the personal to create the impersonal, it is impossible for a nonperson to create a person. Because human beings are persons, the One who imagined, designed and created us, is necessarily a person of superior personality. Personality is not only necessary at the point of creation; it is necessary in order to sustain any real connection or relationship between the Creator and the created. Based on Scripture, human beings are created in the Creator's image. God being Spirit, human beings must be possessed of a spiritual dimension and the capacity for spiritual intelligence as spiritual intelligence is necessary for any meaningful relationship with God, who is Spirit.

If there is to be order in creation, the second question has to be determined by the Creator and not by the created. The Creator is the One who determines the purpose of His creation. Purpose, therefore, has to do with the Creator's Will, which, broadly speaking ultimately brings honor and glory to the Creator. Answer to the third and fourth questions is obvious. If we are created with purpose, then the One who created us will hold us accountable.

Since human beings are not self-created, the Creator must be included in any dialogue about humanity. Having been created by God, human beings are subject to the life, wisdom and power of the Creator. The point is underscored in a series of conversational exchanges between God and the patriarch, Job, in which the absurdity of the created criticizing the Creator is chided (Job 38-42). Many prophets, including Isaiah, have declared the sovereignty of God over creation (Isa. 40:12-31).

As Creator, God has the sovereign right over human beings and thus the authority to determine our value and purpose. Without God, life has no meaning, and without meaning, life has no value and purpose. Purpose and meaning are necessarily established by the Creator. This is not to say that human beings are mindless actors on the stage of life. If design is consistent with purpose, then the fulfilling of purpose is contingent on the ability of the created to accomplish the purpose of its design.

The fulfilling of purpose is a cooperative effort, validated both internally and externally. Of necessity, motivation to pursue purpose must come from within. This means having the freedom to make choices. The presence of volition has made it possible for human beings to participate in personal development and in the determination of our own destiny.

By design, human beings have the freedom to make choices. Freedom of choice, however, does not and could not mean freedom without restraint. Human beings were designed with purpose in mind and, therefore, were designed to function in a particular way, hence boundaries. Life within established boundaries keeps humanity aligned to purpose and enables self-actualization. Life outside established boundaries works against our best interest in that it hinders the fulfilling of purpose and destiny.

Choices determine destiny. This is clear in the account of the history of human origin and throughout the history of humanity. "The Lord God commanded the man, saying, 'From any tree of the garden you may eat freely; but from the tree of the knowledge of good and evil you shall not eat, for in the day that you eat from it you will surely die'" (Gen. 2:16-17, NASB). "The prohibition itself was a reminder to man that his freedom is freedom under authority" (Hughes, 1989, p. 142).

The restriction imposed upon humanity was a real test of character and was essential to wholeness and the fulfillment of purpose. Appropriate choices would have affirmed personhood, enabled purpose and destiny. Inappropriate choices would have conceivably degraded personhood; caused a splitting of human personality, disintegration, and the consequent denial of purpose. It is wholeness which positions humanity to enjoy the freedom to fulfill God's purpose and enables self-actualization.

Based on Scripture, Adam was oriented to fulfill his purpose. However, fulfillment was contingent on obedience to the Creator. Adam was God's steward and therefore accountable to God. As long as Adam's will harmonized with the Will of the Creator, his potential would have been fully realized.

In choosing his own way, Adam did not only violate God's laws, Adam violated his own personhood and cheated himself of personal fulfillment and destiny. So although volition is part of the human framework, there is constraint to operate intelligently – in conformity with God's design and in tandem with established natural and spiritual laws evident throughout creation.

Notion of Worship

Of note is the fact that wherever human beings are found there is the sense that there is a Supreme Being, supernatural in nature and deserving of worship. Where did this sense come from?

In Old Testament literature, worship is commanded and there is prohibition against false worship (Ex. 20:1-5). The command to worship implies the capacity to worship and the intelligence to discriminate between worship that is false and worship that is true, hence the need for spiritual intelligence. In New Testament literature, Jesus indicates true worshippers worship the Father "in spirit and in truth" (John 4:23-24).

If worship is part of the acknowledgment due deity, then worshippers are presumed able to worship intelligently. There being one God, worship is due Him and there ought indeed to be one true religion.

Worship is synonymous with religion. Like music, religion is a universal language spoken by every nation and, as such, impacts cultures everywhere. From ancient civilization to the present, religion has been a significant part of every culture. In addition to the five major religions (Judaism, Christianity, Islam, Buddhism and Hinduism), there are several other religions, thousands of denominational groups and religious cults worshipping a deity or deities. Supporting evidence of religion, religious practices and beliefs are found among the biblical data of both Old and New Testament Scriptures (Gen. 4:1-16; Exod. 34:14; Deut. 6:4-18; Ps. 2:10-12; 66:1-4; Matt. 15:9; Acts 17:21-34; 25:18-19; 26:4-8; Phil. 3:1-3; Rev. 4:4-11), and among other sacred and secular literature.

Religion and religious practices such as worship are universal. Since worship is universal and God is the object of worship, a Spirit Being who should be worshipped in "spirit and in truth," then the ability to relate to God and to worship God intelligently or truthfully, must be a characteristic of spiritual intelligence. Assuming worship of a common Creator is possible, universal spiritual intelligence is needful and plausible.

Notion of the Fall

Although given dominion over the earth (Gen. 1:26-31), the authority devolved was delegated authority, constrained by the ability and willingness of Adam to reflect the nature and character of God, who is Final Authority. Knowing evil was never part of God's design (Gen. 2:15-16).

God designed human beings to know only good. Knowledge of evil would have conceivably corrupted human personality leading down a trajectory contrary to the best interest of the individual and society, not to mention the dishonor and misrepresentation of the Creator.

It is apparent that the first humans knew only that which was good; that by the level of interaction with God and the level of responsibility enjoyed, our ancestors had the intelligence to operate in harmony with the Divine Will and purpose.

Evil was introduced in the mindscape due to the unlawful exercise of volition. The inappropriate exercise of volition disempowered and degraded humanity. In exercising self-will over Sovereign-will, personhood was abused; the image of God in humans was defaced and, as a result, humankind became disabled and dysfunctional spiritually. This meant that the first human beings no longer enjoyed spiritual life and intelligence. Spiritual disconnection from God resulted in spiritual death.

Spiritual death introduced corruption in the human system. Instead of operating from a place of purity, innocence and goodwill, human nature became corrupted, the operating principle of sin affecting our will, emotions, intellect and behavior: body, soul and spirit have been affected. The Fall resulted in the corruption of human nature passed down from Adam to posterity (Gen. 2:15-17; Rom. 3:23; 5:12), inclining toward self-destruction, the destruction of fellow human beings and the environment.

Human depravity is a result of the Fall. Catholic theologians, such as Augustine (2002), and Protestant theologians, such as Calvin (2008), agreed on the doctrine of the Fall and that the Fall brought moral evil into the world. "The sin of Adam and the corruption it introduced were the sin and corruption of our nature, our humanity, for our human nature is one with the human nature of the first man" (Hughes, 1989, p. 132).

In addition to being created in the image of God, we are also created in the image of man. As such we are connected to human ancestors spiritually, physically, and psychologically. At the physical level, ancestors pass on genes which affect development physiologically and psychologically; at the spiritual level, beliefs and values are passed on throughout the developmental stages, affecting development morally and spiritually.

Theologians and psychologists are in agreement concerning etiological linkages between a person and their forebears, and that unresolved conflicts result in dysfunction throughout a person's generation and beyond. Psychologically, the emotional state of one generation may be passed on to the next. "The individual does not stand in isolation, but is anchored in a guilt-connection with his forebears" (Koch, 1972, p. 286).

> Most psychologists believe that babies are born with genetically determined temperaments, physiological dispositions to respond to the environment in relatively stable, typical ways. Such temperaments may later form the basis of specific personality traits. (Tavris & Wade, 2001, p. 108)

Emotional systems of previous generations live on in the emotional systems of current generations (Bevcar & Bevcar, 2003). Psychic and "spiritual gifts" may also be passed on from one generation to the next (Koch, 1972). No mind is an island.

Since the Fall, a pure sinless nature has been displaced by an impure sinful nature, resulting in fragmentation and disintegration. Changes occur in thoughts, attitudes and behaviors, affecting relationships at every level, namely our relationship with God. According to the Bible, disobedience of the first human beings resulted in severe challenges spiritually, psychologically, physically, socially, and intellectually (Gen. 3). Spiritually, Adam and Eve experienced death, meaning that they became disconnected from God. Having been disconnected from God spiritually, humankind no longer enjoyed a personal and close relationship with God. Whereas formerly humans welcomed the presence of God, our forebears no longer enjoyed God's presence. Psychologically, Adam and Eve experienced guilt, shame, fear and insecurity.

Physically, sin brought pain in childbirth (Gen. 3:16) and pain in physical labor (Gen. 3:17-19). As the physical environment was also impacted by sin, the soil became harder to till and the ground yielded thorns and thistles.

Socially, interpersonal relationships were affected. Because of disobedience, humankind became fearful and hid from God. The impact of the Fall on social relationships is seen in the way human beings relate to God and in the way human beings relate to each other. Very early in ancient civilization we find the unprovoked and callous murder of a man at the hand of his own brother. Cain killed his brother Abel (Gen. 4:1-8).

Intellectually, the mind was corrupted, subjecting humanity to a life of ignorance and futility. Hence the declaration: "My thoughts are not your thoughts, neither are your ways my ways. . . As the heavens are higher than the earth, so are my ways higher than your ways and my thoughts than your thoughts" (Isa. 55:8-9, NIV). This is not just a factor of the Infinite versus the finite; this is due to the exchange of a spiritual mind for a carnal mind handed down from physical forebears.

A person with a carnal mind is neither able to apprehend spiritual truths nor attain God-likeness. Instead, the carnal mind is hostile toward God and is incapable of subjecting itself to the law of God (Rom. 8:5-8; 1 Cor. 2:14).

Separation from God has resulted in disharmony within and among human beings, and has resulted in meaninglessness and diseases of meaning. Zohar and Marshall (2000) averred that many sicknesses and diseases may be traced to a life beset by meaninglessness:

Much of our suffering, even chronic physical conditions consist of 'diseases of meaning.' Cancer, heart disease, Alzheimer's and other dementias that may be preceded by depression, fatigue, alcoholism or drug abuse are evidence of the crisis of meaninglessness brought home to the very cells of our bodies. Ultimately death, too, is experienced with pain and terror because we have no meaningful context in which to place the natural ending of this life, no way to die with blessedness, peace or grace. (Zohar & Marshall, 2000, p. 29)

In addition, for exchanging Sovereign-will for self-will, human beings enabled an alien master, known as the devil. Subjection to the devil has resulted in increased sicknesses, diseases and meaninglessness rooted in forces of evil.

The Christian description of the universe as abnormal applies not only to the seen world which has fallen but also to an unseen world in which there is a devil and evil spirits who in their own rebellion against God have an active influence in the world and affairs of men. (Guinness, 1973, p. 309)

Human sinfulness unwittingly facilitated influence of the forces of darkness in the world and the expansion of Satan's kingdom. Disconnected from God, people unwittingly (and often unknowingly) share membership in Satan's kingdom (Acts 26:18; 1 John 2:17-30; 3:7-8).

Notion of a Devil

In addition to a natural inclination to do wrong (due to the Fall), evil is believed by Christians to be rooted in a supernatural devil. Many will agree that there is evil in the world. The majority are impacted by evil in one way or another. Evil is encountered personally and vicariously and in various ways. The experience of evil includes demonic attacks, demon possessions, unprovoked and unmitigated hatred, sicknesses, diseases, hauntings and certain forms of violence.

The Creator being good, where did all this evil come from? According to the sacred writings of Scripture, Satan, also known as Lucifer, was an extremely bright and powerful angel in heaven. On account of his brilliance and power, Satan got puffed up with pride and became envious of God's position. This motivated an attempt to usurp God's authority. As a result, Lucifer and his followers were cast out of heaven (Isa. 14:12-17; Ezek. 28:11-17).

Being cast out of heaven, however, did not mean the end of Satan's ambition. Although failing to usurp authority in heaven, Satan succeeded in usurping authority in the earth, and thus has established his own kingdom in rivalry to God.

Establishment of a rival kingdom was achieved by deceit or trickery. The first humans were tricked into disobedience by the devil. For disobeying God and submitting to the devil, human beings lost dominion in the earth to Satan. Satan therefore became de facto ruler in the earth.

Based on Scripture, Satan epitomizes and promotes evil. Through acts of deception and flagrant attacks, Satan influences, intimidates and coerces people into evil activities. Among the many titles used to describe him are:

1. The ruler of the world (Eph. 2:1-3; 1 John 5:18-19).

2. The serpent (Gen. 3:15; Rev. 20:2).

3. The father of lies and a murderer (John 8:44).

4. The god of this age who inflicts spiritual blindness (2 Cor. 4:4).

5. The enemy (Luke 10:18-19).

6. The adversary and a ferocious lion (1 Peter 5:8).

7. The accuser (Rev. 12:10).

8. A false messenger disguised as an angel of light (2 Cor. 11:14-15).

9. The tempter (Matt. 4:1-11).

10. One who persuades people to do wrong (John 13:2).

11. One who defeats and ensnares some Christians
    (1 Tim. 3:7; 2 Tim. 2:26; Rev. 2:10).

12. The devil (Matt. 4:1; Eph. 6:11; Rev. 12:9; 20:10).

So there are two spiritual kingdoms in the world: one ruled by God and the other by Satan. Satan's kingdom is the antithesis of everything the kingdom of God represents. The kingdom of God is marked by light and good; the kingdom of Satan by darkness and evil.

According to the sacred writings, Satan is head of a well-organized hierarchy of demons responsible for certain territories and activities in the world (Eph. 6:12). Demons are evil spirits possessing supernatural abilities. For example, demons can possess people and cause problems such as dumbness (Matt. 9:32-33; 12:22), blindness (Matt. 12:12), grievous vexation (Matt. 15:22; Mark 7:24-30), epilepsy and suicidal mania (Matt. 17:15-18; Luke 9:37-43), insanity (Mark 5:1-18; Luke 8:26-39) and uncleanness (Luke 4:33-36).

If indeed there is a real devil – a spirit being who is the epitome and source of evil – there is need for spiritual intelligence in order to take a stand against him.

Notion of Spiritual Warfare

The Bible likens the Christian pilgrim to a soldier embroiled in a spiritual battle, engaging spiritual foes (Eph. 6:10-19; 2 Cor. 10:3-5). Every piece of equipment needed to do battle with the enemy is described in spiritual terms. The Christian soldier is described as a spiritual person fighting a spiritual war with spiritual means (2 Cor. 10:4), and receive teachings by the Holy Spirit (1 Cor. 2:13).

The notion of spiritual warfare makes spiritual intelligence plausible. If the battle is spiritual, the enemy is spiritual, the weapons are spiritual, and Christian soldiers are spiritual, then Christian soldiers must have spiritual intelligence to wage a good spiritual warfare.

Notion of Spiritual Birth

The source of life and wellness is both physical and spiritual. In addition to natural and physical forebears, we also bear a connection with the spiritual and supernatural, having been created by God. As such we carry within us both the image of God and the image of man.

There is a physical and natural dimension to us, enabling connection to the physical and natural world. And there is a spiritual and supernatural dimension to us, enabling connection to the spiritual and supernatural world.

Based on biblical literature, there is natural birth and there is spiritual birth (John 1:12-13; Titus 3:5; John 3:5-6). "Flesh gives birth to flesh, but the Spirit gives birth to spirit" (John 3:6, NIV). Natural birth is the basis for physical life; spiritual birth is the basis for spiritual life.

A person of natural birth shares the likeness of natural forebears and produces fruit consistent with the natural and physical. A person of spiritual birth shares the likeness of spiritual forebears and produces fruit consistent with the spiritual and supernatural.

In Scripture, Jesus made a distinction between relationships based on physicality and relationships based on spirituality, and averred people who are truly connected to him are those who are related to him spiritually (Matt. 12:46-50; Luke 8:19-21). The apostle Paul echoed similar sentiments (Rom. 4:13-18; 9:1-8; Gal. 3:22-29). Scripture emphasizes spiritual life as the basis for a genuine relationship with God (Rom. 8:9; 9:8).

If physicality is the basis for physical life and relationships, then spirituality is the basis for spiritual life and relationships. If physical life is governed by natural intelligence, then spiritual life is governed by spiritual intelligence. Physical birth equips for physical life; spiritual birth equips for spiritual life.

In addition to physical senses associated with the nature of flesh, the spiritually reborn operate by spiritual senses associated with the nature of the Spirit (Rom. 2:28-29; 9:6-8; John 15:18-19).

Since people born of natural descent operate by natural and physical senses only (John 3:18-21; 2 Cor. 6:14-18; Eph. 5:6-21), they cannot comprehend the things of the Spirit. In the natural, human beings are described as spiritually dead, blind and foolish (Eph. 2:1, 5; Matt. 15:14; 23:17-19; 2 Cor. 3:14; 4:4; 1 John 2:9-11).

"The man without the Spirit does not accept the things that come from the Spirit of God, for they are foolishness to him, and he cannot understand them, because they are spiritually discerned" (1 Cor. 2:14, NIV). For example, for not understanding the logic of Christianity as explained by Paul, Festus shouted "You are mad, Paul! Your great learning is driving you mad!" (Acts 26:24, GNT).

The spiritually dead cannot relate to things of the Spirit and to spiritual people, can they? It is therefore natural for people who have not experienced spiritual rebirth to believe that those who have are foolish or crazy. The spiritually dead and ignorant will always be at loggerhead with the spiritually alive and intelligent.

This was not so in the beginning. Harmony was disturbed because of the Fall. The Fall resulted in spiritual death passed down from primal progenitors. The result is that instead of the physical being circumscribed by the spiritual, human beings operate chiefly from physical capacity. Without the spiritual informing the physical, sin is inevitable.

Human beings were created with intelligence and integrity, enabling us to live and work in harmony with God, with each other and with the rest of creation, as per design. Contrary to God's design, sin entered the world. The principle of sin having become our default perceptual lens and processor, we became corrupted: sin inclined to unrighteousness, thereby undermining our development. In addition to doing things contrary to our own wellbeing, we do things contrary to other human beings and to the environment created for our enjoyment and sustenance, all of which flies in the face of our Creator.

Sin initiated moral declension, causing us to dishonor ourselves, dishonor each other and dishonor the God who created us (Romans 1). This is why sin is such a horrible mistake and is so reprehensible to God.

In God there is absolutely no darkness (1 John 1:5). God is Light and the Source of light. Without light sinners are lost along a trajectory of increasing darkness. Light in Scripture represents truth, knowledge and right-eousness; darkness is figurative language for evil, ignorance, lies and other forms of unrighteousness.

Sin darkens the soul, taking sinners further and further away from the light of God. Sin places a cloud on spiritual perception thereby warping our mind and personality.

Human dysfunction is rooted in sin. Subsequent to the Fall, everyone is born disconnected from God, hence lacking spiritual life and intelligence. Like food bad for the biological system of the body, sin has a negative affect on the ecosystem of the mind and spirit, and as such degrades the image of God in us.

Having been degraded due to disobedience, reimaging needs to take place. This is made possible by the obedience of Christ. In fact, people who love God are predestined to be conformed to the image of Christ (Rom. 8:29).

> And we all, who with unveiled faces contemplate the LORD's glo-ry, are being transformed into his image with ever-increasing glory, which comes from the LORD, who is the Spirit. (2 Cor. 3:18, NIV)

Sin results in inauthenticity and lack of authority. If human beings lost authenticity and authority in the earth by default via disobedience, it follows that the same might be regained by obedience. In Romans 6:16-23, Paul reminds us that we have a choice in deciding whether or not we are going to remain in bondage to sin or be liberated from it.

In order to regain authenticity, the stronghold of sin affecting our will, emotions, intellect and behavior must be brought down by spiritual means (1 Cor. 2; 2 Cor. 10:4-5). This necessitates rebirth by the Spirit and renewal of the mind (Titus 3:5; Rom. 12:1- 2).

Once corrupted, the mind needs to be reset in order to be restored or renewed. Since the mind cannot reset itself, reset has to be initiated by a Higher Power, namely our Creator. This is why salvation is by grace through faith (Eph. 2:8-9). When God's gift is accepted (John 1:12-13), the Holy Spirit initiates the reset process thereby enabling renewal (Titus 3:5).

The Spirit enables holiness and wholeness to become a real possibility, over time displacing inherent corruption. As we willingly walk in step with the dictates of the Spirit, we will cease our sinful deeds and instead manifest the fruit of the Spirit (Gal. 5: 16-26).

Based on Scripture, people who are not spiritually reborn are understood and described relative to physicality – based on the capacity and restrictions the physical nature imposes. Such persons operate chiefly by the energy and impulses of the flesh and by natural intelligence.

The Bible makes a distinction between natural birth and spiritual birth (John 3:1-7); states there is a corresponding intelligence in operation (1 Cor. 2:14), and differentiates between wisdom received naturally and wisdom received supernaturally (1 Cor. 2:1-13; 3:18-20).

Spiritual understanding and discernment are unique features of people related to God spiritually (Rom. 8:9, 16; 1 John 4:13). The physical and spiritual have their own operating system – the operating system of the flesh and the operating system of the Spirit respectively – influencing cognition and personality. A person who functions chiefly by the operating system of the flesh is described as a "natural man." One who functions chiefly by the operating system of the Spirit is described as a "spiritual man."

Notion of Spiritual Life and Death

Based on Scripture, in the natural human beings are disconnected from God and are therefore spiritually dead (Eph. 2:1, 5); spiritual death is the result of sinfulness (Rom. 6:23); pride is at the heart of our sinfulness (Rom. 1:18-23; 1 Cor. 1:18-21; 8:1); and everyone is a sinner (Rom. 3:10, 23).

Death means separation and is viewed relationally and qualitatively – transitioning from one type of existence to another. The relativity of life and death in various aspects of humanity is apparent. For example, a person may have perfectly good eyes yet cannot see. For a number of reasons, including brain damage, one may be intelligent intellectually and dumb emotionally. There may be life in one area of one's body and death in another.

The difference between physical life and death and spiritual life and death is illustrated in the following: "Jesus said to her, "I am the resurrection and the life. The one who believes in me will live, even though they die; and whoever lives by believing in me will never die. Do you believe this?" (John 11:25-26, NIV)

Biblically, there are three types of death: physical death, spiritual death and eternal death. Physical death takes place when the spirit of a person is separated from their body (James 2:26; Acts 7:59; John 19:30). So death is viewed as transition from one form of existence to the next (Jn. 5:24; 11:21-26; 14:1-3).

Spiritual death takes place when there is disconnection or separation spiritually between man and God (Eph. 2:1-5), meaning that the person does not have a personal relationship with God. Eternal death takes place when the whole person (body, soul and spirit) is separated from God forever in hell (Rev. 20:14).

Life in hell is qualitatively different from life in heaven. Existence in one domain is disempowering and unfulfilling; existence in the other is empowering and fulfilling. In hell, there is perpetual sorrow and suffering; in heaven, there is joy and peace, hence the description of hell as a place of eternal death and heaven a place of eternal life.

Based on the teachings of Scripture, escape from hell is avoidable via spiritual rebirth. Illustrated symbolically in baptism by immersion and practically in daily life, spiritual rebirth results from identification with Jesus' death, burial and resurrection (Rom. 5:12-6:14). Whereas formerly a person was dead to righteousness, yielding the members of their body to unrighteousness, the spiritually reborn is alive to righteousness and yields the members of their body accordingly.

Since by the deliberate unrestricted exercise of volition human beings became slaves to sin and subservient to the devil, by the grace of God, human beings can make the decision to be free. Volition is a key feature of human design, and the ability to exercise volition responsibly is integral to human development.

Life is a series of decision-making and corresponding consequences. Accordingly, choices either enable health and spiritual development or undermine them. All choices are not equal, are they? Since there are things right and not right for us physically, it is reasonable to expect that the same holds true in the spiritual domain.

Spiritual health is largely determined by moral and spiritual choices. There being a spiritual dimension to humanity, human beings need to be fed with the right spiritual food (Matt.4:4; 1 Peter 2:2), if we are to be healthy spiritually. Spiritual health is not just important (3 John 2); it is far more important than physical health (Matt. 10:28), and hence has been the major focus of God's intervention in human history.

Throughout history, God has acted in various ways to deliver humanity from spiritual ill-health. The Law had been the most common means but could not save anyone. No one was made righteous by keeping the Law (Rom. 3:20-31). The law was like a schoolmaster (Rom. 7; Gal. 3 & 4). As schoolmaster, the law increased awareness and understanding of God's standard of righteousness but could not enable the attainment of righteousness. Jesus, however, made this possible (Acts 13:39; Rom. 3:21-25; 8:1-4) and has established a new covenant.

Instead of the legalism of the old covenant, which sought to enforce the requirements of the Law – the attaining of "self-righteousness" – the new covenant granted grace. The new covenant is centered on the efficacy of the blood of Jesus to save from sin. On account of his sinless life and sacrificial death, the righteousness of Jesus may be imputed to sinners, who by faith have repented and have embraced the sacrificial death of Jesus as satisfaction for sin.

Biblical spirituality is defined by the Cross. The Cross is the bridge that enables human beings to cross over from spiritual death into spiritual life. In Christianity, the Cross is the symbol of redemption, forgiveness, reconciliation and salvation.

Although available to all, salvation is applicable only to those who believe or have embraced Jesus as their Savior. Being saved is a personal affair. Salvation is not automatic, as people have a choice in the matter. Human beings are able to exercise volition in accepting God's grace or in rejecting it. When accepted, we are reconciled to God and have become members of God's spiritual family. Among other things, this means deliverance.

For delivering us from the Law and the curse of sin (John 3:16; Rom. 1:16; 1 Cor. 5:1-4; Eph. 1:7-10; 2:18), Jesus is described as the perfect law of liberty (James 1:25; 2:12). This is a fitting description, as Jesus has not only increased awareness and understanding of God's righteousness, Jesus has made it possible for righteousness to be attained (1 Peter 1:24; Eph. 1:7).

Righteousness is important because it reflects God's design for humanity and mirrors God's character (1 Peter 1:16). God is about righteousness and truth. Truth is lived out in righteousness. Righteousness integrates human personality thereby liberating us to fulfill our destiny.

There is nothing more liberating and fulfilling than righteousness and truth (John 8:32-36); no one embodied or exemplified this more than Jesus. In the Bible, Jesus is presented as the perfect bearer of the image of God, the supreme archetype of personhood and the prime model for human identification and aspiration.

Unlike other humans, Jesus fully expressed the glory of God (Heb. 1:3). This is why Jesus could declare: "I am the way and the truth and the life. No one comes to the Father except through me" (John 14:6).

Jesus succeeded where the first man, Adam, had failed (Rom. 5:12-21). In Adam, all died; in Christ, all have been made alive (1 Cor. 15:22). Jesus regained for humanity spiritual life and intelligence. But this is not automatic. One needs to identify with Jesus. To identify with Jesus is to experience him personally; it means to be liberated by him and to be empowered by him (2 Cor. 5:17; Gal. 2:20). People connected to Jesus:

- Have redemption and forgiveness of sins (Eph. 1:7).
- Are made alive spiritually (Rom. 5:12-21).
- Are new creatures (2 Cor. 5:17).
- Are children of Light (John 1:1-12; Eph. 5:8-10).
- Have spiritual blessings (Eph. 1:3).
- Are connected to other believers and are being built up (Eph. 2:19-22).
- Are sealed with the Holy Spirit (Eph. 2:18).
- Have access to the Father (Eph. 2:18).

- May approach God with freedom and confidence (Eph. 3:12).
- Have divine power and participate in the divine nature (Eph. 3:21; 2 Pet. 1:3-4).
- Are destined to bring glory to God Matt. 5:16; 1Cor. 6:20; 10:31; Col. 3:17).

Apart from Jesus, "all have sinned and fall short of the glory of God" (Rom. 3:23). For being the only person to have never committed any form of wrongdoing (Heb. 4:15), Jesus alone qualified as sin bearer for humanity (2 Cor. 5:21). However, Jesus did not die just that people might escape condemnation caused by sin; he died chiefly that human beings might experience regeneration caused by righteousness.

The veil of darkness caused by sin is only removed when people turn to Jesus in repentance and faith (Acts 20:21; 2 Cor. 3:16-18; 4:6-7). Rejection of Jesus means continued spiritual death and perpetual darkness (John 3:18-21, 36). Genuine repentance results in forgiveness. Forgiveness entitles one to begin the spiritual journey, but that's only the beginning. In order to achieve success along the journey, by faith a person must daily repent of known sins and daily conform their life to the life of Christ. Although important, the major effect of repentance is not forgiveness; it is the transformation which accompanies a change of mind.

Unfortunately, some people are more interested in forgiveness than in forsaking their sinful lifestyle; and some see confession as the right to forgiveness. But confession is not repentance, and being sorry for sin is not enough to avoid consequences. One who truly repents changes their mind about doing wrong and goes in a new direction. The power of genuine repentance is in the change of mind and the related change in the lifestyle of the converted. Repentance presumes a change of mind; it involves a sincere desire for and commitment to change.

Confession without repentance neither leads to forgiveness nor enables regeneration. It is repentance and faith that enable forgiveness of sins and the impartation of righteousness to the forgiven. Some refer to this experience as *conversion*. Others describe it as being *saved* or *born-again*, because of the spiritual rebirth that has taken place.

The experience of being born-again spiritually results in the restoration of the divine faculty of spiritual intelligence. According to the Scriptures, the natural man (unregenerate human beings) does not and cannot know the things pertaining to the Spirit, because these things are spiritually discerned (1 Cor. 2:14). It takes a spiritually enlightened person to know spiritual things.

When connected to God by the Spirit, spiritual life and light is enabled (Rom. 8:9; John 14:17; 1 John 4:13). God is Light and there is no darkness in Him (1 John 1:5-6). People connected to God are therefore spiritually alive and issue forth light, and are described accordingly as "light of the world" (Matt. 5:14; John 8:12).

The Holy Spirit is the source of power, enabling believers to bear witness of God and to be witnesses for God (Acts 1:8). In order to do this spiritual intelligence is necessary, God being Spirit. As in other areas of life, an appropriate role model is helpful.

The Christian model of spiritual intelligent living is Jesus. Jesus is also described as light and life of the world (John 6:51; 9:5). Jesus is the archetype of a fully functional human being and the embodiment of spiritual intelligence. Based on Scripture, a personal relationship with God through Jesus is the means of enabling the human mind to cohere with the Divine Mind (2 Cor. 10:3-5).

The mind of Christ is developed in human beings as the Holy Spirit reveals the mind of God and the things of God to the people of God (1 Cor. 2:4-16), and as that knowledge is applied in daily life. Spiritual intelligence enables sanctification. "The sanctification of man consists in the union of his will with the will of God" (Tart, 1976, p. 401).

The term sanctification simply means to be made holy or righteous. Righteousness is both instantaneous and progressive. The moment a person surrenders their life to God, the righteousness of Christ is imputed to their account. This means the person is no longer a condemned sinner, Jesus having satisfied the righteous demands of the Law for sin on their behalf. Imputed righteousness enables salvation from the penalty of sin.

A person is also made righteous through the regenerating work of the Spirit and the willing cooperation and commitment of the converted (John 17:17; Rom. 6:22; 15:16; 1 Cor. 1:30; Col. 3:5-17; 1 Thess. 4:3; Heb. 12:14). Having received the Spirit at the point of conversion (Eph. 1:13), the person thus endowed is enabled to be God-like as far as moral attributes are concerned. Submission to the dictates of the Spirit leads to sanctification (Rom. 8:3-5; Gal. 5:16).

Righteousness achieved through personal efforts, enabled by the Spirit, is the essence of progressive sanctification. In this case, righteousness is being imparted or inculcated leading to spiritual growth.

Spiritual growth enables deliverance from the power of sin. Whereas salvation from the penalty of sin is totally due to the grace of God in declaring the guilty sinner righteous based on what Jesus did for him, salvation from the power of sin involves the work of the believer in translating imputed righteous into real life experience. In this regard, in addition to submitting to the dictates of the Spirit (Gal. 5:16-18), submitting to the dictates of the Scriptures is crucial (Psa. 119:1-3, 9, 11, 98-105; 2 Tim. 2:15; 3:15-17). The "breath" of the Word is just as important as the "breath" of the Spirit.

When a person willingly submits to the dictates of the Scriptures and of the Spirit, he progressively becomes more righteous. Progressive sanctification is the process of being made holy or Christ-like, and is the fruit of spiritual intelligence.

Spiritual intelligence is a means of sanctification; it is not the same as sanctification. Although a well-developed spiritual intelligence leads to sanctification, spiritual intelligence includes other things, such as spiritual discernment, inspiration and illumination.

At this juncture, a distinction needs to be made between spirituality as a capacity and spirituality as an experience. As a capacity, spirituality describes the incorporeal or spiritual dimension of a person, enabling spiritual consciousness or awareness. How-ever, consciousness does not imply intelligence; spiritual consciousness implies the need and the potential for intelligence, but does not necessarily indicate the actual presence or possession of spiritual intelligence.

Intelligence is contingent on life and health in a given capacity. Although everyone has a spiritual capacity, not everyone is spiritually alive or healthy. According to the Scriptures, it is possible to enjoy health in one capacity area and experience ill health in another (3 John 2); it is possible for decay to take place in one area and renewal in another (2 Cor. 4:16); and it is possible to be physically alive and spiritually dead. (Luke 9:59-60). Except for a few, the world to which Jesus came was not spiritually alive, hence the declaration: "I have come that they may have life, and have it to the full." (John 10:10)

To be spiritually dead does not mean a person no longer exists in the absolute sense. Spiritual death in Scripture means the absence of light and life; albeit, death is a relative term. This accounts for the relative interest in things spiritual and in various *spiritualities*, including *spiritualities* that are godless and non-transformative. Indeed, some people are spiritually dead, and some are *more dead* than others.

As an experience, spirituality describes a personal relationship with God, commitment to a worldview that shapes one's thinking and behavior, and commitment to the Holy Spirit as Supreme Guide and enabler of spiritual living. The Spirit motivates along a trajectory that includes repentance, spiritual growth or godliness via spiritual intelligence.

Spiritual intelligence implies a new way of knowing, thinking, acting and being:

> You were taught, with regard to your former way of life, to put off your old self, which is being corrupted by its deceitful desires; to be made new in the attitude of your minds; and to put on the new self, created to be like God in true righteousness and holiness. (Eph. 4:22-24, NIV)

Although a personal relationship with God implies spiritual intelligence, this does not mean everyone who has a relationship with God is at the same level spiritually. Spiritual intelligence does not imply perfect or complete knowledge, or perfect behavior. Knowledge is received in part over time, and imperfect human beings are involved. And since mistakes are part of the maturation process, the more matured are expected to help the not so matured in a gentle and humble fashion (Gal. 6:1-5; James 5:19-20).

To be spiritual does not mean that a person has all the answers and that life is trouble free. Spirituality is a journey; it is a process. Some of the godliest who ever lived went through agonizing moments of pain, suffering, uncertainty, and perplexity. The list includes David, Joseph and Jeremiah, to name a few. Struggle is part of the development process; not knowing is part of the intrigue of growth; and failure is part of the learning curve and motivation for success.

Moreover, although important, churchgoing is not necessarily a sign of spiritual intelligence. Attending church may indicate that a person is religious, but this does not mean that one who goes to church regularly is more spiritual than one who does not. Some people may not be able to attend church due to illness or persecution. In addition, people go to church for different reasons; plus a person may go to church for years and not be affected by its teachings.

Being religious or having religion is not to be equated with spiritual intelligence. Religious traditions show us how we might construct our attitudes and behaviors in spiritually significant ways, but of themselves do not have the power to transform anyone. Put another way, religion may be a means of raising and developing spiritual consciousness, but religion does not impart spiritual life and intelligence. This is the purview of God.

Spiritual transformation is uniquely a work of the Spirit. It is a spiritual journey beginning with a personal relationship with God, enhanced by the development of spiritual intelligence enabling maturity, and is a never-ending quest.

It is apparent in the way life is lived that not everyone has spiritual life and intelligence. There is an intelligence associated with the people of God via the Spirit, teaching, guiding, enlightening and so on, that is not associated with the people of the world (John 14:16-17, 26; 15:26-27; 16:13-15). The Scriptures describe some people as spiritually alive, spiritually wise and capable of spiritual growth (1 Cor. 2:4-8; 3:1-3; Col. 1:9; Gal. 6:1; James 1:5-7; 3:13-16; 1 Pet. 2:1-3), and some people as spiritually dead (Matt.

8:21-22; 15:14; 23:17-19; Luke 9:60; Eph. 2:1-5).

In Scripture, the spiritually dead are labeled the "natural man," and the spiritually alive as the "spiritual man." The natural man (animal man) is spiritually obtuse, has no appetite for spiritual things, perceives things of a spiritual nature as foolishness, and is therefore unqualified to appraise the spiritual.

> The man without the Spirit does not accept the things that come from the Spirit of God, for they are foolishness to him, and he cannot understand them, because they are spiritually discerned. (1 Cor. 2:14, NIV)

On the other hand, although operating at different levels of competency, people who are spiritually alive appreciate the spiritual and have the ability to appraise things that are carnal and things that are spiritual: "The person with the Spirit makes judgments about all things, but such a person is not subject to merely human judgments." (1 Cor. 2:15, NIV).

Notion of Spiritual Dimension to Humanity

The biblical data present human beings as multidimensional: as having a body, soul and spirit (Deut. 4:29; Job 7:11; Ps. 84:21; 1 Sam. 1:15; Isa. 26:9; 1 Thess. 5:23; Luke 1:47). The spirit is the life agent. It is the basis for spiritual and physical life. Although intricately connected to the body, the spirit is a separate entity. Moreover, the spirit and the body (flesh) do not operate at the same level and are not always in sync with each other. Based on biblical literature:

- The spirit may be willing while the flesh is weak (Mark 14:38).
- The flesh may be perishing while the spirit is being renewed (2 Cor. 4:16).
- The spirit may be alive while the flesh is dead (Jhn.1:25-26; 6:47; 1 Cor. 5:5).

Like the spirit, the soul is viewed as the essence and substance of human life

(Matt. 10:27-28; Mk. 8:36-37). The soul leaves the body at death (Gen. 35:18); it may return to give life to the deceased (1 Kings 17:21-22) or remain with God until the resurrection (Luke 14:12-14; Rev. 6:9-11; 20:4-6; Jhn. 5:28-29). "Much of the popular and theological understanding of the essential properties of humanness and personhood has been tied to the concept of a soul" (Brown, 2004, p. 59).

Based on the Bible, the soul:

1. Can be distinguished from the body and spirit
   (1 Thess. 5:23; Heb. 4:12; Gen. 2:7; Luke 1:46)

2. Can be warred against (1 Peter 2:11)

3. Can be hunted (Ezek. 13:18)

4. Can be sinned against (Hab. 2:10)

5. Can be lost (Matt. 16:26)

6. Can be held accountable (Luke 12:20)

7. Can be saved (Heb. 10:39; Acts 2:41; James 1:21; Peter 1:9)

8. Can be resurrected (Rev. 20:4)

9. Can experience rest (Matt. 11:29)

The Bible distinguishes between body, soul and spirit (1 Thess. 5:23) and highlights these features as components of personhood. However, there is disagreement among theologians as to whether human beings are trichotomous – have a body, soul and spirit. Nonetheless, there is agreement that human beings are comprised of both a physical and spiritual dimension.

Life in a given dimension is manifested by fruit consistent with the nature of life. "Flesh gives birth to flesh, but the Spirit gives birth to spirit" (John 3:6, NIV). Accordingly, there is fruit of the Spirit and fruit of the flesh (Gal. 5:19-23), or fruit of light and fruit of darkness (Eph. 5:8-12).

If a natural and physical dimension bears fruit via natural intelligence, then a spiritual and supernatural dimension bears fruit via spiritual intelligence. "As power of some kind belongs to every substance, the power which belongs to spirit, to the substance self, is that of thought, feeling, and volition" (Hodge, 1982, p. 378). The notion that human beings have a spiritual dimension implies the capacity and need for spiritual intelligence.

Notion of Reward and Punishment

Everything we do has consequences. There is reward and punishment in this life and also in the afterlife. Concepts of reward and punishment span every age and are present in every culture. Notions of reward and punishment are deeply imbedded in the human psyche and are common themes of scripture.

According to the Bible, both the righteous and the unrighteous will be judged (Prov. 14:32; Eccl. 3:17; 12:13-14; Jhn. 5:24-29; 1 Jhn. 4:17) and rewarded/punished. Reward and punishment are based on the righteousness and justice of God, who sees and knows everything. "Nothing in all creation is hidden from God's sight. Everything is uncovered and laid bare before the eyes of him to whom we must give account" (Heb. 4:13, NIV). Not even a cup of cold water given in the name of Jesus goes unnoticed and will go unrewarded (Matt. 10:42).

Since everyone is ultimately accountable to God, everyone should be prepared to be judged. The prophet Amos talks about a preparation essential for meeting God in the judgment (Amos 4:12). The writer of Hebrews sees death and judgment as appointments all are obliged to keep (Heb. 9:27). The concept of reward and punishment after death resonates with the apostle Paul (Rom. 2:16; 1 Cor. 4:5; 2 Cor. 5:10) and the apostle John (Rev. 19-22). These views are also supported by John the Baptist (Jhn. 3:31-36), and are, in fact, major themes of Jesus' teachings (Jhn. 3:10-21; 5:19-30).

There is more to life than physicality. St. Paul describes the physical body as a tent or clothing in which the soul dwells (2 Cor. 5:1-3). Moreover, physical death is not final. After death the corrupted body will be redeemed (Rom. 8:23). Redemption of the body will take place at the resurrection. The resurrected body will be reunited with the soul and spirit (1 Cor. 5:3; 15:12-26; 1 Thess. 4:13-18; Job. 19:25-27) and will be in a form capable of immortality. There will be a new quality of life; the physical body will be changed to a spiritual body and from mortality to immortality. So death may be viewed as a bridge enabling the crossing over from one dimension to the next.

Death is not final. This is why God is able to judge both the living and the dead (2 Tim. 4:1). If death were final, God would not be just as there would be no way of rewarding good and punishing evil, would there? Faith in God would be an exercise in futility, as ultimately all die – good and bad alike. What then would be the purpose of life, if irrespective of our deeds or the path taken there is no reward or punishment?

Belief in the resurrection and in life after death is fundamental to a sense of purpose, and to the Christian faith:

> For if the dead are not raised, then Christ has not been raised either. And if Christ has not been raised, your faith is futile; you are still in your sins. Then those also who have fallen asleep in Christ are lost. If only for this life we have hope in Christ, we are to be pitied more than all men. (1 Cor. 15:16-19, NIV)

> Do not be afraid of those who kill the body but cannot kill the soul. Rather, be afraid of the one who can destroy both soul and body in hell. (Matt. 10:28, NIV)

> ...man is destined to die once, and after that to face judgment. (Hebrews 9:27, NIV)

Neither Jesus nor his disciples spoke of death in absolute terms. Jesus, for example, indicated that the time will come when the dead will not only hear his voice but will also be resurrected (Jhn. 5:25-29). The resurrection is a common theme of the Bible and is a popular belief among various religious groups. Most major religions believe in the resurrection of the dead and in final judgment involving reward and punishment.

Reward and punishment are integral to notions of purpose, growth and meaning, and are critical to the promotion of law and order. Every institution – be it family, religion, education, business or government – exist for a reason and has rules and principles by which it operates.

Rules and principles facilitate the achievement of goals and support the reason for existence or the fulfillment of purpose. Purpose is more likely to be fulfilled when motivated by reward and punishment.

According to the Bible, human beings will be judged both in the present life and in an afterlife of eternity (Jhn. 5:19-30; Acts 17:31; Rom. 6:23; 2 Cor. 9:6; Gal. 6:8; Heb. 9:27) based on choices made. Choices have consequences.

Choices play an important role in promoting order internally and externally – in our inner and outer world (spiritually and physically), and as we interact with others and with the environment. Appropriate choices not only enable order but also enable growth and the fulfillment of purpose. In a just system, good choices are rewarded and bad choices are punished.

If inappropriate choices had no consequences, what would be the motivation for doing good, learning, aspiring toward excellence or attaining wisdom? What would be the point of life or existence? If moral choices have no relative value or do not really matter, human life does not matter; does it?

Whatever the purpose and meaning of human life, reward and punishment are interwoven in the fabric. Rules and regulations provide the necessary foundation on which to build; are integral to the growth and success of people and institutions; encourage fair play and provide a sense of justice.

Besides being a compass to determine the path and manner in which things are done, rules and principles form part of what is called an appraisal system. Whether done formally or informally, people and their institutions are constantly being appraised.

Appraisal is done internally at various levels by gatekeepers and externally by the court of public opinion, inclusive of customers, clients and associates. If human beings are constantly appraising behavior in business and in several other areas of life, should we not expect the Creator to do the same where moral and spiritual behaviors are concerned?

The tendency to appraise self, others, organizations, situations and events is a human instinct, a reflex action hardwired in our genes for our survival and wellbeing, and for the survival and wellbeing of others. The ability to make these judgments implies intelligence.

Spiritual Intelligence: A Christian Perspective

It may be argued that the tendency and ability of humans to appraise behavior in every area of life and at every level reflect God's image in humanity, though an imperfect reflection. The ability and need to appraise behavior of all kinds is a critical feature of God's design, is an important aspect of personhood and a human right, which should never be denied or suppressed.

It is critical that people are encouraged to evaluate beliefs and behaviors, as evaluation allows for informed choices. Choices determine effectiveness, growth and health at the individual, corporate and societal levels, supported by reward and punishment.

Reward and punishment are necessary consequences in every civilized and just society. In a just and normal system, everyone plays by the same rules. Rules are clearly defined and commonly understood. Compliance to rules and principles leads to success; noncompliance leads to failure. One reaps what has been sown.

Appraisal is a way of evaluating choices and of providing a basis for reward and punishment. Religion does not escape these facts any more than other disciplines and institutions.

In the physical and natural realm, physical and natural laws are accepted and promoted by scientists and others as inviolable, as in addition to maintaining order, laws enable purpose to be fulfilled. Although flawed, the same holds true for the legal system where society is concerned.

If we accept laws as inviolable and integral to maintaining order in the natural and physical realm and to the wellbeing of society, why should it be inconceivable that there are divine laws crucial to order and wellness in the moral and spiritual domain? In this regard, whatsoever holds true in the natural domain also holds true in the spiritual.

Morally and spiritually speaking, it is commonly believed by the religious that we are stewards of God and that God rewards the faithful and punishes the unfaithful. It is also believed our character should mirror the character of our Creator.

God's grand design . . . can be meaningfully interpreted only in relation to the touch of a purpose extending beyond the confines of our individual lives and beyond the limit of our racial lives. . . It implies that anything and everything you do today can be truly interpreted and justly valued only against standards and criteria operative beyond the limits of the temporal universe. (Blamires, 1980, p. 145)

Christianity teaches that since God created human beings, humanity is accountable to God in this life and in an afterlife of eternity. In 1 Corinthians 15, St. Paul has made a strong case for the resurrection, pointing to it as the basis for hope and meaning, immortality and eternal life in heaven being the ultimate reward. Final reward and punishment are predicated on the existence of a soul and/spirit capable of immortality.

Reward and punishment are based on the character of God and on human efforts to faithfully represent God in the world, hence moral and spiritual laws. Spiritual laws are enforceable by a loving God who has a vested interest in preserving integrity in His creation. Compliance is best encouraged internally and externally: by encouraging responsibility and enforcing accountability.

Responsibility and accountability are critical to human life and development: to the life and development of individuals, institutions and society on the whole, and are critical to the minimization of corruption. No matter the race or culture, no matter the institution or nature of the relationship, responsibility and accountability are our firewalls of protection from corruption, and are the best ways to promote health, foster learning and growth and motivate appropriate behavior.

Appropriate behavior presumes an acceptable standard of righteousness and the ability to discern right from wrong, hence reward and punishment. Being Creator, God is Lawgiver and Final Judge. God will make final judgment in the afterlife. "If God does not exist and there is no immortality, then all the evil acts of men go unpunished and all the sacrifices of good men go unrewarded" (Craig, 2000, p. 49). This indeed would be a travesty. The need to live in such a way that we will be rewarded in this life and in an afterlife of spiritual existence implies spiritual intelligence.

Spiritual Intelligence: A Christian Perspective

Summary

Several biblical teachings, religious beliefs, concepts and practices support the theory of spiritual intelligence. Biblical teachings that support the notion of a spiritual reality and, by extension, the concept of spiritual intelligence, include: (a) the creation of the world by God, who is Spirit, (b) religion and religious practices such as worship, (c) the creation of human beings in the image of God, (d) the Fall, (e) the devil, (f) spiritual life and death, (g) a spiritual dimension or capacity associated with humanity, and (h) reward and punishment. In Scripture, death is not regarded as final or viewed in the absolute sense. It is possible for the spiritually dead to come alive spiritually and for the physically dead to be brought back to life (John 5:21-29). The teachings of Scripture may be summarized thus: Human beings were created by God and in the image of God. In the original state, human nature included spiritual life and intelligence so human beings could relate to God and fulfill the purpose for which we were designed. Human nature became corrupted due to the Fall (original sin), resulting in the loss of spiritual life and intelligence. Spiritual life and intelligence was regained for us by the life, death, burial and resurrection of Jesus, but are activated in human personality when a person embraces Jesus by faith. The Bible describes this as spiritual rebirth. When Jesus is embraced, the Holy Spirit reconnects the human spirit to God, thereby enabling spiritual life and intelligence. "The man without the Spirit does not accept the things that come from the Spirit of God, for they are foolishness to him, and he cannot understands them, because they are spiritually discerned" (1 Cor. 2:14). Since everyone does not embrace Jesus or has a personal relationship with God, everyone does not possess spiritual life and intelligence. And since there are consequences based on choices in the natural realm, it should not surprise us that there are also consequences based on spiritual and moral choices. Christians believe that human beings are comprised of a spiritual dimension capable of immortality, that there is an afterlife of spiritual existence and that God who is Spirit is our Creator, Lawgiver and Final Judge. God has made universal coherence and sustainability of moral values possible through the establishment of moral laws and the impartation of spiritual life and intelligence.

CHAPTER 6

Uniqueness of
Spiritual Intelligence

In the previous chapter, biblical literature, as a major authority on spiritual matters, was examined for evidence in support of spiritual intelligence. In this chapter, some of the unique features of spiritual intelligence will be identified and discussed.

New and Old Testament literature attribute spiritual life and intelligence to a relationship with God. Since God is Spirit (John 3:23-24), the relationship between God and humanity must, of necessity, be spiritual in nature. This presupposes that human beings have the capacity to relate spiritually. Based on Scripture, human beings are comprised of both a physical and spiritual dimension. The ability of human beings to operate spiritually is due mainly to the work of the Spirit in imparting spiritual life and intelligence.

There is a major difference, however, in the operations of the Spirit in the New Testament and in the Old Testament. In the Old Testament, not everyone who bore a spiritual relationship to God had the Spirit of God abiding with them or possessed spiritual abilities. Based on Old Testament literature, the Spirit came upon special individuals or groups of persons such as prophets, priests and kings and remained with them to enable the fulfillment of purpose (Judg. 6:34; 11:29; 13:25; 1 Sam. 10:9-10; 16:13; 1 Chron. 12:18; Num. 27:18; Dan. 4:8; 6:3; Exod. 31:3; 35:31). However, this was temporary. The Spirit departed from persons thus favored if they were later rejected due to disobedience or sin (1 Sam. 16:14; Psa. 51:11). Old Testament data reveal God's presence mediated in the form of the Spirit as having been among His people or with them, not necessarily within them.

The New Testament paints a different picture. Whereas the Holy Spirit came upon or dwelled with Old Testament believers, New Testament believers receive a permanent indwelling. The difference between being present with believers of the Old Testament dispensation and indwelling believers of the New Testament dispensation is highlighted in John 14:15-17.

In the New Testament, people connected to God are indwelt indiscriminately and permanently. Permanent indwelling of believers by the Spirit was initiated at Pentecost (Acts 2:1-4), as promised by Jesus and some of the prophets (Joel 2:28-32; John 14:15-31; 16:5-16; Acts 1:8; 2:38-39).

Since Pentecost, everyone who embraces Jesus is indwelt by the Spirit and has membership in the family of God (John 1:12-13; 3:3-6; Eph. 1:13-14). Members of God's family are people who are truly connected to God at the spiritual level. People thus connected are possessed of spiritual life and intelligence.

Based on Scripture, it is the Spirit who enables spiritual life and intelligence and imparts spiritual gifts (Rom. 8; 12:3-8; 1 Cor. 12-14; Eph. 1:13). According to Nee (1968), the work of the Holy Spirit is threefold: (a) to regenerate, (b) to indwell, so believers might produce the fruit of the Spirit and (c) to enable people of faith with power to witness for Christ.

But why are some people spiritually connected to God and others are not? Scripture indicates that the Fall resulted in spiritual disconnection from God, leading to the immediate loss of spiritual life, and that human personality became corrupted. Every area of human personality was affected: the will, emotions and intellect were affected. Behavior was affected. Wholeness and integration formerly experienced by our primal progenitor were displaced by fracture and disintegration, passed down to posterity, thereby severely impacting the ability of humanity to achieve full potential.

Spiritual disempowerment resulted in the spirit being displaced by the flesh as the governing life principle: "Man's spirit is originally the highest part of his being to which soul and body are to be subject" (Nee 1968, p.

43). Having been disempowered in the area of spiritual capacity, we operate chiefly at the physical level via natural intelligence, informed by the operating system of the flesh, governed by the five senses.

There are two major operating systems, identifiable in human life and experience, influencing thought and behavior – the operating system of the flesh and the operating system of the Spirit. Each operates from a different area of capacity. One system is empowered by the physical dimension and operates from the capacity of the flesh; the other is empowered by the spiritual dimension and operates from the capacity of the spirit, enabled by the Holy Spirit. To this I must add a third, the operating system of the devil, influencing people directly or indirectly using diabolic means. Based on the fact that different principles or laws are at work, different fruit are produced in human personality, resulting in the classification of human beings as natural, carnal, and spiritual (Rom. 8:1-9).

Natural Man

The natural man is a reference to the unregenerate or unredeemed: one who has not yet experienced the grace of God by way of a spiritual rebirth. Such a person is in the dark spiritually, is unable to discern and appraise spiritual truths, and has difficulty in accepting the spiritual. In fact, things that are spiritual are regarded foolishness (1 Cor. 2:14) by the natural man.

To those who prided themselves on being wise according to the flesh, supported by the development of natural intelligence, Paul reminded them that because "the world through its wisdom did not come to know God, God was well-pleased through the foolishness of the message preached to save those who believe (1 Cor. 1:21, NASB). Earlier he remarked that "the word of the cross is foolishness to those who are perishing, but to those who are being saved it is the power of God" (1 Cor. 1:18, NASB).

Based on Scripture, the natural man (unregenerate) does not have the Spirit of God (Rom. 8:9); is worldly and accordingly manifests deeds of the flesh (Gal. 5:19-21).

Spiritual Intelligence: A Christian Perspective

Carnal Man

Although reborn spiritually, the carnal person is a spiritual babe, is therefore immature (1 Cor. 3:1-3; 1 Pet. 2:1-2), and as a consequence is not tremendously different from the unregenerate (natural man). Used in this sense, carnality is a factor of spiritual immaturity. Immature Christians are spiritual babes needing to grow up or develop spiritually: not much has been added to their faith, since being saved or redeemed. People who do not add to their faith stymie growth, and are thus described as unfruitful, short-sighted and blind, and in need of spiritual milk (2 Peter 1:3-11; 1 Peter 2:1-2).

Since the spiritually immature are unable to digest solid food or grasp deep spiritual truths, they need to be fed with milk or simple truths (1 Cor. 3:1-3; 1 Pet. 2:1-2). Failure to apply simple truths when revealed makes it impossible to move on to deeper truths and to develop their spiritual capacity (Heb. 5:13, 14). Unwillingness to learn, ignorance, indiscipline, disobedience and predisposition to live by the influence of the flesh, result in a cycle of spiritual stupor. In biblical terms, immature believers are perceived as having a carnal mind.

Carnality is a factor of ignorance and disobedience. Carnal people are spiritually "dark" or ignorant: They "are darkened in their understanding and separated from the life of God because of the ignorance that is in them due to the hardening of their hearts" (Eph. 4:18, NIV). Ignorance is a major cause of darkness and unwholesome behavior, and may become systemic on account of arrogance.

Carnality has to do with a particular worldview – a mind set on walking according to the dictates of the flesh, governed by rules and principles by which the world operates. Carnality describes an obsession with the world's system as the source of thought and action, and obsession with the world's goods. Self-aggrandizement and pleasure are the motivations for living.

Another word used to describe carnality is "worldliness." Worldliness is a way of thinking and being which places man at the center of life and God, if acknowledged at all, at the periphery. As a system, worldliness promotes godlessness and self-centered living, hence the biblical injunction against conformity and love for the world's system (Rom. 12:2; 1 John 2:12

-3:34). As a philosophy, pleasure is the ultimate goal, hence hedonism.

Paul is unequivocal in noting that the sinful nature of the flesh is not eradicated when a person is reborn spiritually. Being alive physically means that the sinful nature of the flesh is a source of constant conflict with the new divine nature of the Spirit (Rom. 7:15-20; Gal. 5:13-26; 2 Peter 1:3-5). Consequently, there is often a huge gap between head knowledge and behavior. Unless a practitioner, nothing is really learned. The Spirit helps to bridge the gap and resolve the conflict by enabling spiritually intelligent choices. Accordingly, believers are admonished to walk in step with the Spirit.

Spiritual Man

Walking in step with the Spirit is the essence of spirituality. This involves identifying with God by faith; representing God in the world by doing good and by a lifestyle of holiness.

As opposed to self-centered living, which is the essence of carnality, the spiritual is motivated by Spirit-centered living. Among other things, spiritual life involves a positive response to the impulses and dictates of the Spirit.

Although not necessarily in the same order for everyone, the following path toward spiritual enlightenment and growth may be discerned:

1. Awareness of God
2. Conscious acknowledgement of God's existence
3. Surrender to God's authority and rule
4. Acceptance of God's means of salvation
5. Regeneration
6. Commitment to walk according to spiritual laws
7. Application of spiritual laws
8. Practice of spiritual disciplines
9. Increasing knowledge of the spiritual
10. Increasing spiritual growth

The spiritual man is a mature Christian who has a deep relationship with

God. Such a person is able to discern the spiritual, walks according to the influence or dictates of the Spirit, and manifests the fruit of the Spirit (1 Cor. 2:12-15; Gal. 5:22, 23).

Spirituality vs. Carnality

Life lived according to the dictates of the flesh is different from life according to the dictates of the Spirit (Rom. 8:5). There are therefore discernible differences between the natural/carnal person and the spiritual person. Whereas the Spirit exercises control over the mind of the spiritual person, the mind of the carnal person is controlled by the flesh. Each mindset is in opposition to the other (Rom. 8:1-17; Gal. 5:13-26; 6:7-10).

There are little or no discernible differences between the carnal person and the natural person; both are characterized by worldliness, and thus walk according to the dictates of the flesh. In summary, the natural man has no spiritual intelligence, the carnal man has a low level of spiritual intelligence, and the spiritual man has a moderate to high level of spiritual intelligence.

The natural and carnal are set apart from the spiritual by virtue of the nature or type of intelligence informing behavior. Intelligence is consistent with the nature of being. Morally and spiritually, there is a way of thinking and acting, influenced by the flesh, which is consistent with the way the world's system and the flesh operate; and there is a way of thinking and acting, influenced by the Spirit, consistent with the way the Spirit operates. There is a mind associated with physicality, and there is a mind associated with spirituality; there is physical consciousness, and there is spiritual consciousness. Natural intelligence is associated with the physical nature of the flesh. Spiritual intelligence is associated with the spiritual nature of a renewed spirit.

The Bible associates transformation with regeneration by the Spirit and renewal of the mind (Titus 3:2-5; Rom. 12:2). Renewal of the mind is enabled by the Spirit and the sacred Scriptures (Col. 3:5-17; 1 Pet. 2:1-2; 2 Pet. 1:3-11). When the mind is renewed, people generally make more spiritually intelligent choices (Rom. 12:1-2; Phil. 4:8; Hosea 4:6), hence spiritual growth.

Having been corrupted, renewal of the mind is integral to spiritual life and development (Rom. 12:1-2; Eph. 4:23). As the mind influences every aspect of human personality and capacity, the mind is a major battle field. The war on spirituality is a war on the spirit of the mind: it is spiritual and ideological warfare.

Because the operating system of the flesh and the operating system of the Spirit are diametrically opposed to each other, there is constant conflict internally and externally. In addition to personal struggles with the old man, people born of the Spirit are in conflict with the people of the world, sometimes the war escalating from ideology to other forms of warfare, leading to the persecution and death of believers.

The spiritual and the carnal man will always be in conflict, for a number of reasons, including:

1. Life by the operating system of the flesh promotes spiritual ignorance. Life by the operating system of the Spirit promotes spiritual intelligence. (1 Cor. 2:12-14)

2. Life by the operating system of the Spirit promotes spirituality as the ultimate reality, as the basis for human life and development and God as the center of life around whom the world revolves. Life by the operating system of the flesh promotes physicality as the only reality and human beings as the center of life around whom the world revolves.

Disconnected from God, the human spirit is spiritually dead, is unredeemed, is under the influence of the flesh, and may also be under the evil influence of demonic spirits or the devil. In Scripture, unspiritual thinking is associated with the unredeemed or the natural man; spiritual thinking is associated with the redeemed or spiritual man (Eph. 1:7; 5:8-12). The unredeemed is at enmity with God (Rom. 8:7-8), is in darkness (Rom. 1:21) and engages in futile thinking (Eph. 4:17-19).

When connected to God, the human spirit is redeemed, is possessed of spiritual life and intelligence, is under the influence of the Spirit, enabling recovery from the power of sin. However, because the sinful nature of the flesh is not eradicated at conversion and the mind is not renewed overnight, it is possible for the redeemed to experience moral lapses and display spiritual ignorance. Despite the ability to overcome the world (1 Jhn. 4:1-6; 5:4-5), the redeemed may conform to the pattern of thought and behavior established by the world (1 Cor. 3:1-3; 5:1-13), and may therefore be described as carnal.

As volition and human effort is involved, some struggle more than others in the quest toward spiritual maturity. There is constant pressure to live a superficial spiritual life or become worldly. The Bible discourages conformity to the world:

> And do not conform to this world, but be transformed by the renewing of your mind, so that you may prove what the will of God is, that which is good and acceptable and perfect (Rm. 12:2, NASB).

The above Scripture implies a tendency to conform to the system of thought which governs the world, that there is something patently wrong with how the world thinks or operates, and that people of the world do not accept the will of God as "good," "acceptable" and "perfect," hence the need for transformation.

Transformation begins with renewal of the mind. It is critical that the mind be renewed, because the mind is the control center of everything and is the gateway to the body, soul and spirit. And since human dilemma is rooted in the spiritual and is the foundation of everything, spiritual intelligence is integral to the process of transformation. A renewed mind supported by spiritual intelligence has the potential to radically change a person's thoughts and behavior, enabling knowledge of God's will and acceptance of it as being good and perfect.

It is possible for human beings to operate in sync with the will of God because we were created by God and in the image of God. The notion that human beings are created in the image of God (Gen. 1:27) implies the ability to reflect the thoughts, emotions, actions and character of God. Based on the Bible, God desires holiness (1 Peter 1:15-17) and is angry with unrighteousness (Romans 2:1-11).

The character of humanity is to mirror the character of God. Conformity to the character of God is possible via submission to the Rule of God and the Will of God. Independence of God and self-rule produce a life of its own – one which is contrary to the Will of God and contrary to human design and destiny. Obedience signifies recognition and respect for God's authority; disobedience signifies rebellion and disrespect, and associates the disobedient with the enemies of God. Furthermore, since sin is ultimately against God, in addition to aligning sinners with evildoers, sinfulness makes us pliable to manipulation and control by the devil, and herein lies our dilemma.

The Fall established a new spiritual order. Whereas formerly obedience to God was the norm, obedience to the devil has become the new norm, a trajectory initiated by our primal progenitor, Adam. The will, emotions and intellect of our federal head, having been corrupted, the principle of sin has become an inherent feature of human nature, making it impossible to reach our full potential and fulfill our destiny. As every aspect of the decision-making faculty has been compromised since the Fall, human beings are inclined toward inappropriate moral and spiritual choices.

Because the Fall made inappropriate choices inevitable, the mind needs to be redeemed. A redeemed mind connected to God, inclines a person to make appropriate moral and spiritual choices (Phil. 2:13). St. Paul averred the power of God is at work in the people of God (Eph. 3:20-21).

The mind of the unredeemed (unspiritual) and the mind of the redeemed (spiritual) are influenced by opposing sources of wisdom, identifiable in the fruit of their character (James 3:13-18) and scope of influence (1 John 4:1-6). One source of wisdom is below or earthly, and the other is above or heavenly. Earthly wisdom is associated with human beings in their natural state and may manifest as natural intelligence or a perverted (diabolic) form of spiritual intelligence, influenced by demons. The wisdom which is from above gives the heavenly or godly perspective, and is associated with the redeemed and with spiritual intelligence associated with God.

Spiritual Intelligence: A Christian Perspective

Based on biblical literature, the wisdom of God is greater than the wisdom of men and greater than that which is associated with the devil (1 Cor. 1:20-31; 3:19-20; 1 John 4:4). True wisdom comes from God and begins with showing respect for God (Ps. 111:10; Prov. 9:10; James 1:5-6). The Spirit of God or the Holy Spirit is the true source of wisdom (1 Cor. 2:1-16). The word of wisdom is a spiritual gift (1 Cor. 12:18).

In James 3:13-18, James compares wisdom that is unspiritual with wisdom that is spiritual, and points to opposing sources and contrasting fruit: the former is attributed to the devil, and the latter to God. Spiritual wisdom is aligned with truth and produces the fruit of righteousness. Unspiritual wisdom is aligned with ignorance (or pseudo-spirituality), and produces the fruit of unrighteousness. Biblical literature makes a correlation between wisdom and righteousness (Prov. 23:24; 24:7; Eph. 5:1-17), and between ignorance and unrighteousness (Prov. 14:16; 15:21; 1 Peter 1:13-15).

Reproof and discipline originating in fear of God leads to wisdom and are life-giving (Prov. 8:1-36; 14:12; 15:31-33). Permissiveness and undisciplined behavior lead to ignorance, and are life-taking (Prov. 15:31-33).

Unfortunately, ungodly philosophies based on human traditions and elementary principles of the world, promoting permissiveness and unrighteousness are the order of the day. Paul warned of a cultural prism leading to a hollow and deceptive philosophy of life. He also indicated that the philosophy of Christ and all that Christ represents supersedes culture (Col. 2:8, 23). Culture that does not cohere with the Will and Word of God produces unrighteousness.

Unrighteousness is antithetical to the best interest of human beings and, therefore, reflects spiritual ignorance. Whereas spiritual ignorance has brought disgrace and instability, spiritual intelligence has empowered, enabled and uplifted human beings (Prov. 14:34).

Spiritual Intelligence as Divine Enablement

Spiritual intelligence may be viewed in terms of a divine enablement. Biblical data reveal a number of instances of divine enablement in human life and experience. Examples of spiritual enablement in the biblical literature include:

1. Enabling joy in the face of persecution and death (Acts 13:49-52)
2. Enabling effectiveness in ministry (Acts 14:1-7, 19-22; Rom. 15:17-19; 1 Cor. 2:1-4)
3. Enabling boldness and confidence (Daniel 3:13-18; 6:4-11; Acts 4:31; 2 Cor. 12:1-4; Eph. 3:12; Hebrews 11)
4. Enabling visions, dreams and interpretation of dreams (Gen. 40, 41; Dan. 5:11-12; Acts 10:1-23; 16:6-9)
5. Enabling miracles (Rom. 15:19; 1 Cor. 12; Heb. 2:3-4)
6. Enabling discovery of danger and escape from danger (Acts 14)
7. Enabling steadfastness in service (2 Cor. 1:12, 21-22)
8. Enabling wisdom in the appointment of leaders (Acts 14:23)
9. Enabling grace and wisdom through the disciplines of prayer and fasting (Acts 14:23)
10. Enabling wise council through debate and discussion (Acts 15)
11. Enabling spiritual direction (Acts 10:1-22; 16:6-11)
12. Enabling analysis of the spoken word (Acts 17:10-12)
13. Enabling grace in the face of death (Acts 9)
14. Enabling spiritual gifts (Rom. 1:11; 1 Cor. 12:1, 14:1, 12)
15. Enabling spiritual fruit (Gal. 5:22-23; 6:7-8)
16. Enabling spiritual sacrifices (1 Pet. 2:5)
17. Enabling Christ-like character or holiness (Rom. 1:4; 8:1- 4; 2 Cor. 1:12; 3:18; 2 Thess. 2:13; 1 Pet. 1:2, 22)
18. Enabling revelation (1 Chron. 28:12; Acts 1:28; 11:28; 21:4; 1 Cor. 2:9-15)
19. Enabling salvation (2 Cor. 1:21-22)
20. Enabling discernment (Acts 5:1-11; 1 Cor. 12:10)
21. Enabling spiritual understanding (Isa. 11:2; John 14:26; 1Cor. 2:14; Col. 1:9)
22. Enabling spiritual blessings (Eph. 1:3)

23. Enabling spiritual songs (Eph. 5:19; Col. 3:16)

24. Enabling spiritual leading/direction (Neh. 9:20; Acts 11:12; 16:7; Rom. 8:14)

25. Enabling spiritual power in various situations (Mic. 3:8; Luke 24:49; Acts 1:4-8; Heb. 11)

26. Enabling success in spiritual warfare (Eph. 6:10-18)

27. Enabling love (Rom. 5:5; 15:30)

Spiritual Intelligence as Love

Someone once said "the heart of the matter is the matter of the heart." It is apparent that the heart is a source of wisdom: some people describe it as intuition; some as a sixth sense; some as the seat of the emotions; and others associate the heart with emotional intelligence.

Although belief needs to be evaluated, knowledge may be belief-based; that is, a person may know intuitively, separate and apart from instruction or learning. This view is supported in Scripture. For instance, Jeremiah predicted a time when the Word of God will be written on the hearts of Jews (Jer. 31:33). In Romans 2:14-15, Paul talks about the Law written on the hearts of Gentiles having as much value as the written Word.

It is important that focus be placed on the heart, because from the heart springs a number of negative and positive emotions, affecting human life and development. Because of the important role the heart plays, we are admonished in Scripture to guard our heart (Prov. 4:23) and to walk in love (Eph. 5:2).

Although at times used interchangeably, the heart and mind have intelligence of their own. Experience tells us that the heart may be darkened or enlightened, and that the condition of the heart has nothing necessarily to do with education or academic level. As a result, an ignorant person may do something extremely noble and a well-educated person may be guilty of ignoble acts. The reality is: the intellectually underdeveloped may be more compassionate and better adjusted emotionally than the intellectually brilliant.

The compassionate and self-controlled may have been brought up in an environment of love, may have chosen this path intuitively, or may have done so due to the influence of significant others, including spiritual caregivers. Despite the reason for intelligence connected to the heart, theological support makes love a more sustainable and desirable quality. In the Bible, love is highlighted as a fruit of the Spirit (Gal. 5:22), hence the notion of love as an expression of spiritual intelligence. In fact, love is the highest expression of spiritual intelligence and is the law that liberates us to be all we were meant to be.

Spiritual intelligence is best demonstrated in acts of love: love for God and love for people. This view is echoed by James, who delimits religious practices to two things: helping the needy and moral purity (James 1:27). This resonated with the apostle Paul (Romans 12:9-21; 13:8-10).

In light of the fact that we share a common humanity and a common Creator, we have an obligation to love God and to love members of the human family. Jesus agreed that the foremost commandments are love for God and love for our neighbor (Mark 12:28-34). Love for God and love for our neighbor are inextricably linked:

> Whoever claims to love God yet hates a brother or sister is a liar. For whoever does not love their brother and sister, whom they have seen, cannot love God, whom they have not seen. (1 John 4:20, NIV)

Hatred and oppression of people based on religion, race, politics and social class, etc. are unacceptable. In Scripture:

- Love for God is commanded (Mark 12:29-31)
- Love for believers is commanded (John 13:34)
- Love for enemies (unbelievers) is commanded (Matt. 5:43 - 47)
- Love is a debt that can never be fully discharged (Rom. 13:8 - 9)
- Love does no wrong to its neighbor (Rom. 13:10)
- Love fulfills the law (Rom. 13:8-14; Gal. 5:14)

- Through love we are to serve one another (Rom. 5:13; Heb. 10:25)
- Love overlooks, covers and saves from sin (Prov. 10:12; James 5:20; 1 Peter 4:8)
- We are to treat people the same way we would like to be treated — with love (Matt. 7:12)

When people are loved, opportunities are sought to help them; when hated, needs are ignored, there is indifference to social ills, and opportunities are sought to hurt them. People who hurt others spark a vicious cycle of retribution and unending insanities, making the world an insecure and unsafe place to live. Indeed, "hurting people hurt people." It makes sense to love God and to love each other, because the alternative is disempowering and destructive. Hate is wasted and destructive energy, is the source of all kinds of evil, sicknesses and diseases.

Loving God and loving other members of the human family make the world a secure and safe place for all to live. Love enables peaceful coexistence and aligns us with God. Love mirrors the very character of God for God is love (1 John 4:7-12).

Love is the most excellent way (1 Cor. 13). Love is the supreme gift: it does indeed undergirds all the other gifts, giving them value and meaning, causing them to function effectively for the good of all, thereby enabling the fulfillment of our potential.   In the Bible, Christians are described as members of one body (Rom. 12:4-5; 1 Cor. 12:13), possessing different spiritual gifts, distributed by one Spirit (1 Cor. 12), that we might live together in love (1 Cor. 13). Love for God is key to spiritual intelligence and key to overcoming the world:

> This is the love for God: to obey His commandments. And His commandments are not burdensome, for everyone born of God has overcome the world. This is the victory that has overcome the world, even our faith. (1 John 5:3-4, NIV)

The world is fragmented due to lack of love, and every other form of deviance is rooted in the failure of human beings to love God and to love one another. This is why love and unity were chief concerns of Jesus and received so much attention from the spiritually intelligent. Jesus prayed that his disciples, both present and future, would be one (John 17:20-23). David declared: "How good and pleasant it is when God's people live together in unity" (Psalm 133:1, NIV). The writer of Hebrews exhorted believers to "Continue in brotherly love" (Heb. 13:1). Paul exhorted believers to keep the unity of the Spirit (Eph. 4:1-6).

Unfortunately, love does not come naturally for most. Even among family members love may be lacking (Matt. 10:36; 1 John 3:11-12). And where love is lacking there is hate and fragmentation. This is why we are commanded to love one another (John 15:17) and why love is the greatest commandment (Matt. 22:36-40). Older women are therefore exhorted to teach younger women how to love their husbands (Titus 2:3-5), and husbands are exhorted to love their wives (Eph. 5:25). Being members of the human race and members of the same family in particular, one would think love would be automatic; but we know this is not the case. And instead of getting better, things will get worse (2 Tim. 3:2-4).

What is love? Love means different things to different people; and most who talk about love do not have a clue what they are talking about. They'll love a person as long as the person can help them or fulfill a need. Barring that, the person is just another statistic. Today most relationships are transactional: "I scratch your back and you scratch mine." Ask yourself: do I truly care about others? What motivates my interest in the person or people I claim to love?

Since love is not easily defined, love is best understood in terms of how it is manifested – actions associated with it (1 Cor. 13; Rom. 13:10; John 14:23-24; 15:10-17; 1 John 3:16-17). Love is defined by what love does, not by words and feelings expressed, though important. Genuine love solves all relationship issues, and most importantly, our relationship with God. This is why the command to love is the greatest, for love is the highest expression of spiritual intelligence.

Love is more than feelings. Love is an interest in the total wellbeing of another. Love must be intelligently directed and must be circumscribed by truth. For example, to love righteous is to hate evil. Why should we hate evil? Because evil is not in the best interest of an individual or society. Evil degrades and dehumanizes us, makes us pliable to demonic control and aligns us with the devil. Evil is offensive to God and dishonor's Him. Everything we do should be done to bring honor and glory to God (Coloss. 3:17). We cannot serve two masters (Matt. 6:24). If people who love deeply demand and expect everyone in their circle of love to toe the line or play by the same rules, why should we expect anything less from a loving God?

Spiritual Intelligence as Light

The concept of spiritual intelligence is also supported, defined and differentiated by metaphorical language such as "light" and "darkness." In the Scriptures, light is often used metaphorically to symbolize intelligence, truth, goodness and righteousness, which are essential features of human development.

In religion, light describes a path and is held up in opposition to darkness. Although understanding differs, many religions believe in a Universal Light. Pantheists, for example, are of the view that Universal Light is another name for nature. Christianity teaches that this Universal Light is the reflection of a personal God, who, although He may be seen and experienced in nature, is not the same as nature. God is believed to have existed before nature and is above and beyond nature; God should therefore not be confused with nature. God is not nature. God is the Creator of nature and everything that flows from it. Universal Light is reflected in all of nature.

Human beings, animals and plants are dependent on natural light for their survival. In creating the physical and natural world, the first thing God did was to introduce light into the world (Gen. 1:1-5). Of necessity, there had to be light before there was life. Natural light is necessary for creating and sustaining natural life, such as plant and animal life. It is not accidental that plants grow toward sunlight. Sunlight provides the photosynthesis needed by plants to grow. Photosynthesis is the process by which carbon-dioxide is converted into carbohydrates, the food plants need to grow. Plants in turn produce oxygen and provide food, essential for the survival of animal and human life. The light that sustains and nurtures plants and animals is also integral to the sustenance and enjoyment of human life. Everything in nature is a reflection of the light to which it is exposed and connected.

Nothing exists without light. Light enables life and sustains it. As a form of energy, it enables communication within living cells, among various species and with other aspects of creation. Light is the foundation of the physical and natural world as well as the foundation of the spiritual and supernatural world.

Spiritual light is necessary for creating and sustaining spiritual life. Spiritual light is essential to the survival and wellbeing of human beings. Spiritual light provides spiritual energy necessary for spiritual growth, and is transforming.

In addition to being the Source of natural light, God is also the Source of spiritual light (2 Cor. 4: 6-7). God is the Father of lights (James 1:17), in whom there is no darkness (1 John 1:5). All wisdom, truth and righteousness reside in God.

The Holy Spirit, the third person of the triune-God, is described as light also. As the eye is to the light of the body, so is the Spirit to the light of the spirit. The Holy Spirit is described as the Spirit of truth (John 14:17; 15:26; 16:13; 1 John 5:6), the Revealer of things spiritual (1 Cor. 2:10-11; Col. 1:9), and the Source of spiritual life and intelligence (1 Cor. 2:6-16).

The Holy Spirit is credited with giving spiritual light and life to people who embrace Jesus. Life and light are also attributed to Jesus (John 1:1-10; 8:12; 9:5; 12:35-46; 14:6). In Scripture, Jesus is described as Light of the world (John 3; Titus 3:5; Gal. 4:29; Eph. 1:13; 1 Cor. 6:9-11).

Embracing Jesus results in spiritual rebirth (John 1:12-13; 3:5-6). Accordingly, the spiritually reborn are translated from the kingdom of darkness to the kingdom of light (John 12:35-36, 44-46; Col. 1:13). Darkness describes the realm of Satan; light describes the realm of God. Based on Scripture, God is calling people out of darkness into light (2 Cor. 6:14; Eph. 5:11; Acts 26:18; 1 Pet. 2:9; 1 Thess. 5:4-5). Walking in the light is the basis for fellowship with God and with one another (1 John 1:6-8).

The metaphors, light and darkness, describe opposing paths, different mindsets and ways of life. They are used to distinguish people who are related to God spiritually from people disconnected or unrelated to God in a spiritual sense. Accordingly, people connected to God are deemed children of light; people disconnected from God are deemed children of darkness.

People disconnected from God are spiritually blind (Isa. 56:10; Matt. 15;14; 23;16-17, 24-26; Rom. 2:19; 2 Cor. 4:4; 2 Pet. 1:9; 1 John 2:11; Rev. 3:17). In addition to ignorance and arrogance (Eph. 4:18; John 3:19), spiritual blindness is caused by diabolical affliction (2 Cor. 4:3-4), making it all the more difficult for unbelievers to see the light of the gospel.

Spiritually speaking, the dichotomy of life comprises light and darkness; the former symbolizing truth (knowledge) and righteousness (good) on one hand; the latter symbolizing falsehood (ignorance) and unrighteousness (evil) on the other, represented by God and the devil respectively. Volition enables us to go in one direction or the other.

In the Bible, Paul points to an immediate change in the standing or status of believers and a progressive change in their state morally and spiritually (2 Cor. 5:17; Eph. 4:17-33; 5:8-14). Essentially, believers are being transformed into the image of Christ and are moving away from darkness to light (Rom. 13:11-14). The closer we get to the light, the more like God we become.

It is not accidental that the people of God are called children of light (Eph. 5:8-9) and are expected to produce the fruit of light (Matt. 5:14-16; Phil. 2:12-15). The ability to reflect the light of God is an important feature of human design. The more brilliant the reflection, the more the glory of God is revealed.

Unfortunately, the only person to have done so successfully is Jesus. However, for fully revealing the glory of God, Jesus has made it possible for people connected to him (his spiritual offspring) to do the same (Col. 1:27; Rom. 5:12-21). Christ living in us, enables the fulfillment of our potential.

Fulfilling our potential includes glory for ourselves and glory for our Creator (Coloss. 1:27). Based on Scripture, the redeemed are to glorify God in body and spirit (1 Cor. 6:20), to do all things to the glory of God (1 Cor. 10:31), and are being changed from glory to glory (2 Cor. 3:18).

A fully functioning human being vividly reflects the glory of the Creator. Reflecting the glory of the Creator includes the ability to think or reason, the ability to experience a wide range of emotions and the ability to exercise freely one's will consistent with the nature and character of God.

The ability to live in a manner that brings glory to God is a factor of spiritual intelligence. As a reflection of the nature and character of God, human beings have been designed to produce good works. And we have been recreated in Christ for the same purpose (Eph. 2:10). Good works bring glory to God (Matt. 5:16).

Doing good works is described in Scripture as "walking in the light." Walking in the light enables harmony with God and harmony with fellow human beings (1 John 1:5-7). Saint Paul saw spiritual light in terms of a spiritual armor (Rom. 13:12-14), for spiritual light provides safety via spiritual direction.

Biblical data reveal that people are destroyed for lack of knowledge (Hosea 4:6; Prov. 4) and that evil is associated with ignorance (1 Peter 1:13-15). Walking in darkness, however, is not always based on ignorance; it is often based on arrogance – a mind set on evil (John 3:19-20).

Spiritual intelligence is able to save from evil and from moral filth, hence James' admonition: "Therefore, get rid of all moral filth and the evil that is so prevalent and humbly accept the word planted in you, which can save you. Do not merely listen to the word, and so deceive yourselves. Do what it says" (James 1:21-22).

As in the natural, truthfulness in knowledge is crucial and reaps tremendous benefits when applied. Truth sets us free (John 8:32) from ignorance and associated consequences. Spiritual intelligence helps in avoiding costly mistakes and enables spiritual growth and development.

Spiritual Intelligence as Spiritual Direction

Both Old and New Testament literature support the concept of spiritual leading or direction as normative for people associated with God. In fact, Scripture presents the leading of the Spirit as a distinguishing mark or chief characteristic of people belonging to the family of God: "For as many as are led by the Spirit of God, they are the sons of God" (Rom. 8:14, KJV).

The Holy Spirit is the chief agent of spiritual direction (John 16:13). Spiritual direction assumes competence or the intelligence to lead. Spiritual intelligence may therefore be assumed. Based on Scripture, the Holy Spirit has been given indiscriminately to members of the family of God as a source of influence, leading God's people in the right direction (Eph. 1:13-14). In addition to providing comfort, encouragement, power and assurance of victory (Matt. 28:20; John 14:15-18; 16:7; Acts 1:8), the Holy Spirit provides guidance (John 16:13).

The role of the Spirit as spiritual guide in the lives of believers is underscored by the need for guidance. There is need for guidance in the natural domain and there is need for guidance in the spiritual domain. The Spirit's role as guide is critical particularly since we live in a world beset by darkness and falseness. The presence of false apostles, false prophets, false teachers, false Christs, false religions, false cults, false doctrines, false science, false philosophies, false ideologies, false direction and lying spirits, make it imperative that believers are guided by the Spirit and have a way of discerning truth from error.

Spiritual discernment plays a critical role in enabling clarity and in enabling an effective witness to the world. It is against this background that the Holy Spirit was promised as guide and the revealer of truth to believers (John 14:15-17; 16:13-15). The Spirit's presence in us and with us indicates spiritual life and intelligence (Rom. 8:9; 1 Cor. 2:12-14; Gal. 5:16-26). The opposite is also true.

Since every child of God has the Spirit (Rom. 8:9; Eph. 1:13-14), the leading of the Spirit is characteristic of children of God. Response to the Spirit's leading, however, varies. Thus spiritual development is contingent on the exercise of volition or on the cooperative efforts of the people of God with the Spirit of God.

Experience and expression of spiritual life and intelligence are not homogenous. As in other areas of life, people operate at different levels of competency. Levels of spiritual growth and intelligence are relative to levels of cooperation with the Spirit.

Cooperation is not automatic, as by virtue of volition we have a choice in the matter. The leading of the Spirit may be accepted or rejected, hence the exhortation of the Apostle Paul (Gal. 5:16-18). Spiritual intelligence is the experience of walking according to the leading of the Spirit (Rom. 8:14-16). Ways in which the Spirit leads include: the written Word or Scripture, the spoken word of others, inspiration, illumination, dreams, visions, circumstances, impartation of spiritual wisdom and understanding, revelation and spiritual discernment.

In addition, the Spirit enables a heightened level of spiritual consciousness, openness to spiritual direction, practical wisdom and decision-making skills. Clearly some people are more disciplined in their efforts toward spiritual development than others, hence levels of spiritual growth and intelligence. In the final analysis, the Spirit must be submitted to, if growth is to take place.

However, submitting to the leading of the Spirit does not mean mindlessness; and faith is not opposed to reason. For example, Jesus offered proof of his resurrection (John 20:19-28; Acts 1:1-3); Paul admonished believers to be prepared to give a reason for their faith (1 Peter 3:15-16), Paul and others reasoned from the Scriptures (Acts 17:1-17) and encouraged and expected growth (Eph. 4:14-15).

Some things are hard to understand (2 Peter 3:16) and therefore demand a lot of reasoning or explanation. And some things may not be understood using natural means (2 Cor. 2:14). Spiritual intelligence is needed.

In the natural, some things really do not make sense, as in the case of Noah's Ark (Gen. 5:32-10:1). At the time building an ark was laughable. The ground was watered by a mist, and there were no prior experience of rains or floods, so there were no need for an ark. There was nothing natural about building an ark. You see, the building of an ark was not based on natural intelligence or common sense; it was based on spiritual intelligence and uncommon sense.

Spiritual Intelligence: A Christian Perspective

Uncommon sense is not unique to religion. Advance in science and technology has made many things possible, which were laughable prior invention. To some people, guns were laughable, televisions were laughable, planes were laughable, and the list goes on. As someone once said, "You don't know what you don't know."

Notwithstanding, in the area of the spiritual, natural intelligence is extremely limited. Some things lie in the realm of the supernatural and therefore require spiritual lens (1 Cor. 2:12-16). In order to perceive the spiritual and supernatural, spiritual intelligence is needed.

Operating on the basis of spiritual intelligence does not mean putting the brain in recess or in a state of inertia. Although faith is involved, faith without works is dead (James 2:14-20; 1 John 5:4; Matt. 17:19-21). Believers are therefore expected to:

- Prove their faith (James 2:14-26)
- Add to their faith (2 Peter 1:5-11)
- Grow in grace and knowledge (2 Peter 3:18)
- Increase in spiritual wisdom and understanding (Philipp. 1:9-10)
- Examine themselves (2 Cor. 13:5)
- Renew the mind (Rom. 12:1-2)
- Engage the mind (1 Cor. 14:10-19)
- Prepare the mind for action (1 Peter 2:9)
- Gird up the loins of the mind (1 Peter 1:13)
- Study the Word/Scriptures (2 Tim. 2:15; Col. 3:16)
- Be ready to give an answer for their hope (1 Peter 3:15)
- Be vigilant (1 Peter 5:8; Gal. 6:1-10)
- Encourage positive thoughts (Philipp. 4:8)
- Walk worthy of their vocation (Eph. 4:1)
- Make sure of their calling (2 Peter 1:10)
- Walk in newness of life (Romans 6:4)

- Walk in the light (John 8:12; Eph. 5:8; 1 Peter 2:9)
- Guard the heart (Prov. 4:23)
- Train the conscience to discern good from evil (Heb. 5:14)
- Prepare for war (Eph. 6:10-19)
- Train ourselves to be godly (1 Tim. 4:7-8)

Meaningful action is always required, even if prayer and fasting are the only actions to be taken at a particular moment in time (Matt. 17:19-21). Albeit, being human, we have limitations; plus it was never God's will for humanity to know everything (Deut. 29:29; Romans 11:33-36). Nevertheless, development of spiritual intelligence is necessary, if we are to grow spiritually. Spiritual growth is desired and expected (2 Pet. 1:5-10; 2:2; 1 Cor. 3:2).

Growth takes time and effort and involves struggle. Because the sinful nature of the flesh is not eradicated at the time of conversion, there is constant struggle between the outward man and the inward man, or between the sinful nature of the flesh and the sinless nature of the Spirit (Gal. 5:16-17). Each operating system functions by different principles (Rom. 7:21-23), hence conflict.

Although there is conflict, a person who is born-again is not schizophrenic. Positive change often involves conflict and takes time. Old habits die hard; plus it takes time and effort for the flesh to adjust and submit to the Spirit as the chief operating officer.

Successful spiritual living is not realized unless a person willingly submits to the influence of the Spirit (2 Cor. 10:3-5; Gal. 5). Albeit, being spiritually intelligent does not mean relinquishing the right to volition, the need to accept responsibility and to be held accountable for choices made.

While reminding us that it is God who enables the willing and doing of "His good pleasure," Paul exhorts believers to work out their own salvation with fear and trembling (Phil. 2:12-13). The spiritually reborn are to work out in daily practice the salvation God has already by the Spirit wrought in us. "Although the Spirit determines the goal and path, children of God must by their own efforts advance toward it" (Warfield, 1968).

Spiritual Intelligence: A Christian Perspective

Subsequent to being saved, there is a lot of things to work out, involving the exercise of spiritual intelligence. Exercising and developing spiritual intelligence are contingent on a number of factors, namely presenting one's body as a living sacrifice to God and renewing one's mind (Rom. 12:1-2).

Renewing the mind involves developing a spiritual mindset, which includes positive actions of the will, emotions and intellect (Col. 3:1-2; Phil. 4:8; 2 Pet. 1:3-9). A spiritual mindset is crucial to knowing and doing the will of God, and is essential to spiritual transformation (Rom. 12:1-2; 1 Cor. 6:19-20; 3:16-17). Spiritual transformation is a factor of spiritual intelligence.

Spiritual intelligence is a divine ability to receive knowledge supernaturally or by spiritual means; and the ability to use spiritual means to identify and solve spiritual and other problems. Based on Scripture, people connected to God have divine power and participate in the divine nature (Eph. 3:21; 2 Peter 1:3).

Intelligence plays a crucial role in the lives of people everywhere. Mental intelligence yields knowledge to navigate the natural domain. Spiritual intelligence yields knowledge to navigate the spiritual domain. (Psalm 119:105-112; John 17:17).

In addition to special revelation, God reveals Himself through the things which He has created, including nature (Psa. 19:1-4; Rom. 1). God also uses the lives of others, prayer and instruction to bring people to knowledge of the truth (Matt. 28:18-20; Rom. 10:12-17; 1 Tim. 2:1-8; Titus 3:3-7, Jude 24).

God uses various means to get our attention or knock at our heart's door but will not force Himself on anyone (Rev. 3:20). God does not violate our will. God respects our freedom. God has been gracious and wise in granting volition, as the ability to make personal choices is integral to human development. Since the Creator is the one who has granted volition and other liberties, God alone is legally and morally justified where withdrawing these freedoms is concerned. Anyone claiming to be representing God and wanting to take away what God has freely given is indeed a false prophet.

In Scripture, intimidation, force and manipulation are discouraged (2

Tim. 2:24-26). It makes absolutely no sense to force a person to embrace someone or accept a religion against their will. Outward conformity may be an expression of hypocrisy or complicity, in order to avoid persecution. Someone once said "Unwilling obedience is still disobedience." Obedience to the letter of the law must be balanced by obedience to the spirit of the law.

God desires obedience form the heart (Luke 10:27; John 14:15, 23-24), not just outward conformity. Furthermore, God comes into people's heart by invitation, not by force and manipulation. Any religion, therefore, through deliberate force or manipulation, that undermines a person's ability to make their own choices cannot possibility be of God.

In relating to God and others, sincere love must be the litmus test. Righteousness is a willing expression of the heart based on a relationship with the Law Giver. God is not fooled or impressed by outward conformity to the law or by legalism. Genuine conformity to the Law based on love for the Law-Giver is desirable.

Based on Scripture, God is patient with sinners and gives sinners time to repent (2 Peter 3:9). Patience is one of the most enduring evidence of love and concern for sinners, and is indeed a virtue; another is mercy. In Scripture, mercy is promoted and rewarded, and is recognized as an act of righteousness (Matt. 7:5; Isa. 58:6-11).

People who know God have an obligation to be merciful toward unbelievers, to pray for and gently instruct them, bearing in mind that only God can change their hearts and bring them to their senses (2 Timothy 2:25-26). Although God warns of consequences, God shows respect for choices made. Notwithstanding, the spiritually ignorant are obliged to seek God for themselves and respond willingly and appropriately when knowledge of God is discovered or revealed.

Unfortunately, many suppress knowledge of God. People who suppress spiritual truths or refuse to retain knowledge of God when revealed, degrade themselves and are thus inclined to foolish and unnatural behavior (Rom. 1:18-32; Prov. 1:29-33). Such persons fall in the domain of fools (Ps. 14:1; Prov. 1:22). Foolishness and stupidity are associated with evil (Jer. 4:22).

Spiritual Intelligence: A Christian Perspective

On the other hand, spiritual challenges exist even in religion. These challenges have been the bases of religious wars, persecutions and religious disputes. Religious disputes are not uncommon. Jesus, for example, was in constant dispute with the religious scholars of his day. Although he strongly repudiated the views of those with whom he disagreed, Jesus did not deny religious liberties or encouraged persecution of dissidents. On one occasion differences were met in the following way: "Let them alone; they are blind guides of the blind. And if a blind man guides a blind man, both will fall into a pit" (Matt. 15:14, NASB).

While not denying religious liberties, Jesus and his disciples confronted evil and ignorance in religion. They were not afraid of offending anyone, and therefore did not concern themselves with political correctness. They were more concerned with elevating truth and exposing ignorance, in order that people may come to knowledge of the truth. Not even religious scholars were spared exposure.

Jesus publicly contradicted the erroneous teachings of religious experts and their way of life. Truth is religious scholarship or professional religious designation does not necessarily qualify anyone as being spiritually intelligent. People claiming to be the most knowledgeable where religious matters are concerned, despite professional status and qualification, are sometimes severely challenged spiritually. Examples abound both in secular and religious literature.

There is no correlation between religious scholarship with spiritual life and intelligence necessarily. For example, despite religious scholarship, Nicodemus was spiritually obtuse and bore no connection to God spiritually. Such was the case because Nicodemus had not experienced what Jesus called a spiritual rebirth. Intelligence is necessarily consistent with the nature of life. Jesus explained: "Flesh gives birth to flesh, but the Spirit gives birth to spirit" (John 3:6).

The point needs to be underscored that religion does not necessarily makes a person righteous or spiritually intelligent. Some religions are associated with evil and are disempowering. In addition to the misguided, there are religions purposefully dedicated to devil worship. There are many religions, religious denominations and cults. Based on divergence in doctrine and practice, is it possible for all to be equally right? Are all religious choices equal?

Since it is possible to have religion and not be righteous, there is need to discriminate in the area of religion. The ability to discriminate spiritually implies spiritual intelligence. Beginning at rebirth, spiritual intelligence is developed as knowledge is increased, evaluated, validated and applied.

Regardless of the discipline, progress is predicated on knowledge, and knowledge is not complete until lived out or put into practice. As far as application goes, ignorance does not excuse from responsibility and accountability. In the legal domain, we are told "Ignorance of the law is no excuse for breaking the law." The spiritual domain is not exempted.

Ignorance of spiritual laws does not excuse a person for breaking them. Ignorance ought to be avoided, because without knowledge religious zeal has the potential to motivate even the most sincere to do the bizarre and unthinkable (in the name of God and religion). Ignorance is against the best interest of everyone, for it leads to unwholesome thinking and acting. We have seen throughout history that spiritual ignorance has led to all kinds of atrocities, even in the Christian Church.

Religious ignorance is a major cause of underdevelopment and insecurity in the world. Due to the negative impact of ignorance on the individual and on society, the Apostle Paul and others sought to open the eyes of the spiritually blind (Acts 26:18). Paul could identify with spiritual blindness because, prior his conversion, although a zealous religious scholar, in ignorance he persecuted the Christian Church (Acts 26:9-18; Gal. 1:11-24; Phil. 3:1-11).

Religious zeal and sincerity do not necessarily indicate the presence of spiritual life and intelligence (Matt. 23:23-37). It is possible to be sincere and sincerely wrong, hence the many bizarre ways in which people try to impress or appease God. St. Paul indicated that many Jews had zeal for God but "not in accordance with knowledge" (Rom. 10:2).

Though important, sincerity and zeal are not to be equated with spiritual intelligence, for they neither draw a person closer to the truth nor closer to

God necessarily. Spiritual intelligence is needed. In the matter of religion, intelligence is needed to discern truth from error and to balance faith with reason. Spiritual zeal is important, but should be validated and supported by truth (John 4:24). The ability to worship in spirit and in truth demands spiritual intelligence.

Spiritual life and intelligence are contingent on spiritual rebirth (John 3:3-5). In addition to qualifying a person as member of God's family (John 1:12, 13; 1 John 3:1-3), spiritual rebirth qualifies one as member of the Christian Church (John 1:13-13; Acts 2:37-47).

There is a big difference between membership in the family of the world and membership in the family of God or the Church (Eph. 2:1-22; 1 John 3; Coloss. 1:21-22), affecting the relationship they have with one another (John 15:18-20).

> The followers of Jesus make up the Church, the body of Christ, and are thereby a distinct society in tension with the world. The existence of the Church as Church makes it possible for the world to know itself as the world; that is, as unredeemed and in need of grace. (Carter, 2006, p. 114)

The command to make disciples (Matt. 28:18-20) and the admonition to be salt and light to the world (Matt. 5:13-16) underscore the distinctiveness between the Church and the world. The Church and the world represent opposing spiritual principles and principalities, and are warring factions. Distinctiveness between the Church and the world makes membership in the Church desirable and salvation of the world plausible.

If the Church is to have an effective witness, differences between the Church and the world must therefore be understood and appreciated. Ideally a spiritually intelligent Church community is the light and salt of the earth. This includes:

- Providing moral and spiritual direction
- Acting as a restraining force against all manner of evil
- Providing hope for the hopeless

- Setting captives free
- Healing all manner of sicknesses and diseases

Differences exist between the people of God and the people of the world. Alignment with laws and principles associated with God as opposed to laws and principles associated with the world conceivably and practically impact relationships at every level.

Besides differences in beliefs, there are differences in behavior. The more steeped in evil, the more opposed people in the world are toward the people of faith, especially toward the seriously committed. Alliances are formed relative to character. In the words of Jesus:

> This is the verdict: Light has come into the world, but men loved darkness instead of light because their deeds were evil. Everyone who does evil hates the light, and will not come into the light for fear that his deeds will be exposed. (John 3:19-20).

The metaphors, light and darkness, vividly underscore the fact of spiritual differences. They represent different poles of the spiritual spectrum (Matt. 4:16; Luke 1:79; Eph. 5:8). Conflict is therefore inevitable.

Based on Scripture, moral and spiritual battles began in the Garden of Eden, where volition was first tested. For believing a lie, the first humans yielded to temptation and disobeyed the Creator. Having disobeyed God, humanity became corrupted, a condition described by theologians as the Fall.

The ability to make choices was hardwired in our DNA, enabling participation in the creative process and other creative endeavors. This made it possible for human beings to contribute to their own evolution and have a say in the determination of their destiny.

As choices have consequences, volition provided the basis for responsibility and accountability. Moreover, since we did not create ourselves, standards of behavior are the purview of the Creator, and ultimate judgment resides in the Law Giver and Final Judge.

For disobeying a specific command, humanity became corrupted, along with every system reachable by direct or indirect influence. Every form of conflict, unnaturalness and abnormality in human beings and in the world at large may be traced to human footprints – the inappropriate exercise of volition (James 1:13-15). Since evil became part of our *moralscape*, there has been internal and external conflict – a real struggle between good and evil.

The battle between good and evil is fundamentally spiritual, forcing us to choose between two opposing principles (light or darkness) and two opposing principals (God or the devil). The choice we make between one or the other, determines destiny.

Albeit, freedom of religion is a human right, consequences not withstanding. However, the right to freedom of choice does not extend to infringing on the liberty of others to make similar choices. The right of each person/organization to make their own decision should be respected and safeguarded.

Notwithstanding, the point needs to be underscored that all religions are not the same and therefore should not be expected to yield the same spiritual fruit. All roads do not lead to heaven. "...broad is the way that leads to destruction, and there are many who go by it" (Matt. 7:13, KJV). Differences are apparent in every area of life, including religion. Spirituality that does not recognize differences is not only irrational; it undermines human development on the whole.

There are standards or established protocols in every discipline. Conformity advances the cause and nonconformity hinders or undermines it. When things are done in the right way, everyone benefits; when done in the wrong way, everyone gets hurt. Accuracy in knowledge in terms of its truthfulness and efficacy is extremely important. And the best way to promote that while safeguarding the rights of others is to allow divergent views to freely contend in the market place of public opinion.

Conflicting truth claims in religion is common. Yet there is more to religion than subjective experiences. Objective data are relevant in supporting or not supporting truth claims. (John 14:3; 1 John 1: 5-7; 4:20-21). This is why study is so crucial in knowing truth from error (2 Tim. 2:15).

In religion, truth (symbolized by light) and error (symbolized by darkness) are diametrically opposed and yield different results. The tension created on account of spiritual differences is good, as long as religious freedom is respected.

Jesus predicted that moral and spiritual differences between the people of God and the people of the world would result in the people of God being objects of hatred and persecution (John 15:18-19; 16:33; 17:14-18). He also predicted a time when many would murder true servants of God thinking that they are doing God a service (John 16:1-4). This prophetic word has been realized in the past and continues to be fulfilled up to the present time. Other prophets prophesied of sufferings due to persecution (2 Tim. 3:10-13).

Life is comprised of forces of good and evil, light and darkness, truth and lies, wisdom and stupidity. Why should it surprise us that representatives are constantly at war with polar opposites, and that those on the journey do not matriculate without internal and external struggles? Despite pressure to conform to the world's system of thought and way of life, many Christians remain true to the gospel.

On the other hand, some do buckle under the pressure or make compromises. Today spirituality is informed by a consumer-driven society, by the word of man and not by the Word of God. The aim is to satisfy human desires and increase comfort levels over questionable issues in exchange for endorsement, popularity and monetary gain. In many circles, spirituality is not based on what God legislates or defines as right and wrong. Spirituality is relative to the whims of humanity, undergirded by a misguided view of tolerance. Commenting on Christianity in America, Horton (1994) noted weaknesses in the message communicated by evangelicals, due to compromise.

Not only have evangelicals been shaped by secularism in their theology; they have adopted the patterns of thinking that have opened them up to participate in the idolatry of their contemporaries. Believing in the essential goodness of humanity and its moral *perfectability* through ethical education, legislation, self-help, and political pressure, evangelicals have also accepted the idea of secular progress. (Horton, 1994, p. 73)

Spiritual Intelligence: A Christian Perspective

Based on what is called "the prosperity doctrine," a significant part of the Christian community equates secular progress with spiritual progress and has become just as materialistic as the people of the world. It is apparent that not everyone in religion sees a difference between progress based on humanism or secularism and progress based on spiritual enlightenment. Although in some areas results may be similar, there is a vast difference between secular progress and sacred progress in terms of philosophy, interpretation and motivation. The truth is even the sincerely religious may be sincerely wrong and may be motivated by the same philosophies as the people of the world.

Spiritual intelligence is manifested in the wisdom of God's Word (2 Tim. 3:15-17). God's Word is unalterable, and is supported by signs, wonders, miracles and gifts of the Holy Spirit (Heb. 2:1-4). Man's word may be trusted only insofar as it is in alignment with God's Word.

Sincerity and zeal may not be used as leverage against ignorance, hence Paul's prayer for his country men (Rom. 10:1-3). In this regard, diligence is encouraged (2 Tim. 2:15). Religious zeal based on misinformation or ignorance creates dysfunction, even in religion.

Religion may be either true or false. Accordingly, biblical literature warns against false prophets; acknowledges that there is a Spirit of truth and a spirit of falsehood; and has established criteria for discerning truth from error (John 14:17; 15:26; Acts 26:16-18; Eph. 2:1-3; 1 Tim. 4:1; 1 John 4:1-6). As was the case in Jesus' day, there are "blind guides of the blind" (Matt. 15:14).

Despite sincerity and zeal, blind leaders and their followers will fall into the same ditch. In Scripture, growth in knowledge is expected and encouraged (1 Cor. 3:1-4; Heb. 5:12-14; 1 Peter 2:2; 2 Peter 3:18); so also is zeal (2 Cor. 7:11; 9:2; Col. 4:13; Titus 2:14). There is therefore need for balance. Sincerity and zeal are to be mediated by truth. It is truth that sets people free (Jhn. 8:32). In addition to delivering from ignorance, truth delivers from a path that is self-destructive and from a way of life which contributes to the destruction of others. The truth delivers from a path which aligns itself with the father of lies and source of evil. It delivers from the kingdom of darkness and places a person into the kingdom of light (Acts 26:1-32; Coloss. 1:12-14).

Despite the many religions, there are only two spiritual kingdoms in the world – the kingdom of darkness ruled by Satan and the kingdom of light ruled by God. A person belongs to either one or the other. Accordingly, there are spiritual descendants of Satan (Gen. 3:15; John 8:44; Eph. 2:2; Rev. 12:13-17), and there are spiritual descendants of God (John 1:12-13; Rom. 8:9, 14-17; Col. 1:13).

Members of God's kingdom are described as light (Eph. 5:8) and are expected to be the light of the world (Matt. 5:14). When Jesus said to his disciples "You are the light of the world," he meant they were to be a source of life and organizing influence in the world, because that's what light does. Light describes the path of righteousness leading to wholeness and truth. Walking in the light enables human beings to relate to God and others appropriately (Jhn. 1:7; Prov. 4:18-19). Letting one's light shine brings glory to God and helps in expanding God's kingdom.

Early Christians understood the building of the kingdom of God to be their foremost priority (Matt. 6:33). As the people of God, they were regarded as ambassadors, to whom God committed the message and ministry of reconciliation (2 Cor. 4:1-6; 5:14-21). The message and ministry of reconciliation included taking the good news of God's love (the gospel) to others, as commanded (Matt. 28:18-20; Acts 1:8). The gospel emphasizes the truth about the death, burial and resurrection of Jesus (1 Cor. 15:1-4; Rom. 10:9-17).

Christians directed worship to the God of creation and repudiated worship of other gods (Acts 13:49-52). Allegations of upsetting the world were therefore brought against them (Acts 17:1-6). But Christians were neither concerned about political correctness nor popular culture or dissent; they knew the transformative power of the gospel, and believed the gospel had power to bring salvation to its hearers (Rom. 1:16-17). Courage of convictions motivated them to proclaim the gospel as they received it (1 Cor. 15:1-11).

By preaching the gospel, Christians were instrumental in leading people to salvation. Salvation meant transformation (1 Cor. 6:9-11). Various aspects of culture were affected (Acts 17:6). Many people gave up their ungodly lifestyles, including their false gods, and began proclaiming the gospel they once rejected. Life revolved around God and God's kingdom.

Biblical literature reveals a way of life uniquely and fundamentally different from that of people in the world. The people of the world live chiefly by the operating system of the flesh. Life is lived based on physicality – by the impulses of the flesh and revolves around the outward man. People who have a personal relationship with God chiefly live by the operating system of the Spirit. Life is lived based on spirituality – by the impulses of the Spirit and revolves around the Spirit's work in the "inner man."

However, this is not to say that everyone who makes claim to a personal relationship with God is at the same level spiritually (1 Cor. 3:2; 1 Pet. 2:2). Some people are spiritual babes, are therefore immature and are still driven by the dictates of the flesh.

The flesh, though important, through its impulses and natural senses, cannot adequately govern human behavior, and was not designed to function independently of the spirit. From the time of creation, the spirit is the highest aspect of personhood to which body and soul are to be subject (Nee, 1968).

The Fall, however, disrupted the natural order of things. Due to the Fall, the spirit of man became disconnected from the Spirit of God and has been supplanted by the flesh as the governing life principle.

We have already seen that human nature has been severely compromised, sin influencing everything issuing from physicality and has mutated. In addition to being corrupted absolutely, sinners have a corrupting influence, making everyone guilty of sin.

Beginning with the first humans, like a virus, sin has become a spiritual pandemic, affecting every single human being, making it impossible to heal ourselves. As a consequence, sinfulness may only be resolved by reconnecting spiritually to the Divine or Holy Spirit. In other words, in order to regain its rightful role and reclaim authenticity, the spirit of man needs to reconnect with the Spirit of God and once again become the principle operating system. According to Scripture, people who have reconnected to God are re-born spiritually. The experience of spiritual rebirth results in spiritual enlightenment, manifesting as spiritual growth. As this is true in some and not in others, there are differences in the way life is lived.

Differences between life by the Spirit and life by the flesh are illustrated in Table 2 below.

	LIFE BY THE FLESH	LIFE BY THE SPIRIT
TYPE OF LIFE	Physical	Spiritual
TYPE OF BIRTH	Natural	Spiritual
TYPE OF BEING	Unregenerate	Regenerate
FOREBEARS	Physical/Natural	Spiritual
IDENTITY	In Adam	In Christ
NATURE OF BEING	Carnal	Spiritual
POWER SUPPLY	Flesh	Spirit
TYPE OF MIND	Carnal	Spiritual
OPERATING INTEL	Natural Intelligence	Spiritual Intelligence
MORAL COMPASS	Man/Society	God/Bible
TYPE OF FRUIT	Deeds of the flesh (Unrighteousness)	Fruit of the Spirit (Righteousness)
SPIRITUAL CATEGORY	Spiritually dead	Spiritually alive
SPIRITUAL DOMAIN	Kingdom of darkness	Kingdom of light
SERVANT OF	Sin, self, Satan	God and others
REWARD	Death	Life

Table 2: *Physical and Spiritual Life Comparison*

Spiritual Intelligence: A Christian Perspective

Life by the Spirit is lived qualitatively differently from life by the flesh. In life by the flesh, physicality and man-centered living determine morality. In life by the Spirit, morality is determined by spirituality and God-centered living. The nonspiritual person operates from the outer self; the spiritual person operates from the inner self (Phil. 2:13; 2 Cor. 4:7). The outer self is regulated by the law of the sinful nature of the flesh; the inner self, by the law of the righteous nature of the Spirit (Rom. 7:21-25; 2 Pet. 1:3-4).

A profile of the unspiritual, culled from the book of Jude, reveals that the unspiritual: change the grace of God into a license for immorality; deny Jesus Christ; pollute their own bodies; reject authority; slander the divine or spiritual; speak abusively of things they do not understand; are grumblers and faultfinders; follow their own evil desires; are deceived by 'profit;' are hypocritical and pretentious; are unfruitful; are boastful; flatter others for their own advantage; cause divisions; follow their natural instincts; and do not have the Spirit.

In Ephesians 4:17-19, unbelievers are described as:

1. Futile in their thinking
2. Darkened in their understanding
3. Excluded from the life of God
4. Hard-hearted or calloused
5. Sensual
6. Practice impurity with greediness

In John 14, Jesus made a distinction between the people of the world and the people of God – his disciples. One of the differences highlighted is the presence of the Spirit with them, promised also to be within them, operating as Helper. This unique relationship sets us apart from the people of the world. Believers:

◆ Are born of the Spirit (John 3:1-6; Titus 3:5)

◆ Are inhabited or indwelt by the Spirit (Rom. 8:29; 1 Cor. 3:13; 6:19)

◆ Are sealed (validated) by the Spirit (Eph. 1:13-14; 4:30)

- Are gifted by the Spirit (1 Cor. 12:1-11; 1 Peter 4:10; Rom. 12:3-8)

- Are cleansed by the Spirit (1 Cor. 6:11)

- Are anointed by the Spirit (Luke 4:18-19; 1 John 2:27)

- Are taught by the Spirit (John 14:26; 1 Cor. 2)

- Are empowered by the Spirit (Acts 1:8; Eph. 3:16-17)

- Are warned by the Spirit (Acts 20:22-23; 21:3-4)

- Are led by the Spirit (John 16:13; Acts 8:29; Rom. 8:14-16)

- Receive witness/testimony of the Spirit (John 15:26; Rom. 8:12-17; Heb. 10:15)

- Bear fruit by the Spirit (Gal. 5:22-23)

Based on the forgoing, believers are admonished:

- Not to grieve the Spirit (Eph. 4:30-31)

- Not to quench the Spirit (1 Thess. 5:19)

- To walk in step with the Spirit (Gal. 5:16-26)

- To be controlled by the Spirit (Eph. 5:18-21)

For the Christian, life by the Spirit is the way life is to be lived (2 Cor. 10:1-5; Col. 1:29): "We have this treasure in earthen vessels, that the excellency of the power may be of God, and not of us" (2 Cor. 4:7, KJV).

Our connection with the Spirit enables us to be spiritually intelligent, to grow spiritually based on the influence and power of the Spirt, thereby pleasing God. People disconnected from the Spirit are spiritually challenged and therefore cannot please God.

Differences between spiritual intelligence and unintelligence are illustrated in Table 3.

Spiritual Intelligence: A Christian Perspective

SPIRITUAL INTEL	SPIRITUAL UNINTEL	SCRIPTURE
God	Devil	1 Jhn. 3:10; Jhn. 1:12, 13; 8:44
Kingdom of light	Kingdom of darkness	Col. 1:12-14
Children of light	Children of darkness	Matt. 5:13-16; Jhn. 3:19-21; 8:12
Righteousness	Unrighteousness	1 Pet. 1:13-16; 1 Jhn. 3: 10
Assoc. with life	Assoc. with death	Jhn. 3:14-20, 34-36
Heavenly	Earthy	1 Cor. 15:44-49
Spirit	Flesh	Rm. 7:1-13; 2 Cor. 3:13-18
Spiritual nature	Carnal nature	1 Cor. 15:45-50; 2 Cor. 10:1-5
Spiritual man	Natural man	Rm. 7:14; 15:27; Heb. 7:16
Enlightened	Ignorant	2 Cor. 3:14; Gal. 1:11-12
Born of Spirit	Born of flesh only	John 1:13; 3:3-8; 1 John 5:18
Spiritually alive	Spiritually dead	Eph. 2:1-7
Inward man	Outward man	Rm. 7:21-25; 8:1-16
Spiritual mind	Carnal mind	2 Cor. 3:13-18; 4:6; Rm. 7:1-13
New man/self	Old man/self	Eph. 2:12-18; 4:22-24; Col. 3:9
In Christ	In Adam	1 Cor. 1:30; Eph. 1; Phil. 4:6-7
Spirit of God/Truth	Spirit of anti-Christ/ Falsehood	Rom. 8:9; Eph. 2:2-3; 2 Tim. 1:14; 1 John 4:1-5
Law of the Spirit	Law of the flesh	Rom. 8:1-16
Knows God	Does not know God	1 Cor. 15:33-34
Wise	Foolish	Rom. 12:17, 18; Eph. 5:15-17
Spiritual understanding	Natural understanding	Col. 1:9-14; 2 Pet. 1:3-9
Spiritual wisdom	Natural wisdom	1 Cor. 1:18-25; 2; 3:18-20
Fruit of Spirit	Works of flesh	Gal. 5:19-23; James 3:17-18
Spiritual gifts	Natural talents	Rom. 12:6-8; 1 Cor. 12

Table 3 *Spiritual Intelligence and Unintelligence Comparison*

Nature of Spiritual Intelligence

Spiritual intelligence speaks to issues such as openness and obedience to spiritual direction, the use of spiritual gifts in the fulfillment of purpose, moral and spiritual values, enabling reimaging spiritually and coherence with God's will. Essentially, spiritual intelligence enables a sense of meaning and faithful stewardship – living with a sense of purpose and in a way that brings honor and glory to God: "So whether you eat or drink or whatever you do, do it all to the glory of God." (1 Cor. 10:31).

Spiritual intelligence must not be confused with natural intelligence as if they both spring from the same well. They are derived from different sources and are major streams of intelligence. Natural intelligence is associated with physicality and is manifested in natural abilities, behaviors, values and attitudes known as works of the flesh (Gal. 5:19-21). Spiritual intelligence is associated with spirituality, and is manifested in behaviors, values and attitudes known as the fruit of the Spirit (Gal. 5:22-23; James 3:17-18), and in spiritual abilities known as spiritual gifts (1 Cor.12; Rom. 12:6-8).

Spiritual intelligence is the spiritual eye of the understanding, enabling attunement with God. Based on the teachings of Scripture, God is holy (Psa. 99:5; 1 Cor. 3:17), and everything that God does is circumscribed by holiness. If everything God is and does is informed by holiness, it is reasonable to expect the same from people created in God's image.

In the natural, holiness is impossible. This is why people need a spiritual rebirth (John 3:3-5). When reborn by the Spirit, the human spirit becomes alive to God and is activated and empowered to reflect more accurately the divine purpose, image and nature of the Creator (Rom. 8:9-16; 9:8; Gal. 4:4-6; 2 Pet. 1:4-9).

It is not accidental or coincidental that the Spirit, who gives spiritual life, is called "Holy Spirit." Holiness describes the character of the Spirit (Lev. 11:44; 20:7-8). A person attuned to God reflects God's image and character. Attunement with God is essential for fellowship and impinges on a person's ability to truly represent God in the earth. In fact, the people of God are commanded to be holy (1 Peter 1:14-16).

Another word used for holiness is righteousness. Righteousness is predicated on notions of right and wrong, right cohering with natural and spiritual laws, (established by an all-knowing Creator, Law Giver and Final Judge), enabling order and progress, wrong having the very opposite effect.

What is righteousness? Simply put, righteousness means doing what is right morally and spiritually; it is doing the right thing not just because of conscience, laws based on the legal system or social norms, but because it is the godly thing to do. Righteousness ultimately points to God, God being holy, (the epitome of righteousness).

Righteousness is both a moral and spiritual undertaking, as every act of wrong doing is a violation of spiritual laws and an affront to the Law Giver. Notwithstanding, a person may be morally right and not be righteous when the right thing done bears no connection with spiritual values or the motivation is disassociated from notions of godliness. On the other hand, from the spiritual perspective, a person cannot be righteous without being morally right.

Why is righteousness so important?

- Since human beings are God's design and are created in God's image, human behavior should reflect the character of God.

- Righteousness provides the basis for healthy relationships at every level.

- From the divine perspective, righteousness is integral to wellness spiritually, morally, emotionally, cognitively and socially.

- Righteousness enables actualization of human potential, and is a solid foundation for human development.

- Righteousness is crucial to the maintenance of order in the natural and spiritual world.

We have already seen that the Fall made righteousness impossible by human effort alone, that although it is possible for a person to attain righteousness based on religion, the legal system, or standards established by self and society, spiritual intelligent living is impossible without spiritual rebirth. In spite of the best of effort, human beings will fall short in attaining the righteousness demanded by God. This had been the experience of many, including the apostle Paul prior his conversion (Rom. 10:2-4; Phil. 3:1-10).

God's standard of righteousness is exceedingly higher than human standards (Isa. 55:8-9), and proceeds from a personal relationship with God. It is based on a standard of righteousness established by the Creator, and is the ultimate goal of spiritual intelligence. Notice Paul's prayer for the Philippians:

> And this is my prayer: that your love may abound more and more in knowledge and depth of insight, so that you may be able to discern what is best and may be pure and blameless for the day of Christ, filled with the fruit of righteousness that comes through Jesus Christ – to the glory and praise of God. (Philipp. 1:9-11, NIV)

It stands to reason that if by virtue of a physical and natural relationship human beings reflect the nature of natural forebears, by virtue of a spiritual and supernatural relationship human beings should reflect the nature of spiritual forebears also, hence the biblical injunction: "But just as he who called you is holy, so be holy in all you do; for it is written: Be holy, because I am holy." (1 Peter 1:15-16, NIV).

Based on Scripture, human beings have been created in God's image (Genesis 1:27), enabling us to represent God and to be like God. Furthermore, did not the Bible say we are gods? (John 10:34; Psalm 82:6). Unfortunately, human beings want to be like God in every area, except in character. Yet everything rises on the foundation of spiritual intelligence, expressed chiefly through character.

One way in which we are definitely expected to be like God is in the area of morality. Moral likeness is expected and commanded. (1 Peter 1:16; Matt. 5:8). As Creator and Standard Bearer, God requires holiness. Everything that God is and does revolves around His Holiness. Morally and spiritually, human nature is to conform to the Divine nature, hence the biblical mandate to be holy.

Holiness is a state of mind – having a mind predisposed to seek the greater good and to operate at the highest level of integrity, in sync with the Mind of God. Through holiness we become partakers of the Divine nature. (2 Peter 1:3-4). Being holy is to do everything that is pleasing to God; it is to operate in a way that is beyond reproach – with spiritual intelligence.

If we are to honor God and to be like God, holiness is imperative. Holiness is like yeast in the bread of life. We are commanded to be holy, because holiness opens the spiritual eyes of our understanding, enables us to make the best use of our talents and gifts, aligns us to God, and enables a sense of meaning and purpose. It is in holiness that we find ourselves. And it is in finding ourselves that we are able to fulfill our purpose.

Experience of Spiritual Intelligence in N.T.

Righteousness is a factor of spiritual life and intelligence. Biblical literature attribute spiritual life and intelligence to God or to the Holy Spirit (1 John 3:1-10; 4:13-16; 5:18-21). Peter saw the Holy Spirit as a gift from God, and the fount of other spiritual gifts.

The Spirit is received only by people who respond appropriately to God's call to salvation. An appropriate response involves repentance and faith in Jesus (Acts 2:14-41), leading to what is described as spiritual rebirth (John 3:1-8). As spiritual rebirth is not true of everyone, as not everyone who is religious or calls upon the name of the Lord is saved (Matt. 7:21). It is by the grace of God that human beings are saved (Eph. 2:8-9; Titus 3:5; Rom. 3:10).

Without a personal relationship with God, worship and service of God are meaningless (Matt. 7:21-23; 15:8-9; Acts 10; Col. 2:23). Based on Scripture, "God is spirit, and his worshippers must worship in spirit and in truth" (John 4:24, NIV). In addition to drawing people to God (John 6:44), the Spirit joins or unites with the human spirit via an indwelling (Eph. 1:13; Rom. 8:9), at the point of belief, enabling spiritual life and intelligence (Titus 3:5).

Power to bear witness for God is attributed to the Spirit (Acts 1:8; Eph.

3:11). It is the Spirit who enables spiritual life, reveals spiritual things, and gives spiritual understanding and gifts.

The ethos of spiritual life and intelligence is: (a) finding meaning, (b) moral centering, (c) transformative thinking and (d) attunement with God. Spiritual life and intelligence, however, does not imply perfection or infallibility. Revelations can be mistaken or misunderstood; plus it is possible to act on the impulses of the flesh or from the old sinful self instead of from the new redeemed self. Moreover, although supernaturally enabled, developing spiritual intelligence takes time; development is progressive and requires human effort. The need for growth is implied and understood.

From the Judeo-Christian perspective, no one expressed spiritual intelligence more fully and profoundly than Jesus. As man, Jesus amazed religious scholars and others with spiritual wisdom, expressed through discussions, teachings and healing miracles. In addition, Jesus was able to discern people and events, and identify and solve spiritual and other problems via spiritual means.

The success of Jesus as spiritual leader was associated with a spiritual power and intelligence which transcended the natural and physical. It was supernatural.

Jesus' spiritual acumen was understood to be connected with God, the Father and the Spirit (John 1:1-17; 12:28; 14:16; 15:26; 16:7; 17:1-4), whom Jesus represented and embodied (Matt. 3:16-4:1; 1 Cor. 1:30). Isaiah, the prophet, had predicted his birth and spiritual prowess (Isa. 11:1-4).

Jesus himself had made predictions regarding the ability of his disciples to operate in the supernatural (Jhn. 14:12; 16:13-16; Acts 1:5, 8). The promise was fulfilled by the enabling power of the Spirit. As a result, members of the early Christian community were careful to attribute their new-found power to Jesus (Acts 4:1-15).

Jesus and his disciples demonstrated a level of spiritual intelligence and power that defied reason. People were amazed, particularly since members of the new religious movement, save for a few exceptions, did not attend any recognized institution of learning. Jesus himself was of humble beginnings, yet both he and his disciples demonstrated superior ability to identify and solve spiritual and other problems.

Narratives depicting God at work enabling spiritual life and intelligence among members of the early Christian community are highlighted in Table 4.

NAME	EVENT	SCRIPTURE
Apostles	Signs and wonders including healing the sick Boldness to witness Miraculous deliverance from prison	Acts 2:43; 5:12-16 Acts 4:31 Acts 5:17-25
Peter	Healed a cripple Spiritual discernment and judgment Healed a man bed-ridden for 8 years Raised a dead woman to life Received a vision and instruction from the Spirit Escaped miraculously from prison	Acts 3:1-10 Acts 5:1-11 Acts 9:32-35 Acts 9:36-42 Acts 10:9-23 Acts 12:1-18
Steven	Performed signs and wonders Demonstrated wisdom and spiritual power Experienced transformation in countenance Vision of heaven, courage, and power to forgive	Acts 6:8 Acts 6:10 Acts 6:15 Acts 7:55-60
Philip	Delivered others from demons and sicknesses Converted a sorcerer Discerned ulterior motives of Simon, the sorcerer Received a word from an angel Received a word from the Spirit Converted an Ethiopian Transported supernaturally	Acts 8:4-8 Acts 8:9-13 Acts 8:14-25 Acts 8:26-28 Acts 8:29 Acts 8:30-38 Acts 8:39-40
Saul	Encountered Jesus on Damascus Road Converted and struck with blindness Struck Elymas with blindness	Acts 9: 1-9 Acts 13:6-12
Ananias	Received a vision concerning Saul Healed Saul of blindness	Acts 9:10-16 Acts 9:17-19
Church	Experienced increase Led to dedicate Saul and Barnabas to ministry Experienced love and unity	Acts 2:37-4; 5:14 Acts 13:1-4 Acts 4:32-37
Cornelius	Vision of an angel giving specific instructions Experienced conversion	Acts 10:1-8 Acts 10:44-48
Agabus	Prophesied	Acts 11:27-30
Herod	Struck dead for taking glory belonging to God	Acts 12:19-24
Paul & Barnabas	Worked signs and miracles Healed a man crippled from birth	Acts 14:1-3 Acts 14:8-11
Paul	Restrained from going in a particular direction Delivered slave girl from demon spirit Received vision and prophecy Performed miracles Raised the dead Healed sicknesses and diseases	Acts 16:6-10 Acts 16:16-18 Acts 18:9-10 Acts 19:11-20 Acts 20:7-11 Acts 28:7-9

Table 4: *Evidence of Supernatural Power and Intelligence in NT*

Spiritual Intelligence: A Christian Perspective

Are modern-day Christians able to operate in the supernatural? Human needs have not changed; have they? The problems associated with the Fall and with the flesh – sicknesses, diseases, immorality, demonic activity, spiritual warfare and so on – have continued and have taken on added dimensions. How might these and other problems be overcome?

In addition to providing insight into mysteries, Jesus and his disciples healed all manner of sicknesses and diseases, fed the hungry, cast out demons, raised the dead, and performed other signs and wonders. Interestingly, not everyone was delivered supernaturally. The primary focus was on the salvation of souls. Though important, physical healing, etc. played a supporting or subordinate role. Although physical deliverance was of grave concern, saving the inner man was first priority.

Signs represented God's grace in the lives of both the redeemed and unredeemed. Miracles were not to be taken for granted. Invariably, they confirmed the message and messenger of God. In addition to thanksgiving, healing miracles were expected to cause unbelievers to turn to God in repentance and faith (Luke 10:8-16).

Supernatural phenomena are explainable within the worldview of a theistic universe where everything depends on the grace of God. In a theistic universe, it is the prerogative of the Creator to operate naturally or in a general way through natural laws; yet it is also the Creator's prerogative to operate supernaturally or in a special way through spiritual laws. The Creator may even choose a combination of natural and spiritual laws to determine outcomes. As Creator, God has the right to do whatsoever He pleases.

Enabling spiritual intelligence among people of faith is a reflection of God's grace (Luke 8:10; 1 Cor. 1:26-29). It makes good sense that people connected to God would be empowered in a special way spiritually and would live differently from people who are not spiritually alive and thus spiritually unintelligent. There is overwhelming evidence of spiritual light and power associated with people of faith, in ages past and throughout the present century.

Experience of Spiritual Intelligence in O.T.

People of faith belonging to the New Testament dispensation were not the only ones who operated in the supernatural or exhibited spiritual intelligence. Paranormal gifts and people are also noted in the Old Testament portions of Scripture. Biblical records indicate that prophets, priests, judges, kings and others communicated with God, and that God communicated through people of faith to others.

One of the most famous Old Testament example is Daniel. Daniel was a man of prayer and was noted for interpreting dreams. During the reign of Nebuchadnezzar, king of Babylon, the king had a dream, which so troubled him that he could not sleep. The problem was made more grave because the king could not remember the dream, yet demanded an interpretation. Unfortunately, none of the king's "wise men" could help him. This made the king so angry that he commanded their execution. Before the sentence could be carried out, however, Daniel intervened. Daniel responded: "No wise man, enchanter, magician or diviner can explain to the king the mystery he has asked about, but there is a God in heaven who reveals mysteries" (Dan. 2:27-28, NIV). The crisis was averted because Daniel, by the grace of God, told the king his dream and gave the interpretation (Daniel 2:28-48).

When Nebuchadnezzar died, it was reported to the new king "There is a man in your kingdom who has the spirit of the holy gods in him. In the time of your father he was found to have insight and intelligence and wisdom like that of the gods" (Daniel 5:11, NIV). "This man Daniel, whom the king called Belteshazzar, was found to have a keen mind and knowledge and understanding, and also the ability to interpret dreams, explain riddles and solve difficult problems" (Dan. 5:12, NIV-UK).

Daniel's exceptional qualities so distinguished him from the rest that the king decided to make Daniel head of all the governors of the kingdom of Babylon. Knowledge of the king's intent resulted in the other governors deceiving the king into signing a decree outlawing Daniel's religion. However, this did not prevent Daniel from continuing to worship God. Because of the decree, Daniel was cast into a den of lions. Miraculously, the lions did him no harm; yet those thrown in the den afterwards were crushed by the lions

(Dan. 6).

Another notable example is Joseph. Like Daniel, Joseph was associated with the ability to interpret dreams supernaturally. His dreams and ability to interpret dreams were the source of both his troubles and deliverance. As a teenager, Joseph dreamed of becoming so great that even his father and siblings would bow before him one day. For making the dream known, Joseph became the object of hate. His siblings wanted to kill him. Instead, they sold him as slave to an Egyptian. Being sold into slavery did not prevent Joseph's dream from coming to pass. In fact, it turned out slavery was the vehicle used by God to fulfill the dream and deliver Joseph's own family from famine (Gen. 37; 39-50).

While a prisoner in Egypt on a trumped-up charge, Joseph interpreted the dreams of Pharaoh's cupbearer and baker; each dream was fulfilled exactly as Joseph said it would. Later the Pharaoh had a disturbing dream that none of his wise men could interpret. Joseph interpreted the Pharaoh's dream also. The dream warned of wide-scale famine, so Joseph made a proposal to avert disaster (Gen. 40, 41).

> The proposal seemed good to Pharaoh and to all his servants. Then Pharaoh said to his servants, "Can we find a man like this, in whom is a divine spirit?" So Pharaoh said to Joseph, "Since God has informed you of all this, there is no one so discerning and wise as you are. You shall be over my house, and according to your command all my people shall do homage; only in the throne I will be greater than you." (Gen. 41:37-40, NASB)

Solomon was known for his supernatural wisdom and leadership (1 Kings 3). Upon becoming king, Solomon prayed to God for wisdom and received his request, and more (2 Chron. 1:10-12). After seeing with her own eyes the wisdom of Solomon, the Queen of Sheba concurred that the report concerning Solomon's wisdom and achievements was true (1 Kings 10:6).

Moses received revelation from God in flames of fire from within a bush (Exod. 3). He was instrumental in leading the people of God out of bondage (Exod.). As leaders, Moses and Aaron performed miracles by inflicting plagues on Egypt. Through Moses, God parted the Red Sea and enabled the Israelites to escape on dry land. The seabed, however, became the grave of the pursuing Egyptian army. While in hot pursuit of the Jews, the waters of the sea receded and engulfed Pharaoh's army (Exod. 13). Water miraculously came from a rock after being struck by Moses (Exod. 17). Supernaturally, Moses received the Ten Commandments, laws of justice and mercy, and various other laws (Exod. 20; Deut. 5; Lev. 19).

As judge over Israel, Samson was associated with supernatural physical strength (Judges 13, 24, 16:5-12). Noah built an ark – a huge ship – based on instructions given him by God at a time when there was no apparent need for a ship. Noah was ridiculed for it, but the ark later turned out to be the salvation of the world from a massive flood (Gen. 6-9).

For a period of time, God miraculously used a raven to feed Elijah twice daily (1 Kings 17:1-6). On another occasion, God used a poor widow to feed the prophet. For meeting the need of the man of God for food, the widowed woman received an endless supply of food at the hand of God (1 Kings 17:8-16). When the woman's son died, the prophet Elijah raised the boy from the dead (1 Kings 17:17-24). Elijah also prayed fire from heaven, which consumed a sacrifice (1 Kings 18). On the instructions of God, a whale swallowed Jonah. He spent three days in the belly of the whale and survived (John 1-3).

Besides supernatural phenomena involving people, there were supernatural events. For example: a serpent supernaturally spoke to Eve (Gen. 3:1-4). A donkey supernaturally spoke to its master (Num. 22:21). Balaam encountered angels (Num. 22:21-41). Sarah, Abraham's wife, conceived Isaac when she was long past child-bearing age (Gen. 17; 18:1-15; 21). God supernaturally destroyed the cities of Sodom and Gomorrah for their wickedness (Gen. 19).

For a summary of Old Testament evidence of supernatural power and intelligence, see Table 5.

Spiritual Intelligence: A Christian Perspective

POWER	PURPOSE	PERSON/S	SCRIPTURE
Physical	To govern	Othniel	Judg. 3:10
		Gideon	Judg. 6:34
		Jepthah	Judg. 11:29
		Samson	Judg. 13:25; 14:6
Technical	Ship building	Noah	Gen. 6-9
	Garment manu.	Many people	Ex. 28:2-3
	Craft manu.	Bezalel & others	Ex. 31:1-11
Wisdom	To govern/lead	Moses & 70 elders	Numb. 6:17, 25
		Joshua	Num. 27:18-23
		Saul	1 Sam. 10:1
		Solomon	2 Chron. 1:10-12
Knowledge	To govern	70 elders	Num. 11:25
		Saul	1 Sam. 10:6, 10
		David	1 Sam. 15:13
Prophecy	Many reasons	Baalam	Num. 24:2
		Azariah	2 Chron. 15:1
		Zechariah	2 Chron. 4:20
		Micah	Micah 3:8
Miracles	Many reasons	Elijah	1 Kings 18
		Moses	Exodus
		Elisha	2 Kings 4, 5
Dreams & their Interpretation	Many reasons	Jacob	Gen. 28:10-16
		Joseph	Gen. 40, 41
		Daniel	Dan. 2, 4
Visions	Many reasons	Abram	Gen. 15:1
		Isaiah	Isa. 1:1
		Daniel	Dan. 2:19; 7:2

Table 5: *Evidence of Supernatural Power and Intelligence in OT*

Falsification of the Spiritual

It is possible for miracles and other spiritual phenomena attributed to Divinity to have other explanations. According to psychologists, human beings use only a small part of our brain. Unused parts of the brain may become *fired-up* due to an emotionally-charged situation, for example, physical trauma, threat to safety, deep meditation, extreme joy or fear. Under circumstances such as these, solutions to seemingly impossible problems may become clear. While some people attribute solutions to answer to prayer, others make attributions to a higher state of consciousness.

The use of psychoactive substances in spiritual, health-related and various recreational activities, for example, is a global practice going far back into ancient civilization. Psychoactive substances can induce altered states of consciousness, enabling increased insight and awareness.

In addition, some people have mental and psychic abilities, (as in telepathy, clairvoyance and psychokinesis), enabling them to tap into difficult areas of knowledge and use that knowledge negatively. And some people are able to use demonic powers to cause spiritual, physical and emotional harm, as in witchcraft and voodoo.

Atkinson (2007) proffered an explanation for healing and other miracles in psychology. According to Atkinson, suggestions by self and others have the power of getting the brain to effect changes in the body. Therapeutic suggestions under the right circumstances may cause the body to realign or heal itself; unhealthy or negative suggestions may produce diseases and psychosomatic illnesses. These views resonated with Moyers (1993).

Some healing miracles have a basis in hypnotism (Gurveich, 2011). Psychiatrist and neuroscientist, Amen (1988), has added yet another dimension to the dialogue. He proffered an explanation of healing miracles in biology. Based on scientific studies, Amen found that many problems – moral, spiritual, physical and psychological – are rooted in brain damage or brain dysfunction, and are potentially fixable using a medical model or a medical model in collaboration with other therapeutic interventions.

As far as religious "truths" are concerned, many claims to divine revelation are conflicting.

Spiritual Intelligence: A Christian Perspective

If general revelation is open to falsification, so is special revelation. This needs specially to be stressed as both Jesus Christ and the Bible are in danger of being turned into religious symbols beyond the need for verification, defended obscurely in circular reasoning. (Guinness, 1973, p. 354)

There are many ways through which the spiritual may be falsified. The list includes:

- Spiritual wickedness (John 8:44; Eph. 2:2; 6:12)
- Doctrines of devils (1 Tim. 4:1)
- Unsound doctrines (1 Tim. 1:10; 2 Tim. 4:3; Titus 1:9)
- Demon spirits (2 Kings 21:6; 23:24; 1 Chron. 10:13)
- Demon possessions (Matt. 12:22; 17:14-18; Luke 11:14)
- False divination (Ezek. 21:21-23)
- False apostles (2 Cor. 11:13-15)
- False teachers (2 Pet. 2:1-22)
- False prophets (Matt. 7:15; 24:11, 24; 1 John 4:1)
- False prophecy (Jer. 5:31; 29:8-9)
- Hypocrites (Matt. 23:25)
- False signs and wonders (Matt. 24:24; Mark 13:32; 2 Tim. 3:2; 2 Thess. 2:9; Rev. 13:11-18)
- Witchcraft (2 Chron. 33:6; Gal. 5:20)
- Sorcery (Isa. 47:9; 57:3-12; Jer. 27:9-10; Acts 8:9-11)
- Necromancy (Deut. 18:9-12)
- Soothsaying (Josh. 13:22; Isa. 2:6; Acts 16:16-17)
- Magicians (Exod. 7:14-23; Dan. 5:1)
- Mediums (Lev. 19:31; 20:6)

Spiritual phenomena such as prophecy and speaking in tongues, in addition to the possibility of divine origin, may originate in demonic or psychic powers. Yet due to an insatiable desire for religious experience, few question the origin of such experiences. The result is confusion (Guinness, 1973). Guinness bemoaned the fact that, although wider than its legitimacy, experience itself is self-authenticating.

Based on the number of possible sources, experience itself needs to be validated. Biblical sources reveal there is a Spirit at work in the children of God (Eph. 1:13; 3:16, 20; 1 John 4:4) and there is a spirit at work in the children of the devil (Eph. 2:1-2), but the Spirit at work in the children of God is greater (Exod. 7: 8-12; Dan. 2:24; 1 John 4:4; 2 Tim. 1:7).

Children of God are warned of Satan who masquerades as an angel of light (2 Cor. 11:13) and of wolves in sheep's clothing (Matt. 7:15). The people of God are instructed to test the spirits to see whether they are of God (1 John 4:1-6). The gift of spiritual discernment is given to help in this dilemma (1 Cor. 12:10). Confusion regarding the origin of spiritual phenomena underscores the need for spiritual intelligence.

Spiritual practices do not necessarily originate in God and thus are not necessarily signs of spiritual intelligence associated with Divinity. For example, the prophet Isaiah chided members of the religious community for their outward show of spirituality in their multiplied fasts and prayers, while at the same time lacking concern for people in need.

> Is not this the kind of fasting I have chosen: to loosen the chains of injustice and untie the cords of the yoke, to set the oppressed free and break every yoke? Is it not to share your food with the hungry and to provide the poor wanderer with shelter – when you see the naked, to clothe him, and not to turn away from your own flesh and blood? Then your light will break forth like the dawn, and your healing will quickly appear; then your righteousness will go before you, and the glory of the LORD will be your rear guard. (Isaiah 8:6 -8, NIV)

Although useful, religious gestures such as fasting and prayer are hypocritical when they contradict concern for the poor and oppressed. There is a huge difference between *churchianity* or *religiousity* with genuine spirituality.

There is energy connected with the flesh and there is energy connected with the Spirit. Although operating on different frequencies, the energy of the flesh is able to duplicate many things produced through the energy of the Spirit. Unfortunately, many equate every "spiritual" activity with divine spiritual intelligence. The truth is God does not necessarily have anything to do with spiritual activities, although there may be some semblance of good involved. Jesus cautioned:

> Not everyone who says to me, 'Lord, Lord,' will enter the kingdom of heaven, but only the one who does the will of my Father who is in heaven. Many will say to me on that day, 'Lord, Lord, did we not prophesy in your name and in your name drive out demons and in your name perform many miracles?' Then I will tell them plainly, 'I never knew you. Away from me, you evildoers!' (Matt. 7:21-23, NIV)

In addition to knowledge and power associated with the flesh or physicality, (psychic powers included), there is knowledge and power associated with evil spirits, including the devil. Consequently, belief in the existence of God does not necessarily indicate a personal relationship with God or true spiritual intelligence.

♦ Demons believe in God and tremble (James 2:19).

♦ Demons acknowledge God's greatness and superiority   (Acts 10:36-38).

♦ Demons recognize Jesus as the Son of God (Mark 3:11).

♦ Demons recognize the apostles as servants of God (Acts 16:16-18).

♦ The devil can quote Scripture (Matt. 4:4-5).

There is overwhelming evidence of supernatural phenomena associated with the occult. Despite the fact, this does not mean power derived from the occult is legitimate and that all spiritual power is false (Guinness, 1973).

Geisler (1976) has made a distinction between miracles and Satanic signs. He discerned Satanic signs as having the following characteristics: (a) not supporting the truth about God, (b) not bringing about moral good but evil, and (c) as magnifying evil men and the spirits behind them.

There are three sources of wisdom operating in the world: the human, divine and diabolic: the first gives the earthly and human perspective; the second, the heavenly and godly perspective; and the third, the hellish and diabolic perspective, sometimes masked as light.

We have already seen that since the Fall human nature has been corrupted. The corruption of human nature means the corruption of natural intelligence. As such, natural intelligence may cause one to be self-deceived and to be deceived by others. Furthermore, due to corruption, a person may use natural intelligence for selfish and destructive purposes.

Intelligence that comes from the devil is also corrupt and as such does not promote authenticity or wholeness. Spiritual intelligence derived from the devil is evil and is designed to deceive.

Only the intelligence that comes from God is pure and accurate enough to enable authenticity, wholeness and faithful stewardship.

Profile of the Spiritual

A profile extrapolated from biblical data represents the spiritual as:

- Being born by the Spirit (John 3:5-6)
- Being led by the Spirit (Rom. 8:14; Gal. 5:18)
- Being filled with the Spirit (Eph. 5:18)
- Being controlled by the Spirit (Rom. 8:1-4, 9)
- Operating by the law of the Spirit (Rom. 8:1)
- Operating by the power of the Spirit (1 Cor. 2:1-5)
- Living according to the dictates of the Spirit
  (Rom. 8:4, 5, 14; Gal. 5:13, 23)

- Receiving understanding by the Spirit (1 Cor. 2:12-16)
- Receiving confirmation by the Spirit (Rom. 8:16; 9:9)
- Receiving gifts of the Spirit (1 Cor. 12:1-11; James 1:17)
- Receiving the gift of the Spirit (Acts 1:4; 2:1-4)
- Receiving the baptism of the Spirit (Acts 1:5)
- Communicating and worshipping by the Spirit (Eph. 5:19-20; Rom. 12:1-2)
- Receiving spiritual blessings (Eph. 1:3)
- Receiving spiritual rewards (Luke 6:23, 35; Col. 2:18; Rev. 22:12)
- Receiving spiritual restoration (Isa. 58:12; Ps. 23:3; 51:12; Mark 9:12; Gal. 6:1)
- Receiving joy by the Spirit (Acts 13:52)
- Receiving strength by the Spirit (2 Cor. 12:10; Eph. 3:16; Col. 1:9-12; 2 Tim. 4:17-18; Phil. 4:12, 13; 1 Pet. 5:10)
- Receiving knowledge of spiritual things (Rom. 15:27; 1 Cor. 2:13- 16)
- Sowing spiritual seed (1 Cor. 9:11)
- Producing fruit of the Spirit (Gal. 5:22, 23)

See also spiritual traits listed on pages 86 and 87.

Based on Scripture, life without the Spirit means spiritual death and, as a consequence, spiritual unintelligence or darkness. Peter equated life prior spiritual rebirth with ignorance and darkness. Accordingly, Peter reminded converts they were called out of darkness into light (1 Peter 2:9). This reso-nated with Paul (Acts 26:18; Eph. 5:8). Paul associated good with wisdom, implied a correlation between evil and foolishness, prescribed innocence where evil is concerned, and advocated maturity (Rm. 16:19; 1 Cor. 14:20, Eph. 2:1-10). John viewed walking in the light as imperative to having fel-lowship with God (1 John 1:5-10).

Light is a symbol of truth and righteousness, and came to represent spiritual enlightenment, embodied by Jesus. Despite being controversial, Jesus was the most enlightened and transformational leader of his time. As such, he was the light of the world. Both Jesus and his disciples are described as light of the world. In order to shine brilliantly, however, disciples of Christ need to develop their spiritual intelligence.

Developing Spiritual Intelligence

In this section, emphasis will be placed on the Word as a means of developing spiritual intelligence and reintegrating human personality. Developing spiritual intelligence involves the practice of several disciplines, including:

- Faith (Rom. 1:17; 2 Cor. 5:7; Heb. 11)
- Baptism (John 3:22; Matt. 28:19; Acts 2:41; 19:5)
- Communion (Luke 22:19-20; 1 Cor. 11:17-34)
- Prayer (Matt. 6:6; Mark 11:24; James 5:16; 1 Thess. 5:17)
- Fasting (Matt. 6:16-18; Acts 14:23; Esther 4:16; Joel 2:12)
- Fellowshipping (Heb. 10:25; 1 Thess. 5:11; 1 Cor. 12:12-27; Gal. 6:2; Rom. 12:5, 10)
- Thanksgiving (2 Chron. 5:13; Psa. 9:1; Philipp. 4:6-7; Eph. 5:20; Col. 3:16-17)
- Cultivating spiritual gifts (1 Cor. 12; 1 Tim. 4:1-4; 2 Tim. 1:6-7; 1 Peter 4:10)
- Obedience (2 Cor. 10:5-7; Lev. 22:31; John 14:23; James 1:22; Deut. 28:1)
- Walking by the Spirit (Gal. 5:16-18, 22-25; Rom. 8:4-5, 13-14)
- Studying and Meditating on Scripture (2 Tim. 2:15; Psa. 1:1-6).

It appears that prior the Fall spiritual intelligence was intuitive. Disobedience introduced the law of entropy in the human system, causing the dumbing down of the intellect mentally and spiritually, thereby making everything difficult to grasp and control, and as such, requiring hard labor. Albeit, mental intelligence may be developed through natural means and spiritual intelligence may be developed through spiritual means.

The sinful nature of the flesh may be overcome by walking according to the dictates of the Spirit (Gal. 5:16-18) and by putting on Christ (Rom. 13:14; Gal. 3:27; Col. 3:5-14) – by mimicking or imitating the life of Christ; but Christ has to be living in us before he can be lived out by us (Gal. 2:20).

Beginning with regeneration by the Spirit (Titus 3:3-5,8), spiritual intelligence is developed as the mind is renewed, hence the biblical imperative:

> Do not conform to the pattern of this world, but be transformed by the renewing of your mind. **Then you will be able to test and approve what God's will is** – his good, pleasing and perfect will. (Romans 12:2, NIV)

Obedience to God's Word is a sure way of renewing our minds. If disobedience is responsible for darkening the mind, for splitting and disintegrating human personality, and for spiritual and physical death, then obedience is the key to making us whole.

God is our Life Source. When we move away from God, we rob ourselves of His support and protection and diminishes our ability to flourish. This is why love for God expressed in willing obedience is the highest expression of spiritual intelligence (John 14:31; 15:7-10).

Importance of the Word

Since we did not create ourselves, human beings have an obligation to honor our Creator (Gen. 1-2; Eccl. 12:1-2). One of the best ways to do so is to know the Mind of God, expressed in the Written Word. Many biblical writers advocated meditating and memorizing the Word (Joshua 1:8; Psa. 1:2; 119:11), and studying and applying the Word (2 Tim. 3:14-17; 2:15; 1 Peter 3:15).

In Scripture, wisdom and knowledge are deemed extremely useful and begin with respect for God (Prov. 1). Knowledge of God is crucial, and the best way to know God and God's Will is to study and obey His Word. Spending quality time in the Word increases our spiritual IQ, enabling us to "demolish arguments and every pretension that sets itself up against the knowledge of God, and we take captive every thought to make it obedient to Christ (2 Cor.5:10, NIV). The Word has power to:

- Make us wise (Psa. 19:7-11; Prov. 2:1-5; 2 Tim. 3:14-15)
- Enable understanding (Psa. 119:97-105)
- Evoke faith (Romans 10:17; 1 Thess. 2:13; John 20:31)
- Cleanse from sin (John 17:17; Eph. 5:26; Psa. 119:9-16)
- Deliver from sin (Psa. 119:11; 1 John 2:1; 2 Peter 2:9)
- Deliver from shame (2 Tim. 2:15; Rom. 1:16-17; 5:1-11)
- Prevent heresy (2 Tim. 4:1-3)
- Give light and life (John 5:24, 39-40; 6:63)
- Save souls (John 5:24; 2 Tim. 3:14-15)
- Enable spiritual conquests (Eph. 6:11-17)
- Enable freedom (John 8:32)
- Nourish and enable spiritual growth (1 Peter 2:1-12; Heb. 5:12-14)
- Enable reverence and knowledge of God (Proverbs 2:1-22)
- Enable joy and delight (Jer. 15:16; Psa. 119:97-104)
- Enable a good answer or defense (2 Tim. 2:15; 1 Pet. 3:15)
- Enable hope (Rev. 15:4; Isa. 43:10)
- Lengthen life and enable peace (Prov. 3:1-2; Psa. 119:165)
- Enable direction and discernment (Psa. 119:105; Heb. 4:12)
- Profit us in many ways (2 Tim. 3:16-17)
- Enable healing (Matt. 10:1; Psa. 107:20; Prov. 20-22)
- Enable security (Hosea 4:6)

- Enable blessings (John 13:17; Psalm 1:1-6; Rev. 1:3)
- Make us successful (Josh. 1:8)

Notice the importance of the Word in the life and ministry of Jesus (Matt. 4:1-11; John 17:13-19). The importance of the Word in enabling spiritual life and in developing spiritual intelligence cannot be overemphasized. In addition to other Scriptures, the book of Proverbs is totally devoted to teaching wisdom.

Based on the Bible, God created human beings and established our boundaries, according to His own design and purpose. Being Creator, it was God's prerogative to decide the meaning and purpose of life and on matters of right and wrong. The effects of the inappropriate use of volition by the first humans led to spiritual death and dysfunction, manifesting in diseases of meaning. This has been passed on to posterity.

Was God wrong in creating humanity with volition? Who am I to question the wisdom of the Creator? From beginning, the Creator intended active participation in the fulfilment of destiny, hence volition being part of our mindscape. Had God desired automatons, God would have created robot-like creatures, not humans able to participate in their own development and responsible for their own choices.

God made us humans with intelligence and volition. Intelligence equips us with the ability to reason and acquire knowledge. Volition empowers with the ability to choose between alternatives, giving us the opportunity to determine our own destiny. But with this freedom came responsibility and accountable.

As there is light and darkness, there is good and evil, truth and error, and there is right and wrong; so all choices are not equal, are they? It is inconceivable that all choices should produce a common experience or have the same consequence, lead to the same place or fulfill the same purpose. Since all choices are not equal, it is necessary that choices have consequences. Consequences are the best way to motivate appropriate choices and encourage development.

Volition made it possible to participate in our own development. Although there are many facets to development, spiritual development is foundational, as it gives a sense of meaning and purpose. Meaning and purpose are contingent on a personal relationship with God, enabling fellowship and faithful stewardship.

As Creator, God desired willing obedience. Obedience is not relevant unless there are inviolable laws and the ability to accept or reject them. Although given the capacity to agree or disagree, obey or disobey, human beings were obliged to make decisions in reference and in deference to God, hence the notion of stewardship. As stewards, faithfulness and obedience were required.

Disobedience is tantamount to disrespect and dishonor. Plus, showing disrespect emboldens others to do likewise, and in fact causes God's enemies to blaspheme God's name (Romans 2:17-24). We have already seen that in addition to consequences at the personal level (Romans 1:28-32), disobedience has consequences for society in general and the world at large.

Notions of right and wrong and attended consequences are not unique to the moral and spiritual domain. Every discipline has its codes of conduct, laws governing how truth is derived, organizations validating its efficacy and courts mediating its disputes. So obedience is not only relevant in the spiritual domain; it is also relevant in every area of life. There is obligation to obey society's laws, and the various rules governing institutions and groups of which we are a part. The flourishing of individuals, groups and nations is contingent on obedience to various protocols, laws, and governing authorities.

Assuming a common Source, if growth and development is predicated on order and the achievement of harmony through the making of appropriate choices in the natural realm, the same must be true in the spiritual. Conformity to natural and spiritual laws established by the Creator enables human development; disconformity or rebellion undermines it.

Exclusion of spiritual intelligence from our mindscape has made it impossible to achieve our full potential as per design. Spiritual rebirth has made what God had predesigned a possibility via indwelling of the Spirit. Among other things, the reason the Holy Spirit is given (Eph. 1:13-14) is to provide believers with power to be witnesses for Christ (Acts 1:8, Matt. 28:18-20). In other words, possession of the Holy Spirit is the exclusive right of believers, in order that people of faith may, by the energy of the Spirit, truthfully and powerfully represent God in all the earth. Everything that issues from the Spirit is driven by this agenda.

By definition and implication, Jesus was careful to underscore the manner in which He wished to be represented. Two of the main words used to define the scope of the Spirit's influence are the words "Holy" (Acts 1:8) and "Truth" (John 14:17; 16:13). These two attributes speak of the ability to discern right from wrong (good from evil) as far as morality is concerned, and truth from error as far as spiritual beliefs or doctrine are concerned. Both words cohere with notions of integrity and soundness, and as such speak to the highest level of intelligence. Intelligence associated with the Spirit is by definition Spiritual Intelligence.

Although spiritual intelligence is also associated with believers (1 Cor. 2:14), spiritual intelligence is not an esoteric term. The chief mandate of believers is to make this intelligence available to all, as God had predesigned us for wholeness. Wholeness is not possible without spiritual intelligence being an objective reality and a subjective fact. To be convincing, spiritual intelligence needs to be displayed experientially or practically.

Like other intelligence paradigms, spiritual intelligence may be affected by levels of emotional intelligence. When operating at a high level of emotional intelligence, people are inclined to be disciplined in the pursuit of goals and objectives; to feel good about themselves and to demonstrate pro-social behaviors. The opposite is also true. In terms of overall development, spiritual intelligence may be affected by one's character. As practitioner, a person becomes sharper in their understanding and more discerning, thus becoming more inclined to learning via study and revelation. Faith also plays a crucial role. (Matt. 21:22; Mark 11:24; Luke 16:10; 17:6; Rom. 10:17).

Summary

Although the Bible does not speak directly of a spiritual intelligence, the

Bible does speak of spiritual wisdom, understanding, discernment, revelation, inspiration, illumination, and spiritual and supernatural abilities. In Scripture, the concept of spiritual intelligence is supported by metaphors such as light and darkness, emphasis being on light as representative of a path or way of life consistent with truth and righteousness. Other images include night and day, the old self and the new self, and the inner man and the outer man. The concept of spiritual intelligence is supported by narratives of divine enablement in various circumstances, such as the ability to interpret dreams, understand mysteries, and perform miracles. Biblical literature profiles the spiritual as being able to receive, understand, discern and apply spiritual knowledge, and being able to use spiritual means to identify and solve spiritual and other problems. Several commands and allusions in the sacred writings of Scripture imply the existence of spiritual intelligence. References are made to a paradigm shift in one's way of thinking and a shift in domain or sphere of influence informing behavior. There are three major operating systems informing thought and behavior: the operating system of the flesh associated with natural intelligence, the operating system of the Spirit associated with spiritual intelligence, and the operating system of the devil associated with pseudo or counter-intelligence. There are distinct differences in perceptual frameworks, in the way life is lived and levels of competency. Spiritual intelligence is not an innate ability. Due to the Fall, human beings are born spiritually dead, but may become spiritually alive by the Holy Spirit the moment Jesus is embraced as Savior from sin. When connected to God, human beings are empowered to reflect more accurately God's image, will and purpose in creation. A personal relationship with God enables spiritual life and intelligence, and gives a sense of meaning and purpose. Spiritual intelligence is falsifiable by various means, such as psychology, biology, psychoactive drugs and the occult.

The next chapter will focus on benefits and potential benefits of spiritual intelligence.

CHAPTER 7
Benefits of
Spiritual Intelligence

Through the centuries, various religious traditions have developed spiritual disciplines to promote individual and group spiritual maturity. Researchers in cultural anthropology and sociology of religion examine how the spiritual relates and integrates with culture. Scholars in both transpersonal psychology and transpersonal anthropology are investigating concerns raised by spiritual intelligence. Research already reveals support for spiritual intelligence and points to many benefits and potential benefits of a spiritual paradigm.

Personal Benefits

Spiritual intelligence enhances human potential in many ways, such as understanding the spiritual, enabling spiritual growth, enabling access and application of spiritual resources to deal with a host of spiritual and other problems.

As religious people are more likely to have a sense of purpose and to observe laws and norms, Durkheim (1972) attributed the stabilization of the individual and society to religion. Alienation from God leads to a loss of purpose and anomie or lawlessness. Religion empowers by giving a sense of purpose and meaning.

A lack of meaning and purpose is a major cause of deviance and criminal behavior. Without meaning and purpose, personhood is devalued and degraded. Meaninglessness and purposelessness are acted out in inappropriate behavior, affecting relationships with God and others. Indirectly and directly, religion contributes to lessening deviant behavior, including crime.

May (1969) identified four characteristics associated with people disconnected from God and others: (a) an avoidance of close relationships, (b) an inability to feel deeply about anything, (c) a tendency to be cold and detached, and (d) a superior attitude. May stated that these behaviors are mere defense mechanisms against anxiety and a sense of powerlessness.

Spirituality informs values, and builds character. Many people see a connection between spirituality and morality and will agree that moral virtues have the potential for actualizing self.

Family Benefits

Spirituality promotes marriage, faithfulness in marriage and other family relationships. Since the family is the bedrock of society (Clarke, 1999), there are exponential benefits to be obtained. Emphasis on positive emotions – such as love – augurs for better relational, emotional and physical health, and aids in problem-solving. The teachings of Scripture impart values to the socializing context and thus mitigate immoral behavior. Immoral behavior ruins relationships, family life included.

Family members who operate at a high level of spiritual intelligence strengthen the family unit by ensuring a wholesome and stable moral and spiritual environment. Children growing up in such an environment are better able to reach their full potential and are thus better able to contribute more to society. Stable and wholesome family units positively impact society on the whole.

Social Benefits

Many view religion as potentially able to bind people and society together. There are therefore social and relational benefits to be derived from a well-developed spiritual intelligence.

Collins (1999) foresaw deprivation of love among affluent societies as contributing to apathy, and saw a correlation between apathy and crime:

> It seems to me that the contemporary famine of love, which seems to afflict affluent societies, is going to produce a generation of men and women who suppress their painful feelings of insecurity and deprivation by becoming apathetic. It is my observation that many of the mindless crimes that bedevil modern life are committed by apathetic people who are often ruthless, i.e. without care or empathy for others. (p. 121)

Love is critical to spiritual, emotional and physical health, and is an important feature of spiritual intelligence. Zohar and Marshall (2000) attributed diseases of meaning, for example drug abuse and certain forms of crime, to a lack of spiritual intelligence, and averred spiritual intelligence provides the potential for a better and more satisfying life. Vaughn (2002) expressed the view that spiritual intelligence deepens primary love relationships, contributes to healing relationships, helps people to appreciate others, helps them to recognize the power of forgiveness, enhances their capacity to give and receive love, and helps them to learn from mistakes and make wise decisions.

Making wise decisions involve revisiting assumptions and changing attitudes. Attitudes of hate, for example, tend to lead to perceptual issues, relationship issues and issues of injustice. Some aspects of injustice are rooted in sexism, classism, *casteism*, racism and bigotry. Spiritual intelligence potentially undercuts these vices by promoting love (1 Cor. 13:1-13) and the breaking down of racial, social and gender barriers (Matt. 5:43-48; Gal. 3:26 -29).

Tippet (1987) posited that people need to see themselves biologically as the same human beings if they are to live happily together, and that humans need to be right with God in order to be right with each other. People who are rightly related to God tend to relate appropriately to fellow human beings as well (Matt. 22:37-40; Rom. 12:8-10). Because security of the spiritually intelligent is essentially based on a personal relationship with God, unseemly behavior in order to secure self is minimized; individual differences and human diversity are more readily accepted; and interdependence and community spirit are encouraged.

The spiritually intelligent has a sense of stewardship, articulated in helpful concern for others (James 1:27; 1 Pet. 4:10; Acts 2). Most religions emphasize helping the poor and other persons in need. As no one may fulfill God's purpose alone (Warren, 2002), serving God and others is not just a command; it is necessary. In this regard, many prestigious institutions in areas such health, education and charitable organizations, have been founded by people spiritually intelligent enough to respond to needs or had the foresight to anticipate them. The spiritually intelligent have played a tremendous transformative role in societies worldwide.

One who is spiritually intelligent is necessarily concerned not only with personal development but also with the development of others. Accordingly, the spiritual is described as the light and salt of the earth (Matt. 5:13-16). As light and salt, the spiritual points people to God and prevents moral decay in the world.

True spirituality is perfectly modeled by Jesus, and as such Jesus. An appropriate role model is essential for setting a standard worth emulating and for providing a basis for validating and encouraging moral striving. Human beings thrive best where there is an appropriate nurturing environment, including role models and mentors. In the spiritual realm, Jesus is supremely the most qualified. For personifying spiritual intelligence, Jesus is deemed the perfect model of what a human being should be or look like in terms of character.

In being the perfect model of spiritual intelligence, Jesus potentially reconciles the lost world to God (2 Cor. 5:18-20). The entire creation, inclusive of humanity is reconcilable to God through Jesus (Coloss. 1:19-23; Heb. 2:9-11). The life of Jesus points people to God and to authentic personhood. For example, in a world where pride and arrogance were often associated with power and success, Jesus displayed meekness and humility.

Virtues such as meekness and humility are worth emulating (Philipp. 2:5-8), for they promote healthy self-esteem and positively impact relationships at every level. One who has a healthy self-esteem will relate appropriately to God and others. Religious authors on the subject of spiritual intelligence, such as Sager (1990), and nonreligious authors, such as Zohar and Marshall (2000), rank meekness and humility highly on their list of characteristics associated with spiritual intelligence.

Again, the perfect example is found in Jesus. Growing to be Christ-like in one's thinking, attitude and character is the essence of spiritual intelligence (1 Pet. 2:1-2; 2 Pet. 1:3-8; 3:18). Spiritual growth and intelligence includes loving God and others (1 Cor. 13; Gal. 5:13, 22; 1 John 4:7-8). Jesus modeled love for the world to see and experience.

Through Jesus, many people have experienced God's love. Motivated by love and compassion, Jesus did right for people in need. Having noticed the cares and concerns of others, Jesus was often moved to do whatever was necessary to relieve human suffering or remedy situations beyond the ability of persons to help themselves. Accordingly, he fed the hungry, healed all manner of sicknesses and diseases, raised the dead, cast out demons, forgave sins, taught multitudes, and provided leadership to people who "were like sheep without a shepherd." The life of Jesus was circumscribed by love.

Love is recognized as the highest expression of spiritual intelligence, and the command to love as the greatest of all the commands (1 Cor. 12:31-13:13; Luke 10:25-29). Love is a commodity that is not diminished by sharing, but is increased (Jones, 1998). Love for God and one's neighbor enables human beings to reflect God's image more accurately, hence the teaching of love was a major part of Jesus' ministry and is a major emphasis of Scripture.

Love is integral to spiritual growth and intelligence. There are many benefits to be derived, especially by the one showing love.

> The first task of love is self-purification. When one has purified oneself, by the grace of God, to the point at which one can truly love one's enemies, a beautiful thing happens. It is as if the boundaries of the soul become so clean as to be transparent, and a unique light then shines forth from the individual. (Peck, 1983, p. 268)

Spiritual Intelligence: A Christian Perspective

Peck noted, however, that reaction to the light might not be the same for everyone exposed to it and warned of possible suffering on account of doing good. Suffering on account of doing good should not be equated with failure (1 Peter 3:13-18). Although not immediately apparent at times, there is always a benefit to be derived, either by the person undergoing suffering, the one inflicting suffering or by others; sometimes the whole world benefits. Good ultimately triumphs over evil.

A good way to make a difference in the world is to treat others the same way you would like to be treated (Matt. 7:12), to treat people with love. Treating each other with love makes the world a better place for all to live.

Spiritual intelligence promotes the expression of positive emotions such as love. Thus the spiritual intelligent seek to build a community of love. This love, however, is not the free, unrestrained and reckless love advocated by the world, where it doesn't matter who or what we love. Love associated with spiritual intelligence takes cognizance of right and wrong, and as such is concerned about behaviors that promote the integrity of the individual and society, and most importantly, behaviors that honor God.

Love is the cradle in which development takes place, enabling purpose to be fulfilled. The proof of love is in the choices we make; it is in loving the things that God loves and hating the things that God hates. To love is to align our character with the character of God, for God is love.

The opposite of love is hate; and we know what hate brings. In summary, hate brings everything that is bad, namely division and destruction. Love does the opposite. Love unifies and protects.

Since love does not come naturally to most and is often misunderstood, there is a number of commands in Scripture instructing us to love, showing us how to love and providing a basis for love. The list includes the following:

1. "We know that we have passed from death to life, because we love our brothers." (1 John 3:14, NIV)
2. "Anyone who claims to be in the light but hates his brother is still in the darkness." (1 John 2:9, NIV)

3. "All men will know that you are my disciples, if you love one another." (John 13:35, NIV)

4. "Love must be sincere." (Romans 12:9, NIV)

5. "Above all, love each other deeply, because love covers over a multitude of sins." (1 Peter 4:8, NIV)

6. "Love does no harm to its neighbor. Therefore love is the fulfillment of the law." (Romans 13:10)

7. "This is love for God: to obey his commands. And His commands are not burdensome, for everyone born of God has overcome the world..." (1 John 5:3,4, NIV)

8. "God is love. Whoever lives in love lives in God, and God in him..." (1 John 4:16, NIV)

9. Love:
    - Is patient
    - Is kind
    - Is not envious
    - Is not boastful
    - Is not proud
    - Is not rude
    - Is not self-seeking
    - Is not easily angered
    - Keeps no record of wrong
    - Does not delight in evil
    - Rejoices in truth
    - Always protects
    - Always hopes
    - Always perseveres
    - Never fails (1 Cor.13:4-8, NIV)

Love for God enables the people of God to overcome the world (1 John 5:3-4), God working all things together for the good of those who love Him

(Rom. 8:28), enabling purpose to be fulfilled.

Purpose is a construct of God's design. Being Creator, God gets to decide our purpose. Specifically, purpose is contingent on a person's spiritual gifts and talents; collectively, it is contingent on God's will for humanity on the whole.

Because God is a God of order, everyone does not have the same gifts (1 Cor. 12). We are uniquely equipped to fulfill our potential, including being a blessing to others. We are blessed by God to be a blessing. Selfishness is to be avoided. As "no man is an island," there is interdependency. Consequently, the spiritually intelligent serve each other in love (Gal. 5:13).

And because God is a God of order, there are natural and spiritual laws supporting order in both the natural and spiritual domain. It is therefore crucial that human beings comply with God's laws as disobedience has the effect of causing disharmony, disaster and defeat. God's laws are designed to enable the fulfillment of purpose. Law and order are expressions of God's love.

God's love is circumscribed by holiness. If holiness enabled God to do the right thing in creating order in the world, the same must be true of human beings. Holiness enables human beings to experience order internally and externally. This is why the greatest commandments are about love for God and love for our neighbor.

We are commanded to love, for God is love (1 John 4:7) and to be holy, for God is holy (1 Peter 1:14, 15). Nothing makes us more whole than love, and nothing integrates us more than holiness; neither can be divorced from the other.

Holiness speaks to wholeness. It means to be attuned with God. There is no incoherence or contradiction in God. Everything that God does reflects order and integrity. People who love God are godly. The best way to show love for God is to obey God (Luke 10:27). Obedience is the platform for holiness. And love is the highest expression of holiness.

Love seeks to create harmony, not disharmony. Love seeks to promote development; it does not undermine it. Having been corrupted by sin, we need to learn how to love. This is a factor of spiritual intelligence. Nothing integrates an individual and society more than love. Love is indeed the most excellent way.

National Benefits

The exercise of spiritual intelligence has made people better citizens. Biblical literature encourages Christians to pray for and submit to the authority of human government (Matt. 22:15-22; Rom. 13:1-7; 1 Tim. 2:1-2; 1 Pet. 2:13-14). The Scriptures, however, do not promote blind loyalty (Acts 13:1; 16:37). There is acknowledgement of governments' responsibility to promote righteousness and justice (Acts 13:1; 16:37). The promotion of righteousness and justice is integral to the survival and wellbeing of any nation (2 Chron. 7:14), and bears a correlation with the type and level of intelligence in operation.

The exercise of spiritual intelligence has not only made people better citizens, but in addition has augured well for integrity at every level of society. Integrity is important to the sustenance and security of human beings: spiritually, physically, psychologically, intellectually and socially. Throughout history, the rise or fall of any nation has been associated with the integrity of its people. A fitting example is found in ancient China:

> In ancient China the people wanted security against the barbaric hordes to the north, so they built the great wall. It was so high they believed no one could climb over it and so thick that nothing could break it down. They settled back to enjoy their security. During the first hundred years of the wall's existence, China was invaded three times. Not once did the barbaric hordes break down the walls or climb over it. Each time they bribed a gatekeeper and then marched right through the gates. The Chinese were so busy relying on walls of stone they forgot to teach integrity to their children. (Maxwell, 1993, p. 42)

Like the people of ancient China, many nations build walls of stone, only to have these walls undermined by corruption. Today walls of stone come in many forms, including military might, education, religion and wealth. None of these walls, however, may endure or redound to anyone's benefit where spiritual intelligence is lacking. Without spiritual intelligence, there is a chink in the walls of protection thereby exposing individuals, families and nations to disaster and defeat. A spiritual paradigm promotes integrity at every level.

Accordingly, there is commitment to peaceful co-existence, and improvement and growth in the lives of others. The spiritually intelligent are active in the development of human potential and in responding to the needs and concerns of others. Religion, for example, has had a long and outstanding history of involvement in areas of social concern such as education, health, community development, social justice and other social services, such as feeding the poor, taking care of the elderly and homeless.

> The high-water marks of Western culture have their origins within the community of faith. In virtually every field of cultural endeavor Christians have played a leading role, discovering norms, creating forms, and passing on their ideas and skills to others. The development of Western art, music, literature, architecture, politics, education, law, and economics – even such modern languages as English, German, Spanish, and French – is inconceivable apart from the contributions of Christians, and the worldview they embodied, in every age. (Moore, 2007, p. 153)

Spiritual intelligence has transformed the lives of individuals and of societies all over the world. There is an apparent correlation between levels of spiritual intelligence and levels of development at the individual and societal levels, though not necessarily. There is also an apparent correlation between corruption and paganism. Nations steeped in paganism are seemingly more inclined to have a distorted view of reality; they are more likely to show less regard for the sanctity of human life, less regard for human rights, less tolerance for the views of others, less regard for freedom of religion, and are more likely to be involved in all kinds of moral perversions, compounded by high levels of illiteracy.

Spiritual intelligence encourages faithful stewardship, thereby enabling development and growth; this in turn augurs well for peace and stability in the world.

Physical Health Benefits

The wisdom of spiritual intelligence is not only seen in the supernatural but also in the ordinary and mundane, such as lifestyle choices. Many diseases and illnesses affecting people today are the result of lifestyle choices. Hypertension, diabetes, certain types of cardiovascular diseases, certain types of cancer, kidney and liver diseases, and HIV/AIDS, to name a few, are sometimes rooted in lifestyle choices.

Unresolved guilt, anger and anxiety are major causes of hypertension, stroke and other diseases (Nezu, Nezu, & Diwakar, 2005). Promiscuity is a major factor in the spread of HIV/AIDS, and a cause of cervical cancer (Bolton & Singer, 1992; Vance, 1993). Gluttony and laziness result in obesity. Obesity is a major cause of diabetes and heart diseases (Hark & Morrison, 2009). Inordinate consumption of alcohol or drunkenness is a cause of liver disease (Worman, 2006). Smoking is a cause of emphysema and kidney disease (Sessa, Conte, & Meroni, 2000). Drug abuse damage people physically, psychologically, socially and spiritually.

By discouraging drug abuse and other ills, health in the individual and society is promoted. Spiritual intelligence encourages proper diet and, therefore, promotes physical health that might prevent illnesses such as obesity and obesity-related illnesses. Spiritual intelligence promotes faithfulness in marriage and discourages promiscuity. Consequently, illnesses caused by sexually transmitted diseases, including cervical cancer and HIV/AIDS, are potentially avoided. The biblical teaching, for example, that one's body is a temple of God encourages greater care for the body, physically and otherwise, thereby increasing the potential for a greater measure of wellness. Spiritual intelligence promotes natural and spiritual healing and a healthy lifestyle.

Because spiritual intelligence encourages better lifestyle choices, there is the possibility of minimizing illnesses and their severity, resulting in a longer and better quality life. Lifestyle choices not only affect us in terms of personal physical health, but may be the onset of genetically transmitted disease. Many diseases, illnesses and deaths associated with poor physical health, may be prevented through spiritually intelligent living.

Moral Benefits

Moral character is germane to human beings and is a reflection of the nature and level of intelligence motivating behavior. Spiritual intelligence is essential to appropriate character formation. Issues of morality affect character and, therefore, profoundly affect human life and existence. Since God is the source of spiritual life and intelligence, people who are spiritually connected to God are empowered with spiritual life and intelligence. Spiritual intelligence promotes moral transformation of the individual and society. It positively impacts values and attitudes and thereby improves personal and corporate integrity. Moral perversions, such as corruption, are held in check by the exercise of spiritual intelligence.

Rauschenbusch (1912) saw religion as having enormous potential to contribute significantly to the moral and social environment:

> Religion creates morality, and morality then deposits a small part of its contents in written laws. The State can protect the existing morality and promote the coming morality, but the vital creative force of morality lies deeper. The law becomes impotent if it is not supported by a diffused, spontaneous moral impulse in community. If religion implants love, mutual helpfulness, and respect for the life and rights of others, there will be little left to do for the law and its physical force. The stronger the silent moral compulsion of the community, the less need for the physical compulsion of the State (p. 374).

Religious Benefits

The word religion is derived from the Latin *religare*, which means to tie or bind together (Chambers Study Dictionary, 2002). Experience has taught us, however, that this is not true of every religion. Some religions are divisive and are inimical to the best interest of the individual and society, due in part to bigotry and levels of spiritual intelligence.

Religious organizations may therefore benefit from higher levels of spiritual intelligence among their membership. Spiritual intelligence enables people to discriminate or make sound judgment in matters of religious concern, such as deciding on religious doctrine and practices. In addition, through a highly developed spiritual intelligence, members of religious organizations may articulate more clearly and convincingly their message. This may in turn lead to greater organizational success and effectiveness.

A lifestyle consistent with the message preached enables a more impactful presence of the spiritual in the world. True religion is not a separate compartment of life. It ultimately underlies all life-affirming activities. Consequently, spiritual activity may not only be found in churches, but in all progressive social causes (Fuller, 2001).

Spiritual Benefits

According to biblical literature, the journey toward spiritually intelligent living begins with salvation from sin (John 3:16-19) and includes the impartation of a divine nature (2 Pet. 1:3-4) and the transformation of one's cognitive capacity (Rom. 12:1-2). Spiritual intelligence is attained because of the Spirit's influence in regenerating and guiding the redeemed sinner (Tit. 3:5; Gal. 5:16-24). By way of the Spirit, the old man is regenerated and the old mind renewed.

A sound mind distinguishes the people of God from the people of the world (2 Tim. 1:7), and is the basis of true spirituality. Redeemed human beings are enabled with spiritual life and intelligence. The redeemed take on the character of God and participate in the Divine nature (Kimbrough, 2002). The potential to improve spiritual awareness and understanding and to inculcate a greater sense of stewardship and of right and wrong are real possibilities. A well-developed spiritual capacity has the potential to solve moral and spiritual problems.

Emotional/Psychological Benefits

There are also potential therapeutic benefits to be derived from spiritual intelligence. Spiritual intelligence is useful in addressing health-related issues such as psychological and social problems associated with negative emotions. For example, by encouraging hope in this life and in an afterlife of eternity, the spiritually intelligent are insulated from self-destructive tendencies and are prevented from committing other atrocities associated with feelings of hopelessness and other negative emotions.

The promotion of positive emotions enables positive behaviors. Positive emotions, encouraged by spirituality, improve mental health, and are regarded as a fruit of the Spirit (Gal. 5:22, 23). Many claims of people, who have experienced healing via a spiritual paradigm, have been validated. Secular psychotherapists are becoming increasingly aware of the potential benefits of religious approaches to health and wellness. Some psychotherapists are therefore including elements of a religious model in what was previously perceived to be the domain of contemporary secular culture (Watts, 2006).

Watts observed that the process of transformation employed by religion is briefer and more dramatic than the process employed by psychotherapy toward emotional health: "For example, someone who has long been troubled by guilt and who eventually makes a sacramental confession may be deeply moved by hearing absolution proclaimed" (Watts, 2006, p. 158). Forgiveness associated with a spiritual paradigm of healing potentially precipitates healing or makes healing instantaneous (Belgum, 1967).

Many sicknesses and diseases are rooted in guilt. Guilt-producing behavior and negative emotions tend to throw the body in the precarious position of being more susceptible to the ravages of germs and bacteria. Consequently, persons afflicted by guilt are more prone to a number of illnesses such as cardiovascular diseases and cancer. Persons afflicted by guilt are also more prone to accidents (Belgum, 1967). Physicians, scientists, therapists and patients see a connection between mind and body, and affirm the ability of the mind to heal the body or to cause physical illnesses (Moyers, 1993).

Peck (1993) has included the spiritual and social as having a relationship with physical wellbeing: "Virtually all disorders are not only psychosomatic but psycho-spiritual-socio-somatic" (p. 59). Due to the insidious nature of guilt, it is not uncommon for persons afflicted by guilt-related sicknesses and diseases to take longer than normal to heal, especially if, while treating symptoms, the source of the problem is not discovered Lord treated as well.

> Resentments and hate are the obstacles that keep many people from clearing up their unfinished emotional business and achieving harmony with others. Transcending fear opens the way to forgiveness of others who have wronged you, and it releases a love that can make you psychologically immune to your environment. Choosing to love and hold on to the meaning of life increases the chances of survival under all conditions. (Siegel, 1986, pp. 113-114)

A fitting example is provided by Siegel (1986), who reported the following story told by Jack Schwarz, a survivor of the Nazi's death camps:

> Jack Schwarz has told how he passed out during a whipping and had a vision of Christ. Filled with love from the image, he said to his torturer, "Ich liebe dich." The guard was so shocked that he stopped, and he was even more astounded when he saw right before his eyes the prisoner's wounds healing within moments. (p. 194)

Medical doctors, pastors, psychiatrists and psychologists agree that negative emotions such as hate, an unforgiving spirit and bitterness are major causes of ill-health spiritually, physically, emotionally and socially (Nezu, Nezu & Diwakar, 2005). Negative emotions affect the integrity of the body, soul and spirit. Hate, for example, affects interpersonal relationships and does more damage to the individual expressing hate than the one to whom hate is directed. The point is underscored by the following narrative:

> I (John) met Agnes Sanford in 1961 in Springfield, Missouri, where she prayed for the healing of my back by asking the Lord to

215

enable me to forgive my mother. (Until I was thirteen, my relationship with my mother had been terrible. But then I forgave her and she was forgiven, and since that time we have enjoyed a good, if imperfect relationship). I knew by my psychological training that Agnes was praying for the inner boy from conception to thirteen whom I could not reach. It worked. I was healed. (Sanford and Sanford, 1982, p. 4)

Biblical literature associates negative emotions with the carnal nature of the flesh and with the devil (James 3:14-16; Gal. 5:19-21). Peck (1993) expressed the view that because of its neglect of spirituality, psychiatry in America is in a predicament. There is failure in diagnosis and treatment, in research and theory, and in the personal development of psychiatrists. According to Peck, "A psychiatry which does not regard humans as spiritual beings may be largely missing the boat" (Peck, 1993, p. 234).

Mower (1961) believed, barring organic involvement, neurotics and psychotics are not sick, they are sinners caught and condemned by their own consciences, and would therefore be better helped by religion than psychotherapy. Belgum (1967) indicated that an increasing number of reputable psychotherapists, such as Eysenck and Szasz (as cited in Belgum, 1967), were discouraged about psychoanalytic interpretation of mental illnesses. Due to not finding any scientific or statistical evidence for the efficacy of psychotherapy as generally practiced, questions were raised regarding the term "mental illness," calling it a "myth." Consequently, some therapists who had previously scoffed at religion were beginning to recognize religion's serviceable efficacy. Based on a spiritual therapeutic paradigm, "deliverance or exorcism may provide the opportunity for decisive change" (Watts, 2006, p. 158).

Wieman and Westcott-Wieman (1935) saw religious faith as a potent factor in psychotherapeutic treatment. According to them, there is a progressive emergence of meaning or value in genuine religious living. Through intelligent religious living, people may become more effectively self-directed, more soundly oriented, and more creatively interrelated with their known universe of life. The authors stated that, because the ethics of religious teachings usually go along with the treatment, religion often gives a firmer foundation for the recovery process.

In addition to religion's serviceable efficacy, the free services rendered by religion are believed more authentic. Because clients were not charged for services rendered, they believed there was genuine concern for them as individuals. This by itself is often therapeutic. Psychotherapeutic services offered by religion included: assistance in resolving inner conflicts, developmental and other problems, relationship issues, and vocational conflicts.

Intellectual/Educational Benefits

Spiritual intelligence potentially impacts people intellectually and educationally. It was said of Blaise Pascal, a mathematician, physicist, psychologist and engineer of the seventeenth-century, that subsequent to his conversion to Christianity "his life blazed with a brand-new light, from a source other than the physical nature or psychic consciousness. It was an experience of the Spirit, the Holy Spirit" (Tart, 1976, p. 398).

Wickett (2007) purported human beings have a spiritual faculty and that the spiritual should be integrated with other aspects of learning. By the promotion and exercise of spiritual intelligence, both educators and learners are potentially able to achieve greater levels of success. An emphasis on spiritual intelligence may help enable children to have a sense of meaning and purpose, a sense of stewardship, and improved self-esteem. Improvement in self-esteem has the potential to lead to improvement in behavior and thus help children to be more focused and disciplined. Disciplined children allow quality time to be directed at teaching. Teachers would therefore not need to spend quality time dealing with disciplinary issues and getting students to be attentive and focused in schools; class time could be used more productively.

The development of children's spiritual intelligence potentially empowers children to live more ordered and disciplined lives and, thereby, facilitates intellectual growth. Children in turn may achieve better academic results and make significantly greater contributions to society, not only in the pursuit of academic excellence but also in the pursuit of moral excellence, particularly in how knowledge is used.

A theory of spiritual intelligence may be used to provide clues to help bridge the gap between knowledge and behavior and thus, balance intellectual growth with spiritual and moral growth. Many people claim that values and attitudes they hold dear today were developed through religious education during their formative years; others see a link between deviance and lack of spiritual training.

The reality is that worldview impacts understanding and influences behavior; each is supported and reinforced by the other. Consequently, whereas unrighteousness hinders spiritual under-standing, righteousness promotes it (Psa. 25:14; John 3:16-21; Rom. 1:18-32; 12:1-2). Without spiritual and moral training, educators run the risk of developing more educated and sophisticated criminals or deviants.

Economic Benefits

The implications of spiritual intelligence also include economic benefits. Massive savings may be achieved by spiritually intelligent living, especially through eliminating vices such as corruption. Corruption has a trickle-down effect and hinders human development in several ways. By diverting public funds or resources to personal use, for example, the poor are made poorer and the rich are made richer. This leads to other forms of social problems, and results in widespread inequalities and injustices in society.

Corruption has the potential to destabilize a country spiritually, socially, economically and psychologically. Harris (2003) averred that even though individual and corporate corruption might never reach the status of illegality, legal corruption is just as damaging to society:

> While an act of corruption by an individual or a private company may not involve conditions that violate a law, it trespasses a moral law between good and evil. Worse, corrupt acts begin a process in which the rules of society are ignored, standards are lowered, and people worry more about their own wellbeing than the general wel-

fare. In short, corruption can weaken the fabric of society until it frays to the point of destruction. (Harris, 2003, p. 8)

The words of Harris (2003) appear evident in every-day life. The spiritual, intellectual, psychological, physical and social fabric of society is being frayed by corruption. Many societies are near destruction because of corruption. Corruption is being manifested at every level and in many of societies' institutions – in sports, schools, businesses, governments and charitable organizations, including churches. Whereas corruption has weakened and destabilized, moral uprightness has strengthened and secured. Personal integrity, coupled with love and respect for all, positively impacts basic institutions such as the family, and filters through to other institutions, communities and nations.

As the spiritually intelligent are potentially more moral and operate at higher levels of integrity, there are implications for crime rates and social services impacted by crime. A more moral population means massive savings derived from the minimization of crime. Less capital would be needed to prevent and fight crime, and less would be needed for building prisons and for dealing with various other security issues. Less capital would be needed, as well, to address health-related issues caused by crime.

Where health is concerned, spiritual intelligence encourages better lifestyle choices, thereby enabling people to live healthier, happier and more productive lives. This in turn has economic benefits for individuals, organizations and nations. For example, by having healthier and happier employees, businesses benefit from less down-time and increasing productivity.

Positively, spiritual intelligence encourages thrift and appropriate use of resources. Careful use and proper management of resources arguably result in massive savings and greater returns on investments.

In addition, businesses that are values-led and seek the common good of others are potentially more sustainable (Zohar & Marshall, 2004). Fair treatment of employees, provision of quality goods and services, proper care of the environment and good corporate citizenship have the potential for significantly impacting the growth of employees, patrons, the business environment and the community in general. The use of spiritual intelligence in businesses makes good business sense. By seeking the good of others, spiritual intelligence creates goodwill, which ultimately secures and sustains everyone.

Environmental Benefits

There are implications for the environment as well. Spiritual intelligence sees interconnectedness in all of nature and advocates faithful stewardship. By virtue of a common Creator, humans bear a connection not only to a supernatural and infinite God, but also to the natural and finite environment. Moreover, the natural environment nurtures and sustains us. Faithful stewardship over the natural and finite environment is therefore in humanity's best interest. As stewards, people who are spiritually intelligent have a sense of accountability to God and others, and, therefore, they protect and preserve the environment for personal use, and for the use of others, including posterity.

There is global acceptance of the need to protect the physical and natural environment. Evidence of global warming, for instance, due to human footprints, is manifested in tsunamis and other catastrophes around the world. Many nations are now more conscious of the devastating consequences of failure to protect the natural and physical environment. In order to facilitate sustainable all-round development and for the sake of posterity, moves are afoot to exercise better stewardship over the planet. In the spiritual and supernatural environment, devastating consequences are also observed, due to human footprints, beginning with the first human beings. There being a spiritual and supernatural environment, shouldn't there be efforts to protect it as well as the natural and physical environment? Indeed! Spiritual consciousness needs to be aroused and spiritual intelligence developed.

Summary

Based on examination and analysis of the related literature, spiritual intelligence is transformational. Both non-biblical and biblical sources yield examples of spiritual life and intelligence at work in the lives of the spiritually minded and records positive effects or benefits. Biblically, this is true of the ancients (persons connected to the Old Testament dispensation) and persons belonging to the New Testament period, including the present time. Nonbiblical sources span the gamut of secular history. There are many benefits and potential benefits of spiritually intelligent living. There are benefits to the individual, the family, the church, the education system, various other institutions, and to society overall. At the organizational levels, spiritually wise people augur for better human relationships, increased morale, increased pro -ductivity and increased general success. Spiritual intelligence benefits people spiritually, morally, emotionally, intellectually, physically, economically, relationally and environmentally.

CHAPTER 8
The Case for
Spiritual Intelligence

The objectives of this study were: (a) to provide supporting evidence for the existence of spiritual intelligence, (b) to build a theory of spiritual intelligence, (c) to describe and explain the nature of spiritual intelligence, and (d) to show some benefits and the possible impact of spiritual intelligence on human life and development.

Chapter one presented the need for spiritual intelligence, and chapter two various challenges to overcome. Findings from the literature review were discussed in chapters three and five. In chapter four, traits signifying the presence of spiritual intelligence were presented and theories of spiritual intelligence discussed.

Three theories of spiritual intelligence were presented and discussed: a theological model, a psychological model and a relational model. The theological model was conceived chiefly from a study of human capacity based on the sacred writings of Scripture. The psychological model was derived from a study of the human mind from the perspective of psychology. The relational model was based on a study of human interaction in social context and was grounded in sociology and psychology. Each theory supported the view of an inner spiritual capacity corresponding to an outer spiritual reality and developmental need.

Maslow's Motivational Theory was used to support the importance of spirituality in enabling peak experiences. Description and explanation of the

223

unique nature of spiritual intelligence were provided in chapter six. Benefits of spiritual intelligence were highlighted and discussed in chapter seven. The current chapter makes the case for spiritual intelligence by marshaling the evidence disclosed in detail in the previous chapters, and includes some additional insights.

Is there a spiritual reality? If so, are natural means sufficiently capable of apprehending and navigating the spiritual? Can natural means be used to identify and solve spiritual problems? Do human beings have a spiritual capacity or dimension? If so, is there a corresponding intelligence. What is spiritual intelligence? How is it acquired, developed and manifested? What is the difference between spiritual intelligence and natural intelligence? Is there any correlation between spirituality and morality? There being a spiritual intelligence, what are some of the benefits and potential benefits? What problem or problems is spiritual intelligence capable of solving.

There is evidence of the supernatural in various aspects of culture. The spiritual is a major theme among artists, playwrights, authors and other creators. Published works narrating encounters (fiction and non-fiction) of hauntings and other horror stories line the bookstores and public libraries. Evidence of the spiritual in literature includes the views of writers and researchers on the subjects of intelligence, spirituality, spiritual intelligence and religion.

A significant number of people are convinced that human beings are inescapably spiritual or religious. Religious scholars, mystics, philosophers and others are of the view that there is indeed a spiritual world. In addition to a long history of institutions designed to promote religious and spiritual development, there is a long history of institutions designed to teach and promote a dark side of the spiritual, such as witchcraft and other occult practices. In addition, the spiritual consulting business is a growing industry all over the world.

Religion and other spiritual paradigms are experienced in every part of the globe. Scientists are conceding that some phenomena are outside the scope of scientific explanation; and some are of the view that there is evidence of the spiritual in all of nature. There is increasing acknowledgment of the spiritual in a number of disciplines, such as politics, leadership, education, business and medicine.

The supernatural has become a preoccupation for some and is largely responsible for the popularity and success of movies and television shows such as **Harry Potter**. The supernatural is so entrenched in cultures worldwide that organizations are established to report on and investigate paranormal phenomena and provide help where necessary.

Christians believe that there is a spiritual side to humanity, needing to be fulfilled, having the potential to connect to the spiritual world. Fulfilment is contingent on which aspect of the spiritual is embraced, as there is a dark (evil) side to the spiritual and there is a bright (good) side. Choice determines whether or not purpose is fulfilled.

Capacity is intelligently designed and is aligned to purpose. The Creator programmed human nature to conform to His Divine Nature, hence natural and spiritual laws enabling control and ecology, thereby enabling purpose to be fulfilled.

From beginning, purpose was the prerogative of an all-knowing Creator. Obedience or alignment to the Creator would have led to purpose being fulfilled. This in turn would have enabled humanity to be fulfilled at every level. Disobedience would have the opposite affect.

Unfortunately, our primal progenitors chose disobedience. Disobedience led to innocence being lost. Whereas humanity knew only good, evil became part of our knowledge base and decision-making framework, hence integrity issues at every level.

The inappropriate use of volition led to the corruption of humanity, making us pliable to forces of darkness. Forces of darkness operate like counter intelligence, attacking and undermining our wellbeing. These forces may manifest as misguided humans or spirit beings called demons.

Demons affect humans similar to malwares on perfectly designed computer systems. Once compromised the gate is opened for the entire system to be corrupted. Corruption or ill health spreads, harming others, especially people closely connected to us.

The corruption of humanity came about by invitation. By misrepresenting God's Word and casting doubt on God's credibility, the devil tricked Eve in making a bad decision. Although not deceived, Adam went along with Eve in doing the forbidden, and as a consequence the devil became de facto ruler in the earth. (Genesis 3:1-7)

In disobeying God and acquiescing to the solicitation of the devil, Adam and Eve enabled the successful corruption of humanity, immediately causing spiritual death. Physical death also became part of their experience, though not immediately.

Corruption of the first human beings meant the corruption of the rest of humanity, as the fallen sinful nature of the first humans was passed on to posterity, inclining us to deviance. According to the Bible, everyone since Adam is born spiritually dead, meaning that we are born disconnected from God spiritually; a personal relationship with God may be regained and spiritual life restored by way of spiritual rebirth. Albeit, spiritual growth is necessary and involves the development of spiritual intelligence.

At this juncture, it is important to make a distinction between spirituality as a capacity and spirituality as a way of life. Everyone has a spiritual capacity but everyone is not spiritually alive or intelligent. As a capacity, there is potential for spiritual life and intelligence; in reality, this might not be the case. As in the case where a person might be intellectually brilliant and emotionally obtuse, it is possible for a person to be physically alive and yet spiritually dead. Jesus once told his disciples to "let the dead bury their dead," meaning that the spiritually dead should bury the physically dead. If there is no life in a given capacity, intelligence cannot be expected.

So what is spiritual intelligence? Let us first distinguish between natural intelligence and spiritual intelligence. Spiritual intelligence is not to be confused with natural intelligence as if both spring from the same well; both are derived from different sources and are major fields with their own streams of intelligences called gifts.

Natural intelligence is inherently natural; it is manifested in behaviours, values and attitudes known as works of the flesh (Gal. 5:19-21) and in natural abilities. Spiritual intelligence is inherently supernatural; it is manifested in behaviours, values and attitudes known as the fruit of the Spirit (Gal. 5:22

-23; James 3:17-18), and in supernatural abilities known as spiritual gifts (1 Cor. 12; Romans 12:6-8).

Spiritual intelligence and natural intelligence operate by different laws. Natural intelligence is connected to the physical, is limited thereto and operates in tandem with natural laws. Spiritual intelligence is operational in both the physical and spiritual world, but mainly operates in tandem with spiritual laws and is unlimited.

Spiritual intelligence is not to be equated with devotion to a particular religion or with sincerity. A person may be sincere and sincerely wrong. Religion may be pure or impure; and there are many shades of grey in between.

Spiritual intelligence is not to be equated with knowledge of the spiritual. Although spiritual knowledge is important, it is possible to have head knowledge or to be aware of the spiritual and show some measure of appreciation and understanding without this knowledge affecting one's life or informing one's behavior. Unfortunately, some people are enamored with religious knowledge, rituals and liturgies without having any serious connection with God, "having a form of godliness but denying its power." (2 Timothy 3:5)

Spiritual intelligence does not imply infallibility or perfection. Spiritual intelligence implies the possibility of spiritual ignorance, degrees of spiritual wisdom, and levels of spiritual competence. Athough everyone may have a measure of truth, everyone does not fully understand or knows how to apply even the measure of truth possessed.

Spiritual intelligence is not about being well-informed or well-educated theologically, or possessing religious credentials, as religious knowledge does not necessarily equate to spiritual intelligence or translate to spiritually intelligent living.

Spiritual intelligence does not involve ascetic practices. It is not about denying physical needs or robbing a person of joy and the pleasures of life (Psa. 16:11; Rom. 14:17; Philipp. 4:4-13). In fact, joy is a fruit of the Spirit (Gal. 5:22-23).

Spiritual intelligence is not the right of a special class or group of people:

> Brothers and sisters, think of what you were when you were called. Not many of you were wise by human standards; not many were influential; not many were of noble birth. But God chose the foolish things of the world to shame the wise; God chose the weak things of the world to shame the strong. God chose the lowly things of this world and the despised things — and the things that are not — to nullify the things that are, so that no one may boast before him. (1 Cor. 1:26-29, NIV)

In addition to having a sense of humour, God is smart enough to ensure there is no room for boasting. So spiritual intelligence has nothing to do with human merit; it is imparted solely based on the grace of God subsequent to salvation. And salvation is also based on God's grace (Eph. 2:8-9; John 6:28-29; 1 John 2:22-25).

So what is spiritual intelligence about? Spiritual intelligence is about being enlivened and enlightened spiritually. This is a work of the Spirit (1 Cor. 2:14; Eph. 1:18; 3:14-21; John 3:1-8). Spiritual intelligence is: (a) the ability to receive, understand, discern and apply spiritual knowledge; and (b) the ability to use spiritual means to identify and solve spiritual and other problems.

There is evidence in both religious and nonreligious literature supporting a supernatural ability to receive, accept, understand, discern and apply spiritual knowledge, and the ability to use spiritual means to identify and solve spiritual and other problems. There is evidence of spiritual intelligence manifested in spiritual direction, wisdom, discernment and other forms of empowerment or enabling.

For example, there is support in Scripture of spiritual intelligence manifested in healing powers:

> Jesus went throughout Galilee, teaching in their synagogues, proclaiming the good news of the kingdom, and healing every disease and sickness among the people. News about him spread all over Syria, and people brought to him all who were ill with various dis-

eases, those suffering severe pain, the demon-possessed, those having seizures, and the paralyzed; and he healed them. (Matt. 4:23-24, NIV)

Jesus did all these great things (and more) and promised his disciples would do greater things (John 14:12).

Evidence in religion supporting the concept of spiritual intelligence includes: recognition of the sacred and spiritual, such as sacred literature, religious objects, places of worship and the act of worship. Human beings have an affinity to the spiritual and a seemingly innate and insatiable desire to worship. This innate desire to worship is believed to be connected to a spiritual dimension or capacity. A spiritual capacity implies the potential to discriminate where spiritual matters are concerned, hence the possibility of spiritual intelligence.

Among the religious, there is evidence of spiritual help and healing in various circumstances. Testimonies of people who had received spiritual and supernatural help such as guidance, deliverance from sicknesses and diseases, emotional healing and divine intervention in difficult circumstances, support the veracity of spiritual intervention. Lucid details are provided by persons claiming personal encounters with the supernatural and by persons claiming to report on the factual experience of others. Evidence of spiritual intervention has made the concept of spiritual intelligence plausible.

Evidence in the occult includes involvement in and attraction to witchcraft, necromancy, *voodooism* and Satanism, practiced worldwide. There are substantial and substantiated claims of sicknesses and diseases, demon possessions and harassments, ritual murders, and other forms of evil and immorality associated with the occult, as well as claims of healing and help through the same means. These realities underscore the need for and plausibility of a spiritual intelligence.

Evidence in theology supporting spiritual intelligence includes biblical teachings that God is Spirit, that there is a spiritual dimension to human beings, and that human beings are created in the image of God. God being Spirit, Spiritual Intelligence where God is concerned is implied. A parallel between the spiritual dimension of human beings and the Creator, a Spirit

Being, in whose image human beings are created, imply the potential for spiritual life and intelligence in humanity.

Christianity presents Jesus as the ideal model of spiritual life and intelligence. The life of Jesus is the perfect standard by which spiritual life may be judged and comparisons made, hence emphasis on being Christ-like or having the mind of Christ. Christ indeed was the most transformational figure that ever graced the planet. Jesus' spiritual acumen and accomplishments were astounding.

Epistemological evidence of spiritual intelligence includes other ways of knowing. Other ways of knowing besides natural intelligence processing data through the five senses of hearing, seeing, smelling, tasting and touching are consistent with human cognitive processing. According to Aquinas (2003), revelation and reason complement each other.

There are other ways of knowing besides the five senses. There is scientific evidence of extrasensory perception (ESP) as found in psychics and mediums, for example. Clairvoyance, telepathy, intuition, precognition, kinesiology, use of pendulums, radionics and dousing rods are recognized sources of knowledge globally. Biblical data support concepts such as inspiration, revelation, illumination, discernment, visions, dreams and interpretation of dreams.

Ontological evidence of spiritual intelligence includes scientific evidence found in Einstein's relativity theories and in quantum physics, supporting the notion of a metaphysical aspect to reality. Einstein (2005) averred subatomic particles do not exist until observed – the behavior of particles changes based on observers' perception and consciousness. Einstein also stated that one has to use different lenses to observe physical matter at the subatomic level and that rules governing what can be seen do not apply to the things we cannot see.

> Einstein's breakthrough was to realize that absolute time and space were…outside the realm of science. We measure space in terms of how far one thing is from another. We measure time in terms of the movement of objects in space. Whenever we measure, however we measure; it can only be in relative terms. But the framework of that

movement, the absolute background, that, he understood, is meta-physics. (Freeman, 2010)

Invisible reality is supported in Scripture. Biblical data reveal the presence of unseen or invisible reality, that what is seen was not made from that which is seen, and that the unseen are eternal and imperishable (Heb. 11:3; 2 Cor. 4:18). Einstein's views also resonated with Zukav (1989). According to Zukav, the most basic elements of matter are subatomic particles, described as waves of light or vibrations of energy, which may manifest visibly and invisibly.

If at the most elementary level, everything is a wave of light or sound vibrating at different frequencies, then regardless of the superstructure, such an object may be affected, acted upon, destroyed, resuscitated, or recreated by energy or sound equal to or greater than the object acted on. Moreover, if the physical is able to manifest visibly and invisibly, it should be possible for the spiritual to manifest similarly (naturally and supernaturally); shouldn't it?

Besides being able to manifest as waves of light or vibrations of energy (sound), another interesting discovery is that subatomic particles are able to communicate with each other regardless of distance. Since subatomic particles are strung together, they may remain in contact with each other over any period of time and distance, and as such are able to influence each other (Bohr, 2010). Bohr, however, could not discern a reason for this maze of connectivity. In this maze of connectivity appears the design of the Creator to facilitate communication and relationships throughout the universe.

The most common means of communication is sound-related, made possible by a boundless quantum energy field: sound travels through air, water and solids at different frequencies. Energy produced by sound is apparent throughout nature. In keeping with the Creator's design, sound takes different forms and may be harnessed and applied in multiple ways. Where human beings are concerned, scientists have found that humans emit tiny particles of light called photons. Photons provide a perfect communication system.

In addition, humans emit vibrations of energy in the form of sound. According to Habib (2019), human beings have what is called a vagal system. The vagal system runs from the brain to every major organ of the body. At the core of the vagal system is the vagas nerve, which may be self-activated or activated externally. In addition to maintaining balance, the vagas nerve control's the body's functions. When operating at a certain frequency, health may be optimized. Referred to as vagal tone, there is a healing frequency, ranging between 85-255HZ. It is believed that many illnesses may be cured by simply increasing a person's vagal tone. This may be done using certain kinds of music and exercises. Ancient vocal rituals attest to the efficacy of healing vibrations of the human voice.

Today sound science is being used in the medical field in a number of ways. For example, SonoPrep procedure is being used to temporarily liquefy skin cells allowing medications to pass, thereby eliminating the need for injection. Histotripsy procedure is being used to force tissues apart, thereby eliminating the need for incision with a medical tool. High frequency sound waves are being used to generate enough heat to close a wound in less than a minute, and seal internal injuries without burning the skin or flesh in between, thereby eliminating the need for stitches. Shockwave therapy is being used to treat tennis elbow and planter fasciitis.

A similar procedure is being used to shatter kidney stones. Vibroacoustic therapy uses low frequency sounds and vibrations to massage deep internal areas of the body. It has been successfully used to reduce neurological diseases such as Parkinson's. Sound waves are being used to destroy bacteria clumped together, in less than 30 seconds. Ultrasound is being used to detect babies and cancer. High-intensity ultrasound (HIFU) is being used to treat some cancers by fragmenting the tumors. (Dubensky, 2012)

In the field of oceanography, sound science is being used to determine the depth of water, study fish – their biomass and distribution – and to navigate, communicate with and detect objects on and under the sea.

Sound science is a major feature in the rapidly growing wireless and telecommunications industries and in cinematography; and is being experimented with in regard to food technology, agriculture and horticulture.

In the field of music, sound science is having a profound affect. The language of music is universal and is used in various ways. Music may be used therapeutically, religiously and socially. It may be used to motivate people to take action (good and bad), motivate unity or solidarity, inspire, entertain and educate. Music may uplift or cause melancholy and reprehensible behavior. Music is sometimes personal or social commentary, aspirational and inspirational, expressed in a number of formats. Despite the many genres, music may be broadly categorized as sacred, secular and Satanic, affecting behavior accordingly.

Music is used in places of worship by both the religious and profane, and as such may be used in worship of God or in worship of the devil. So music may be used for good or evil. Spiritually speaking, the use of chants or incantations, words and beating of drums have been used to effect change, positively and negatively. Some artistes employ a mind-influencing technique called backward masking in their music. Messages promoting witchcraft, Satanism, rebellion, promiscuity and use of illegal drugs, for example, are masked in recordings, received subliminally by unsuspecting patrons, when the record is played in reverse or backwards. (Aranza, 1985; Larson, 1978) Certain types of music degrade personality.

In addition to the energy produced by sound, scientists averred the mind's ability to significantly impact the environment. The ability of the mind to control matter (telekinesis), for example, is no longer regarded as myth. Telekinesis is now being used in areas such as neuroprosthetics and in other disciplines to transform lives.

In New Testament literature, Jesus spoke to winds and waves, a tree, a group of pigs and significantly altered their state. In the Old Testament, Moses struck a rock and it gushed forth water, Elijah prayed and prevented rain from falling and by the same method caused rain to fall.

Communication via sound science is common throughout the animal kingdom, and has been found among mammals such as bats and whales, and among insects and plants. Today a whole new realm of understanding is being propelled by discoveries of the ability of human beings to communicate with animals, plants, and with other aspects of nature, using sound technology and telepathy.

Peppergurg (2008) and Williams (2005) highlighted the ability to communicate with animals. Dog training is apparently the most popular. The ability to communicate with dogs and train them has resulted in service dogs being used in crime fighting, in detecting certain illnesses and diseases, and in the helping industry, such as search and rescue, and in assisting the blind. Birds have been long-used as delivery agents, travelling many miles to deliver mail.

If limited human beings can communicate with birds, animals and trees, for instance, training and subjecting them to their will, it seems possible for spiritual beings, using the technologies of sound and telepathy to do the same.

Scientists are of the view that everything in nature, including humans, vibrates, is comprised of fields of energy, supported by a gigantic energy field, manifesting visibly and invisibly, and may respond to or be acted on via sound and telepathy; messages may be transmitted and received consciously and unconsciously across time and space.

It appears that despite differences, each aspect of nature has its own language supported by laws, enabling communication. The ability of various aspects of nature to communicate with each other and to be impacted by each other suggests interconnectedness in all of nature. Advance in communication technologies, particularly the Internet, underscores how well-connected we are, how easy it is to influence each other in real time and the possibility of causing enormous changes across the globe in a relatively short period.

Although not fully understood, interconnectedness in all of nature has made it possible for various aspects of nature to be affected by sound and telepathy. The key appears to be knowledge of the language, the ability to crack the code, using telepathy, sound or other technologies to create the desired effect.

Radin (2006) believed consciousness can penetrate any barrier and can travel faster than the speed of light, without affecting the quality of the communication. Based on evidence gleamed from scientific research, Radin found that psychic phenomena such as telepathy, psychokinesis and clairvoyance are real. These views resonated with other scientists such as Kaku (2014) and McTaggart (2008).

If communication at the natural level is possible via energy produced by the mind (consciously and unconsciously), and regardless of distance, then it ought to be possible for communication to take place at the spiritual level via energy produced by the spirit regardless of distance. Put another way: If human beings are able to "perform miracles" via psychic and natural energy, there are endless possibilities when spiritual energy is deployed.

As in the natural, energy produced by the spirit may manifest visibly and invisibly. In the Bible, we are told that the Word became flesh (John 1:14) and that the tongue has power of life and death (Prov. 18:21). Is it possible that "word" is a creative force, capable of intervening in nature and of creating its own reality?

If through the science of sound, human beings are able to do amazing things by the application of natural intelligence, it is quite possible for humans to do even greater things by the application of spiritual intelligence (through the science of sound), bearing in mind that we have a spiritual capacity. Communication intelligently directed, through sound or telepathy, at the natural or spiritual level, has power to create the desired affect.

It is not only the spoken word which has power; unexpressed intentions of one person toward another are capable of producing similar results. Attitudes emit their own aura or energy and may have a positive or negative affect. Scientists have proven unequivocally the power of intention. They have found that expressed and unexpressed intentions of people toward others, even when separated by enormous distance, are able to produce the results intended. The intention of humans directed toward plants and objects may also be executed, regardless of distance (Kaku, 2014; McTaggart, 2008).

There is support for the power of intention in Scripture. Knowing that Jesus intended to cast them out of a man, demons begged Jesus to cast them into a herd of swine (Matt. 8:28-34). On another occasion, a centurion's servant was healed through the power of intention many miles from where Jesus met her master and apprised of her condition (Matt. 8:5-13).

Spiritual Intelligence: A Christian Perspective

From the perspective of psychology, we know that the human mind and the things which issue from it (thought, speech and action) have multiple affects. At the personal level, psychic energy and breath are released consciously and unconsciously, thereby creating outward and inward changes, affecting the functioning of the brain and body, and may also impact people and other areas of life.

If the mind has power at the physical level, power may also be expected at the spiritual level. There being a spiritual dimension to humanity, similar things are possible when spiritual energy is deployed or invoked. There is conclusive evidence that persons gifted spiritually are able, through the energy of the Spirit, to gain special insight and address problems normally incomprehensible and impossible to treat by others.

The energy supporting the visible and the energy supporting the invisible has their own breath and may manifest accordingly. The concept of breath as part of invisible reality is in keeping with Spirit, believed to be a powerful intelligent life force with the ability to manifest in different ways. In the Bible, ways in which the Spirit is presented include:

1. Wind (Acts 2:2-4)
2. Sound (Acts 2:2-4)
3. Fire (Acts 2:3-4)
4. Breath (John 20:22)
5. Dove (Matt. 3:16; Mark 1:10; Luke 3:22)
6. The Lord (2 Cor. 3:17-18)
7. God (Gen. 1:2; John 4:24)

Despite the many shapes and forms the physical and spiritual may take, it is to be acknowledged that the dichotomy of life involves the visible and invisible, the natural and supernatural. In light of the fact that we live in both a physical and spiritual world, it seems logical that the physical should be circumscribed by the spiritual, invisible reality being more fundamental and enduring, ranking first in terms of existence and first in terms of power. According to Nee (1968), the spirit is the highest aspect of personhood to which body and soul ought to be subject.

Christians believe the world was created by the Invisible: "By faith we understand that the worlds were prepared by the word of God, so that what is seen was not made out of things which are visible" (Heb. 11:3, NASB).

Since the visible emanated from the invisible, we are forced to attribute intelligence to the invisible on account of the presence of intelligence observable in the visible. Considering intelligent design, the unique personalities, purposefulness, order and intelligence in every aspect of creation, the world could not possibly be an accident of impersonal forces in nature. And since we cannot reasonably argue back to infinitum, we are forced to assume existence of a First Cause of everything and assign Invisibility, Personality, Spirituality, Intelligence and Ultimate Reality to First Cause.

In Scripture, God is described as eternal, immortal and invisible (1 Tim. 1:17), the creator of everything (Acts 17:24-28), who predates the beginning of everything (Coloss. 1:15-17; John 1:1-3). As First Cause, the heavens and earth cannot contain God (1 Kings 8:27), and no one can escape His presence (Heb. 4:13), for there is no place where God cannot be found (Psa. 139:7). Furthermore, God reveals Himself in the heavens (Psalm 19:1-6).

Based on the Bible, everything came into existence through the Word (Gen. 1-2) and is being kept together by the Word of God (2 Peter 3:5-7). If God, who is Spirit (John 4:24), through Word or breath brought the world into existence, it is possible that energy associated with breath is a fundamental part of the world's ecosystem; that regardless of its diverse manifestations, breath is the creative and energizing force keeping everything together.

At the natural level, animals breathe in oxygen and breathe out carbon dioxide; plants breathe in carbon dioxide and breathe out oxygen. Oxygen is critical to animal life; carbon dioxide is critical to plant life. Since at the natural level, the sustaining force in human, animal and plant life is associated with different forms of breath, namely oxygen and carbon dioxide, it is conceivable that the sustaining source of the spirit is another form of breath, enabling spiritual life. In Scripture, "breath" and "spirit" are often used interchangeably. Moreover, breath is the evidence of life.

Notwithstanding, the natural and spiritual are not exclusive: They are interconnected and are being held together by a Supreme Spirit, who is the Source of all things. This Spirit is identified as God (John 4:24), and is described as the Alpha and Omega – the Beginning and the End (Rev. 1:8).

Evidence in psychology supporting spiritual intelligence includes psychology's support of spirituality. Spirituality has been proven effective in: (a) enabling better mental health, (b) being able to address problems outside the scope of psychology, such as demon possession, (c) producing faster and more permanent results in effecting healing than psychology, such as issues rooted in guilt and being unforgiving (Watts, 2006; Belgum, 1967; Koch, 1972), and (d) influencing self-actualization (Maslow, 1964; 1976). Maslow and others noted that there are various levels of consciousness, and perceived religion as enabling greater self-actualization and peak experiences. Psychologists and medical doctors see a connection between mind and body, and have stressed the importance of the mind in healing and in holistic development.

The power of the mind to effect radical changes locally and non-locally has implications for development at micro and macro levels, and thus underscores the need for development of the mind. The mind may issue both good and evil, and as such has the ability to increase or decrease its own light as well as the light within its intended object. Since the mind may be an empowering or disempowering agent spiritually, spiritual intelligence is needed.

There is increasing interest in the ability of the conscious mind to impact the subconscious, and vice-versa. It is argued that through the practice of various disciplines desires may be manifested at the conscious and subconscious level, physically and spiritually. Today there are various theories on Manifesting, and Mindfulness is now a recognized discipline.

Complementing the work of psychics and mediums, secret societies and institutions of wizardry around the globe educate the faithful in the art of casting spells and in using the powers of darkness to accomplish desires, and they are constantly recruiting. The truly spiritual counters with Spiritual Intelligence. The battle is on-going (Matt. 12:28; Mark 16:17-18; Luke 10:17-20). Because to be truly spiritual involves warfare, spiritual intelligence demands preparation for war, active and intentional participation (Eph. 6:10-20).

Psychology's support for the theory of multiple intelligences makes spiritual intelligence plausible. Many researchers have opposed theories of a single or general intelligence and have supported theories of multiple intelligences. Theories of multiple intelligences, namely Gardner's (1983) theory, paved the way for other intelligence paradigms, such as social intelligence (Emery et al., 2008; Albrecht, 2009), emotional intelligence (Goleman, 1995), and spiritual intelligence (Sinetar, 2002; Tipping, 2005) to be included in the mix of intelligences.

Intelligence has been redefined by psychologists such as Gardner (1983) to include several abilities corresponding with the diverse aspects of personhood. In redefining intelligence, Gardner (1999) and Munhall (2001) have recognized the role of culture in identifying and encouraging development of an intelligence paradigm. Since spirituality plays a major role in cultures everywhere, significantly impacting development (positively and negatively), spiritual intelligence is desirable: and since spiritual ability corresponds with a spiritual capacity inherent in humanity, spiritual intelligence is plausible.

Evidence in neuroscience of the supernatural and spiritual includes discovery of God-spots in the brain. Scientists have found that neurons in the frontal lobes of the brain light up in response to religious experiences and beliefs. Neuroscientists and psychologists have long-held the view that the frontal lobes of the brain consist of neurological links to special abilities or skills and that intelligence has a basis in biology/neurology. Discovery of God-spots in the brain having links with spiritual activities and experiences supports the case for spiritual intelligence.

Evidence in medical science supports the concept of spiritual intelligence. Many international documents and professional organizations such as the World Health Organization (WHO) relate spirituality to health and to holistic development. Spiritual care and its implications are now being studied and promoted by health professionals such as Astrow, Puchalski and Sulmasy (2001), Delbanco (1991), Fallot (2007), Koenig (2004), and Vader

(2006).

Medical science supports the spiritual as being able to: (a) provide healing to patients suffering from psychosomatic illnesses, (b) heal physical sicknesses and diseases, and (c) promote better physical health and healing through religious practices, such as faith in God, prayer, love and forgiveness (Sperry, 2001; Schreurs, 2002; Watts, 2006; Pargament, 2006). It is the norm for some doctors to pray for patients before surgery; and in some hospitals, it is the custom for spiritual caregivers to minister alongside medical professionals as part of the care-giving protocol.

Evidence in social science supporting the plausibility of spiritual intelligence includes: (a) social scientists' perception of religion as binding or holding society together (Durkheim, 1972) and (b) as promoting moral goodness, thereby enabling healthy human relationships (Vaughn, 2002). Major differences in terms of character, lifestyle, and spiritual abilities or gifts are observable between people who are spiritual and those who are not (2 Pet. 1:1-11; Kimbrough, 2002). Biblical data reveal transformation is possible via renewal of the mind (Rom. 12:2). Many narratives reveal transformation by way of spiritual renewal or a personal relationship with God.

Evidence in law supporting spiritual intelligence includes the use of certain principles advanced by Scripture, namely aspects of the Ten Commandments (Exod. 20), such as those referring to the sanctity of human life (Exod. 20:13), honesty (Exod. 20:15) and equity (Exod. 20:16-17), as bases for jurisprudence. The establishment of legal systems worldwide and other moral codes of conduct for mediating right and wrong, and for adjudicating specific legal and moral issues speak to a universal sense of righteousness and justice.

Human beings throughout the world have a natural sense of justice, expressed mostly when we become victims of injustice. But where did this sense of righteousness and justice come from? An innate spiritual and moral consciousness as part of human DNA is a plausible explanation. The God who created humankind must have created us with a sense of justice, God being Just. In Scripture, God is described as Just and the Judge of all the earth (Gen. 18:25; Rev. 15:3). People who enter the legal profession do not get involved because it is a game they enjoy playing, but because, in the main, they have a sense of justice.

Evidence in technology supporting the plausibility of spiritual intelligence includes artificial intelligence. Artificial intelligence is present in man-made systems and machines (Minsky, 2006; Brighton, 2007). These instruments reflect the natural intelligence of their creators. If limited human beings can create artificial intelligence in machines, then it is quite possible for an Unlimited Spiritual Being to create spiritual intelligence in humans reflecting the Spiritual Intelligence of their Creator. Artificial intelligence in man-made machines makes spiritual intelligence within the spiritual capacity of human beings plausible.

Evidence in general science supporting the concept of spiritual intelligence includes the support of some scientists for the creation theory. Arguments were based on evidence of intelligent design observable in the universe, orderliness in the universe, and the earth's fine-tuning for life. The evidence led some scientists to conclude that the universe is the product of Supernatural Intelligence and not the result of a freak accident or an impersonal force in nature, as others believed.

The cosmos and the world in which we live could not possibly have come into existence by accident, or formed itself out of nothing, or from chaos, or happened to exist by natural means, or by a physical being with limited powers. The complexity and intricacy of creation's design – the wonder of the solar system, the precision in rotation of the stars in space, the exquisiteness and beauty of the creatures and plants of creation, everything after its kind, the times and seasons, the enduring natural and spiritual laws which govern the natural and spiritual realms, the resources of the heavens and of the earth, the awesomeness of the lands and seas, and the ecosystem – speak of the unlimited powers of the Creator, a Spirit Being, One who knows everything, is above and beyond everything, though present everywhere overseeing everything, and whose imprint is in everything. If God is the Spirit who created the world, Spiritual Intelligence associated with God may be inferred.

Spiritual Intelligence is evident in the intelligent design of creation, enabling orderliness in the universe. The planets of our solar system, for instance, as indicated above, are amazingly precise in their movements, avoiding collisions and creating cycles such as times and seasons. The Creator's presence is established in the intelligence of His design and the intelligence deposited in creation to support and regulate itself.

There is evidence of the spiritual and immaterial in all of creation, including matter. It is argued by scientists that matter is eternal. As such, matter cannot be annihilated, although it may be altered and may manifest in different forms. Even waste matter may be converted to energy or transformed into something else. One may therefore infer that if the physical is indestructible, the spiritual is indestructible also. Indestructibility of the physical and spiritual gives credence to notions of eternal life and eternal death as possible end states.

Evidence in quantum physics suggests the possibility of life after death, where matter is concerned. Based on scientific discovery, colliding neutrons (dead stars) actually produce life: When dead stars merge, they keep getting brighter and brighter.

If dead matter may be energized and become increasingly powerful by a simple act of what appears to be accidental collision, it follows that it is quite plausible for the deceased to regain life when intentionally acted on by a Being described as Omnipotent.

Many narratives of the after-life, death, near-death and other paranormal phenomena support the reality of life after death. Intrigued by testimonies of persons who have had death, near-death and out-of-body experiences, medical researchers and others have conducted research validating their claims. Based on testimonies, researchers such as Moody (2001) and Gallup and Proctor (1982) conceded the possible existence of an immortal soul or spirit and of life after death.

The religious and mystics have long argued for the immortality of the soul. An immortal soul and/or spirit and life after death imply spiritual life and intelligence. Be that as it may, there is evidence of the spiritual and supernatural in virtually every area of life, hence support for spiritual intelligence.

There are chiefly two operating systems governing human thought and behaviour – the operating system of the flesh from which natural intelligence is derived and the operating system of the Spirit from whom spiritual intelligence is derived. Because the spiritual is the foundation for the natural, in addition to working in tandem with natural laws, spiritual intelligence may override natural laws.

Overriding the natural by the spiritual is explained as miracles. As the mind is trained to view reality chiefly through physical and natural lenses, works accomplished through the energy of the Spirit are deemed miraculous even by the spiritual. That which is normal (or should be) from the spiritual perspective is regarded abnormal from the natural perspective.

Albeit, there are ancillary systems attached to the flesh, such as gifts associated with the psyche, for instance, telepathy; and there are gifts associated with the devil and demons, as in witchcraft.

Evidence in the physical and natural domain supporting spiritual intelligence include notions of right and wrong, and laws supporting order in the natural realm. A major focus of spiritual intelligence is spiritual development that promotes moral purity and general goodness. It is commonly accepted that there is good and evil in the world. Evil is the major threat to civilization as it undermines development at every level.

Besides the possibility of being demon-possessed, there is a form of narcissism or inflated ego in people obsessed with evil. Evil people do not like to play by established laws or rules; they like to play by their own rules and desire to be able to change the rules along the way to suit themselves. Yet no one succeeds unless he/she plays by the rules.

In the Bible, evil is described as transgression. Any violation of God's laws is regarded as transgression, and transgressors regarded as evil doers. People who take sides with evil or consent to evil by their silence are deemed accomplices and as such are just as culpable of having committed an offence.

Some people try to get around culpability by declaring "There is no right and wrong," and "To each his own." Albeit, the real world operates on certain principles – on knowledge that can be validated as right, on justice that are intuitively just and rationally verifiable, on morality, that, for the most part, are universally acceptable, and on human rights that are inalienable.

In the natural and physical domain, submission to authority is expected and demanded. Order is predicated on notions of right and wrong. Consequently laws governing behavior, building codes, professional codes of ethics and rules supporting various systems. Where rules are applied, purpose is fulfilled; the opposite is also true. In Scripture, support for law and order extends to human government (Romans 13:1-6). Submission is based on the premise that governments exist to promote order and the wellbeing of citizens, and as such are God's representatives.

If rules are crucial to proper functioning in the physical and natural domain, why would anyone presuppose that rules are not relevant in the moral and spiritual domain? Moreover, if submission to human authority is a necessary feature, enabling the rule of law and order in the natural domain, it is reasonable to expect the same and even greater support for God's rule in the moral and spiritual domain, God being Creator.

AFTERWORD

Is there a spiritual reality? If so, are natural means sufficiently capable of apprehending and navigating the spiritual world? Can natural means be used to identify and solve spiritual problems? Do human beings have a spiritual capacity or dimension? If so, is there a corresponding intelligence enabling apprehension and navigation of the spiritual?

Physical reality is apparent. It is also obvious that human beings are intelligently designed to comprehend and navigate the physical world. In fact, we take this for granted. Some are skeptical however in regard to the metaphysical.

Notwithstanding, most will agree human beings are multidimensional, that in addition to a physical dimension, there is a spiritual dimension to us. Acceptance of a physical and spiritual dimension raises the question of whether or not God intended human beings to operate by the energy of the flesh or by the energy of the spirit, or by both.

Because both the physical and spiritual are integral and essential features of human design, it is reasonable to assign energy and cognition to the spiritual, particularly since holistic development is impossible without the manifestation of life and intelligence in both areas of capacity. It is also reasonable to infer that if natural intelligence is crucial to appropriate functioning at the natural level, there being a spiritual dimension to humanity and a spiritual reality, spiritual intelligence is crucial to appropriate functioning at the spiritual level. Moreover, if every living cell in the body has cognition and responds to the energy of natural intelligence, one may infer a similar influence, where spiritual intelligence is concerned. And if a mind-body relationship exists in the physical realm, it is reasonable to infer a similar relationship in the spiritual realm.

If in the area of the metaphysical, other forms of knowing such as telepathy and premonition, are commonly-accepted, then why not spiritual intelligence? In the Bible, cognition is assigned to the mind operating based on the energy of the flesh and to the mind operating based on the energy of the Spirit (Rom. 8:6-7; 1 Cor. 2:12-14).

The human race is undeniably spiritual: there is a spiritual dimension to humanity, which craves expression and fulfilment. We have seen in previous chapters that the spirit is the foundation and core of being. That being the case, it is apparent spiritual intelligence should take priority in informing natural intelligence and life in general. Working synergistically, natural and spiritual intelligences have the potential to enable the actualization of human beings and accelerate the pace of civilization, as the Creator intended.

Notwithstanding, spirituality is understood differently by various cultures, religious groups and individuals. In the main, spirituality is associated with religion and therefore reflects diverse religious views. Hence various conceptions of spirituality, various spiritual practices and levels of spiritual intelligence informing how spirituality is expressed and operationalised.

There are also non-religious views. Most are sincere, although sincerely wrong. For instance, New Age theology affirms "God is whomever we want God to be." The emphasis is on sincerity. Such a view suggests that God is the creation of the human mind, in which case the notion of God is a myth. Besides being ridiculous, experience tells us that sincerity does not prove anything: a person may be sincere yet sincerely wrong. Atrocities committed in the name of God and religion underscore the point.

Unfortunately, many use sincerity as the litmus test of the validity of a religion. However, sincerity does not necessarily reflect authenticity; does it? If sincerity alone qualified a religion or person as authentic, it would not matter what is believed, or how life is lived. Would it? All religions would have equal status before God.

If sincerity is unacceptable as bonafide proof of authenticity in other disciplines, why should it be acceptable in religion? To be fair, it is hard to imagine a number of ways to God, or various standards based on ethnicity, religion or even sincerity, for that matter, unless God is a figment of the imagination or of human design.

Being a person of faith does not prove anything, as people of faith are not necessarily right with God. Their faith may be shallow. Furthermore, faith may not be in God but in faith itself. When all is said and done, it is not faith in faith that matters; it is the object of faith that makes faith credible. Furthermore, faith without credible support is meaningless (James 2:14-26). If the basis for faith is solid, positive results may be expected. If not, no matter how firmly held or sincerely believed, disappointment is guaranteed. Jesus puts it this way: "If the blind leads the blind, both will fall into a pit" (Matt. 15:14, NIV).

Belief must always be supported by sound intelligence. Supporting the point is the fact that spiritual intelligence is not necessarily part of the mindscape of the religious, as not everyone claiming religion is spiritually alive more so to manifest spiritually intelligence. This was the case of biblical characters and theologians, such as Nicodemus and Saul.

As in any discipline, it is incumbent on truth-seekers to validate knowledge. This has become increasingly important, as religious ignorance and bigotry have been major causes of insecurity across the globe, and are linked to upheavals of epic proportions, particularly in the Middle East.

Albeit, religion is a significant part of culture and a major socializing agency, informing beliefs, values and behaviors everywhere, the reality of which underscores the need for spiritual intelligence. In the spiritual space, appropriate choices are more likely, where there is a high level of spiritual intelligence.

Christians believe underdevelopment of spiritual capacity is the root cause of much of the problems being faced individually and corporately. In fact, lack of spiritual intelligence or low spiritual intelligence has contributed to a lack of meaning and diseases of meaning, manifesting in spiraling cases of drug abuse, suicide and hate crimes such as genocide.

Failure to promote spiritual and moral development have contributed to global social problems and health issues at every level. In the meantime bizarre spiritual practices compete with what may be regarded normal throughout the world. As a consequence, religion for some may be empowering and uplifting, and for others disempowering and oppressive.

It is apparent that all religions are not equal. Whereas in parts of the world religion is enabling development, in other places, progress is being denied by people hell-bent on committing all kinds of atrocities in the name of God and religion. Adding to the conundrum is the misperception that there is only one general intelligence (mental intelligence), enabling competence in all areas of life. Yet experience tells us that a person may be smart in one area and dumb in others.

The multidimensional nature of humanity and of life in general imply the existence of multiple intelligences. So far educators and others have put forward several theories of intelligence. The list includes mental, emotional, social and spiritual intelligences.

Spiritual intelligence is the overarching intelligence as spiritual intelligence validates the other intelligences in terms of assigning meaning and purpose. Among other things, spiritual intelligence gives a person the ability to navigate the spiritual world. Spiritual intelligence is: (a) the ability to receive, understand, discern and apply spiritual knowledge; and (b) the ability to use spiritual means to identify and solve spiritual and other problems.

Morally and spiritually speaking, there is a pattern of thinking and behaving, typical of the world, which does not support spiritual and moral development. According to St. Paul, such persons "are darkened in their understanding and are separated from the life of God, because of the ignorance that is in them due to the hardening of their hearts" (Eph. 4:18, NIV). The mind therefore needs to be renewed, if transformation is to take place (Rm. 12:1-2).

Many biblical writers describe the unregenerate as spiritually dead, hostile toward God (Luke 1:7; 9:60; Rm. 5:10; 8:7-8), and blind (John 3:3; Acts 26:18; 2 Cor. 4:4). Hence the call for spiritual rebirth (John 3:1-7). Spiritual rebirth enables the human spirit – through its connection with God – to transcend the limitations of the physical senses and to develop spiritual senses (1 Cor. 2:13-14). When God is embraced, the door is opened to spiritual life and intelligence (John 3:3-7). Based on Scripture, God is Spirit (John 4:24), and is the Source of spiritual light and life (John 1:4; 3:19; 8:12; 12:46; 14: 6; 14:15-26). Since revelation comes through the Spirit (1 Cor. 2:10), a person needs to have the Spirit (Rom. 8:9) in order to be connected to God (Rom. 8:14-17) and in order to know and understand spiritual things (1 Cor. 2:10-13).

Renewal the mind is crucial, because the mind is the gateway to the body, soul and spirit. When the mind is renewed, transformation in every area of life becomes a real possibility, affecting the spiritual, physical, psychological and social environment. Every form of development may be traced to a renewed or enlightened mind, manifesting in appropriate choices.

In the area of morality, Christians are of the view that belief in God, supported by spiritual disciplines, enable the religious to be more moral than the non-religious. This is not to suggest that morality is coterminous with religion. There are indeed many non-religious persons whom may be described as morally upright, in the broad sense of the term. Albeit, morality is more sustainable when underpinned by a theological framework, emphasis being on a personal relationship with God, and not on religion per se.

Notwithstanding, despite arguments for God, people are more inclined to tap into other sources of knowledge and power, as these sources make no demands morally and spiritually. Besides, everyone is not equally aware of God.

Understandably, development in any area is contingent on levels of awareness and discipline. Plus focus is determined by priorities. Whatever we value, gets our attention and discipline. Accordingly, people succeed in areas that are important, or have meaning to them. Since the physical is most obvious and basic, human beings essentially live based on physicality and the senses associated with the natural and physical. This does not mean everyone enjoys the same physical health; does it? Neither does it mean that life by the natural senses, associated with the flesh, puts everyone at the same level intellectually. There is evidence of levels of underdevelopment and immaturity, and there is evidence of levels of development and maturity. Life by senses associated with the Spirit is expressed similarly.

As in the physical, spiritual birth implies stages of development and the need for growth. Growth, however, is not possible without struggle. The struggle toward maturity is both internal and external. There is competition between the old self and the new self; the sinful nature of the flesh is constantly at war with the sinless nature of the Spirit; there is conflict between competing religious ideologies; there is conflict between the philosophy which motivates how people of the world think and how the people of God think; and there is a raging war between the forces of good and evil. For these and other reasons, emphasis needs to be placed on developing spiritual intelligence.

Although the natural and physical are important, the spiritual is more deserving of attention. The spirit of human beings lives on long after we are dead physically. In addition to being more enduring the spiritual is the foundation for meaning and purpose. Moreover, besides existential benefits, there are benefits which may be carried over into a completely new spiritual existence, extending beyond the grave (Matt. 6: 19-21; 16:25-26).

The spiritual dimension is the core of our being and is indestructible. When connected to the Spirit, there is eternal life; when disconnected, there is eternal death. Disconnected from God, we are spiritually dead, although not in the absolute sense. As long as we are physically alive, there is the possibility of spiritual rebirth, hence Jesus's proclamation to Nicodemus, "You must be born again."

Spiritual rebirth is translated as having a personal relationship with God. A personal relationship with God enables spiritual life and intelligence; the absence of a relationship with God has the opposite effect. Disconnected from the Source of Life means the absence of purpose and meaning, and the presence of diseases of meaning.

Be that as it may, there is natural reality and there is spiritual reality, supported by their own intelligence network. Natural intelligence is crucial to appropriate functioning at the natural level; spiritual intelligence is crucial to appropriate functioning at the spiritual level.

Spiritual intelligence enables *receptability*, perceptibility, *responseability* and applicability of things spiritual and is enhanced through education, especially where the educative process includes application.

Invariably there is incongruity and conflict between the natural and the spiritual, as natural understanding competes with spiritual understanding and self-will competes with God's Will. Albeit, if indeed there is only one

God, everyone must ultimately agree on whom God is, and agree on fundamental concepts, particularly on how one might be rightly related to God and accomplish God's Will.

Nevertheless, in a world in which almost everything is interpreted through physical lenses, some people have difficulty accepting the spiritual; and many who acknowledge the spiritual do not treat the spiritual with the same level of respect given the physical. Moreover, despite the contribution of the spiritual to the wellbeing of society in general, attempts are being made to devalue spirituality and to disregard the efficacy of religion altogether. Instead of downplaying the value of religion, we need to find ways to develop spiritual intelligence that promotes pure religion. Pure religion promotes moral goodness (James 1:27) and love, even for enemies (Matt. 5:43-48; Rom. 12:18-20).

As in every discipline, disagreement in religion is inevitable. However, disagreement should not mean hate for people with whom we disagree. Nor should it mean engaging in techniques designed to silence contending voices in order to enforce conformity. Divergent views should be respected. Divergent views should neither be used as a basis to invalidate religion nor to enforce loyalty to one religion.

Moreover, while separation of Church and State is necessary – for many practical reasons – religion should not be ignored. Freedom of religion should not mean freedom from religion. Religion has its problems, but so do other disciplines. For example, many claims to science may be regarded pseudoscience. We do not disregard or discredit disciplines because they do not fit into our schema, do we?

No subject affects our lives more profoundly than spirituality. Religion is only one expression of spiritual reality. The real issue is — do human beings have a spiritual capacity? If so, why isn't the development of spiritual capacity given equal treatment as the development of natural capacity?

> Until we begin educating the whole person . . . in every area of life and culture, we will continue to drift toward the margins of society, our fervent educational activities notwithstanding (Moore, 2007, p. 85).

Spiritual Intelligence: A Christian Perspective

The positive and negative impact of religion on human life and development necessitates a major focus on religion in general and on spiritual intelligence in particular. There is natural intelligence and there is spiritual intelligence. These streams of intelligences correspond to major aspects of the human framework (our natural capacity and our spiritual capacity), and to the world at large (the visible realm and the invisible realm).

Human beings are multidimensional creatures. There is a physical, emotional, intellectual and spiritual side to us requiring intelligence. However, intelligence is not static. Intelligence needs to be developed in each area of capacity.

Development in any area is impacted by things such as genes, personality, values, the nurturing environment, culture and socio-economic factors. Socio-economic factors, for instance, determine growth opportunities and where the emphasis is placed. People born in poverty, for example, may not have the means to develop their intellectual capacity, so the emphasis may be on physical skills. Due to geography, access to the best schools and to other resources may be denied, and as such slow or hinder the pace of development. If socio-economic factors affect development in the natural domain, it should not be surprising that development in the spiritual domain is affected similarly.

Despite challenges, however, choices play a key role in human development, and may be validated internally and externally. Internal and external interactions cannot be avoided. If purpose is to be fulfilled, successful navigation of a person's inner and outer worlds is crucial. The complex nature of reality implies the need for diverse skills, enabling discernment and development of the world in all its complexity. Since we are both physical and spiritual, intelligence may be developed naturally through the energy of the flesh and supernaturally through the energy of the Spirit.

Spiritual intelligence connects and empowers at multiple levels. Intellectually, specific areas of the frontal lobes of the brain respond to spiritual experiences, thereby facilitating spiritual enlightenment, discernment and problem solving. Biologically or physically, spiritual intelligence enables health by promoting proper diet and exercise; plus there is the potential for physical healing through prayer and other spiritual disciplines. Psychologically, spiritual intelligence enables a positive outlook and stress management, despite circumstances. Spiritually, spiritual intelligence enables connection with God and with one's inner-self or spirit; it enables spiritual transformation and moral centering. The integrity of individuals, groups, organizations and the world at large may be enhanced by sound intelligence, particularly spiritual intelligence.

Unfortunately, the importance of spirituality is being down-played, especially its role in the transformation of the individual and of society on the whole. Some are trying to create an amoral society, meaning that they are trying to create a world in which morality does not factor in our day-to-day affairs, including relationships. According to such persons, we should forget about moral values and embrace any and everything. "To each his own." Love should be the overarching principle.

However, wouldn't such a philosophy create more emptiness, confusion and diseases of meaning in the world? And what would be the purpose of life if there were no meaning to it? What would be the foundation on which we stand, if there were no moral compass or belief system supporting our creative endeavors and way of life?

Are there any universal laws or principles applicable across the board, enabling coherence and human development? Or do we get to cherry-pick the things we love and the things we hate, based on our lifestyle, politics, or religion? What about the legal system to which we all subscribe? Do we get to decide which aspect of the law we obey or disobey, imperfect as that system might be? What about systems in the universe, so intelligently and perfectly designed, enabling order in the natural and physical environment? What about the human system, and even systems designed by human beings? Do these systems not tell us anything about how things "ought" to be?

If there is no system, human nor divine, that operates based on the whims of subjects, what does that tells us about governance in general and about morality in particular? If some things are proper and right, then the opposite must also be true. The reality is everyone has a sense of right and wrong and their own code of ethics, even if not practiced consistently.

Moreover, life is impossible in a world in which there is no right and wrong and no certain way of differentiating truth from error.

The only time issues of right and wrong or morality will not matter is when every cause produce the same effect and every action produces the same consequences; and that my friend will never happen. The real world operates on principles of right and wrong and on cause and effect. These are the only rational bases for order and development in the world. This is true of the natural and physical world and of the spiritual and metaphysical world as well.

A highly developed spiritual intelligence yields major benefits at the personal, interpersonal, family, organizational and societal levels. Spiritual intelligence develops a more moral and responsible citizenry, and promotes health in society by enabling individuals and groups to be healthier physically, socially, psychologically and spiritually.

Even atheists agree. Sheiman (2009), a professed atheist, for instance, averred religion provides psychological, moral, emotional, existential, communal and physical benefits that no other institution can provide. These views resonated with Parris (2012), who made a case for the need for God in Africa. God is needed everywhere and religion has its benefits. However, it is the spiritual intelligence associated with a religion that makes it viable.

This study illustrates a possible revolution and transformation if a society really works toward developing each person's spiritual capacity, as much as it works to develop their natural capacity. Recognition of spiritual intelligence and the integration of the development of spirituality in daily life at the micro and macro levels present tremendous possibilities for the individual and for society at large.

The need for a focus on developing spiritual intelligence is extremely crucial, as spiritual intelligence supports and gives meaning to the other intelligences. Spiritual intelligence is the very foundation of life. It connects us with our Creator and gives us a sense of meaning and purpose.

APPENDIX

Figures and Tables

Africa Needs God

Matthew Parris: As an atheist, I truly believe Africa needs God

By TIMES ONLINE

Reposted from:

http://www.timesonline.co.uk/tol/comment/columnists/matthew_parris/article5400568.ece

Before Christmas I returned, after 45 years, to the country that as a boy I knew as Nyasaland. Today it's Malawi, and The Times Christmas Appeal includes a small British charity working there. Pump Aid helps rural communities to install a simple pump, letting people keep their village wells sealed and clean. I went to see this work.

It inspired me, renewing my flagging faith in development charities. But travelling in Malawi refreshed another belief, too: one I've been trying to banish all my life, but an observation I've been unable to avoid since my African childhood. It confounds my ideological beliefs, stubbornly refuses to fit my world view, and has embarrassed my growing belief that there is no God.

Now a confirmed atheist, I've become convinced of the enormous contribution that Christian evangelism makes in Africa: sharply distinct from the work of secular NGOs, government projects and international aid efforts. These alone will not do. Education and training alone will not do. In Africa Christianity changes people's hearts. It brings a spiritual transformation. The rebirth is real. The change is good.

I used to avoid this truth by applauding - as you can - the practical work of mission churches in Africa. It's a pity, I would say, that salvation is part of the package, but Christians black and white, working in Africa, do heal the sick, do teach people to read and write; and only the severest kind of secularist could see a mission hospital or school and say the world would be better without it. I would allow that if faith was needed to motivate missionaries to help, then, fine: but what counted was the help, not the faith.

But this doesn't fit the facts. Faith does more than support the missionary; it is also transferred to his flock. This is the effect that matters so immensely, and which I cannot help observing.

First, then, the observation. We had friends who were missionaries, and as a child I stayed often with them; I also stayed, alone with my little brother, in a traditional rural African village. In the city we had working for us Africans who had converted and were strong believers. The Christians were always different. Far from having cowed or confined its converts, their faith appeared to have liberated and relaxed them. There was a liveliness, a curiosity, an engagement with the world - a directness in their dealings with others - that seemed to be missing in traditional African life. They stood tall.

At 24, travelling by land across the continent reinforced this impression. From Algiers to Niger, Nigeria, Cameroon and the Central African Republic, then right through the Congo to Rwanda, Tanzania and Kenya, four student friends and I drove our old Land Rover to Nairobi.

We slept under the stars, so it was important as we reached the more populated and lawless parts of the sub-Sahara that every day we find somewhere safe by nightfall. Often near a mission.

Whenever we entered a territory worked by missionaries, we had to acknowledge that something changed in the faces of the people we passed and spoke to: something in their eyes, the way they approached you direct, man-to-man, without looking down or away. They had not become more deferential towards strangers - in some ways less so - but more open.

This time in Malawi it was the same. I met no missionaries. You do not encounter missionaries in the lobbies of expensive hotels discussing development strategy documents, as you do with the big NGOs. But instead I noticed that a handful of the most impressive African members of the Pump

Aid team (largely from Zimbabwe) were, privately, strong Christians. "Privately" because the charity is entirely secular and I never heard any of its team so much as mention religion while working in the villages. But I picked up the Christian references in our conversations. One, I saw, was studying a devotional textbook in the car. One, on Sunday, went off to church at dawn for a two-hour service.

It would suit me to believe that their honesty, diligence and optimism in their work were unconnected with personal faith. Their work was secular, but surely affected by what they were. What they were was, in turn, influenced by a conception of man's place in the Universe that Christianity had taught.

There's long been a fashion among Western academic sociologists for placing tribal value systems within a ring fence, beyond critiques founded in our own culture: "theirs" and therefore best for "them"; authentic and of intrinsically equal worth to ours.

I don't follow this. I observe that tribal belief is no more peaceable than ours; and that it suppresses individuality. People think collectively; first in terms of the community, extended family and tribe. This rural-traditional mindset feeds into the "big man" and gangster politics of the African city: the exaggerated respect for a swaggering leader, and the (literal) inability to understand the whole idea of loyal opposition.

Anxiety - fear of evil spirits, of ancestors, of nature and the wild, of a tribal hierarchy, of quite everyday things - strikes deep into the whole structure of rural African thought. Every man has his place and, calls it fear or respect; a great weight grinds down the individual spirit, stunting curiosity. People won't take the initiative, won't take things into their own hands or on their own shoulders.

How can I, as someone with a foot in both camps, explain? When the philosophical tourist moves from one world view to another he finds - at the very moment of passing into the new - that he loses the language to describe the landscape to the old. But let me try an example: the answer given by Sir Edmund Hillary to the question: Why climb the mountain? "Because it's there," he said.

To the rural African mind, this is an explanation of why one would not climb the mountain. It's... well, there. Just there. Why interfere? Nothing to be done about it, or with it. Hillary's further explanation - that nobody else had climbed it - would stand as a second reason for passivity.

Christianity, post-Reformation and post-Luther, with its teaching of a direct, personal, two-way link between the individual and God, unmediated by the collective, and insubordinate to any other human being, smashes straight through the philosophical/spiritual framework I've just described. It offers something to hold on to those anxious to cast off a crushing tribal group-think. That is why and how it liberates.

Those who want Africa to walk tall amid 21st-century global competition must not kid themselves that providing the material means or even the knowhow that accompanies what we call development will make the change. A whole belief system must first be supplanted.

And I'm afraid it has to be supplanted by another. Removing Christian evangelism from the African equation may leave the continent at the mercy of a malign fusion of Nike, the witch doctor, the mobile phone and the machete.

Review Questions

1. Define spiritual intelligence and discuss its implications for daily life.
2. What support may be found in Scripture for the concept of spiritual intelligence?
3. What support may be found in secular literature for the concept of spiritual intelligence?
4. Describe the nature of spiritual intelligence.
5. How does spiritual intelligence differ from natural intelligence?
6. Compare and contrast spiritual intelligence with spiritual un-intelligence.
7. What are some of the benefits and potential benefits of spiritual intelligence?
8. How may spiritual intelligence be integrated in religion and society?
9. What does having a "personal relationship with God" means   to you?
10. Why is spiritual intelligence crucial to human development?
11. How may a person develop their spiritual intelligence?
12. Compare and contrast the worldview of Christianity with that   of Islam, Hinduism, Judaism and New Age?
13. Discuss the concept "falsification of spiritual phenomena."
14. Review a scenario from life experience (or create a hypothetical one) reflecting a situation or question needing application of spiritual intelligence. Show the steps you have taken (or would take) in solving the problem.
15. Discuss the concept 'sanctification.'
16. What are the essential differences between sanctification and spiritual intelligence?
17. Discuss the concept 'spirituality.'
18. What does it mean to be spiritually dead?

19. What does it mean to be spiritually alive?

20. Write an essay differentiating between spirituality as a capacity and spirituality as an experience.

21. Development of spiritual intelligence is synonymous with spiritual growth. Discuss.

22. Explain the differences between the 'natural,' 'carnal' and 'spiritual' man.

23. Discuss the term 'worldly' or 'worldliness.'

24. Discuss the role of spiritual intelligence in solving spiritual and other problems. Give examples, inclusive of personal experience.

25. Write a five-page paper on the use of sound in healing interventions.

26. If there is one God why are there so many religions?

27. How does a secular understanding of the world differ from a spiritual worldview?

28. How does psychological maturity differ from spiritual maturity, and in what ways are they similar?

29. Are there higher powers that exert casual influence in the world? Give reasons for your answer.

30. Prepare a spiritual profile of the life of Christ.

31. Write an essay showing how you may identify and develop your talents and gifts.

32. Write an essay showing how you are developing your gifts to help others.

References

Alexander, E. (2012). *Proof of heaven: A neurosurgeons journey into the afterlife.* New York: Simon and Schuster.

Albrecht, K. (2009). *Social intelligence: The new science of success.* Misenheimer, NC: Pfeiffer.

Albright, C. (2006). *Spiritual growth, cognition, and complexity: Faith as a dynamic process.* In J. Koss-Chioino & P. Hefner (Eds.), **Spiritual transformation and healing: Anthropological, theological, neuroscientific, and clinical perspectives**. London, UK: Altamira Press.

Amen, D. (1998). *Change your brain, change your life: The breakthrough program for conquering anxiety, depression, obsessiveness, anger, and depression.* New York, NY: Three Rivers Press.

Amman, J. (1979). *Spiritual theology.* Huntington, IN: Our Sunday Visitor.

Aquinas, T. (2003). *Reason and revelation complement each other.* In R. Martin & C. Bernard (Eds.), **God Matters: Readings in philosophy and religion** (pp. 255-265). New Jersey: Pearson Education.

Aranza, J. (1985). *More rock country and backward masking unmasked.* Lafayette, LA: Vital Issues Press.

Armstrong, T. (2009). *Multiple intelligences in the classroom* (3rd ed.). Alexandria, VA: ASCD.

Arterburn, S., and Felton, J. (1991). *Toxic Faith: Understanding and overcoming religious addiction. Nashville, TN:* Oliver-Nelson Books

Astrow, A., Puchalski, C., and Sulmasy, D. (2001). *Religion, spirituality, and health care: Social, ethical, and practical considerations.* **American Journal of Medicine.** 110. Amsterdam, Netherlands: Elsevier.

Atkinson, W. (2007). *Suggestion and auto-suggestion.* Whitefish, MT: Kessinger.

Augustine. (2002). *Saint Augustine: On Genesis.* Hyde Park, NY: New City Press.

Babbie, E. (2001). *The practice of social research* (9th ed.). Belmont, CA: Wadsworth/Thomson.

Backman, S. (2001). *The manners of ghosts: A study of the supernatural in Thomas Hardy's short poems.* (Gothenburg studies in English, 82). Göteborg, Sweden: Acta Universitatis Gothoburgensis.

Baddiel, I., & Blezard, T. (1999). *The Supernatural: Investigations into the unexplained.* Hapauge, NY: Barrons Juveniles.

Badley, L. (1995). *Film, horror and the body fantastic.* Westport, CT: Greenwood Press.

Baker, D. (Ed.) (1983). *Ghosts in country villages: Stories of mystery and the supernatural.* London, UK: Kimber.

Baker, H., & Baker, R. (2007). *Expecting miracles: True stories of God's supernatural power and how you can experience it.* Grand Rapids, MI: Chosen Books.

Bazin, G. (1962). *The loom of art.* New York, NY: Simon & Schuster.

Beauregard, M., & O'Leary, D. (2007). *The spiritual brain: A neuroscientist's case for the existence of the soul.* New York: Harper Collins.

Beck, T. (2011). *10 most profitable films of the decade.* Retrieved from http://www.associatedcontent.com/article/2454882/10_most_profitable_films_of_the_decade.html?cat=40

Belgum, D. (Ed.) (1967). *Religion and medicine: Essays on meaning, values, and health.* Ames: Iowa State University Press.

Bentley, T. (2008). *The reality of the supernatural world: Exploring heavenly realms and prophetic experiences.* Shippensburg, PA: Destiny Image.

Bennett, R. (1997). *To heaven and back.* Grand Rapids, MI: Zondervan Publishing.

Bertrand, M. (2007). *Rethinking worldview: Learning to think, live, and speak in this world.* Wheaton, IL: Crossway Books.

Blackaby, H., & Blackaby, R. (2001). *Spiritual leadership.* Nashville

References

TN: Broadman & Holman.

Blamires, H. (1963). *The Christian mind: How should a Christian think?* Ann Arbor, MI: Servant Publications.

Blamires, H. (1980). *Where do we stand? A Christian res-ponse to secularism.* Ann Arbor, MI: Servant Publications.

Boa, K. (2001*). Conformed to his image: Biblical and practical approaches to spiritual formation.* Grand Rapids, MI: Zondervan.

Bohr, N. (2010). *Atomic physics and human knowledge.* New York: Dover Publications.

Bolton, R., & Singer, M. (1992). *Rethinking AIDS prevention: Cultural approaches.* Amsterdam, The Netherlands: Gordon and Breach.

Booker, M. (2009). *Red, white, and spooked: The supernatural in American culture.* Westport, CT: Praeger.

Bowell, R. (2005). *The seven steps of spiritual intelligence: The practical pursuit of purpose, success and happiness.* London, UK: Nicholas Brealey.

Bradberry, T., Greaves J., & Lencioni, P. (2009). *Emotional intelligence 2.0.* San Diego, CA: TalentSmart.

Bright, B. (1986). *Holy Spirit: The key to supernatural living.* San Bernardino, CA: Campus Crusade for Christ International.

Brighton, H. (2007). *Introducing artificial intelligence.* Cambridge: Icon Books.

Brown, R. (1992). *He came to set the captives free.* New Kensington, PA: Whitaker House.

Brown, W. (2004). *Neurobiological embodiment of spirituality and soul.* In J. Malcolm (Ed.), **From cells to souls - and beyond: Changing portraits of human nature.** Grand Rapids, MI: William B. Eerdsman.

Busoni, F. (1957). The essence of music: And other papers. New York, NY: Philosophical Library.

Butler, D. (1966). *Western mysticism: The teaching of Augustine, Gregory and Bernard and the contemplative life.* New York, NY: Harper & Row.

Buxton, M. (1980). *No earthly reason: Stories of the supernatural.* London, UK: Kimber.

Buzan, T. (2001). *The power of spiritual intelligence: 10 ways to tap into your spiritual genius.* London, UK: Thorsons.

Calvin, J. (2008). *Institutes of the Christian religion.* Peaboy, MA: Hendrickson.

Canning, J. (Ed.). (1988). *50 strange stories of the supernatural.* New York, N.Y.: Bonanza Books.

Capra, F. (1991). *The Tao of physics: An exploration of the parallels between modern physics and Eastern mysticism* (3rd ed., updated). Boston, MA: Shambhala.

Carter, C. (2006). Rethinking Christ and culture: A post-Christian perspective. Grand Rapids, MI: Brazos Press.

Cary, J. (2006). *What is spirituality?* Retrieved from http://www.suite101.com/content/whatisspirituality-a1500

Cavanagh, G., Hanson, B., Hanson, K., & Hinojoso, J. (2003). *Toward a spirituality for the contemporary organization: Implications for work, family and society.* In M. L. Pava & P. Primeaux (Eds.), **Spiritual intelligence at work: Meaning, metaphor and morals,** pp. 111-138. Amsterdam, Netherlands: Elsevier

Chambers Study Dictionary. (2002). Edinburgh, Scotland: Chambers Harrap.

Chambers, P. (1998). *Paranormal people: The famous, the infamous, and the supernatural.* London, UK: Blanford.

Clark, C. (1966). *Scientist and the supernatural: A systematic examination of the relation between Christianity and humanism, with special reference to the work 'Religion without revelation,' by J. S. Huxley and other agnostic writings.* London, UK: Epsworth Press.

Clark, L. (2003). *From angels to aliens: Teenagers, the media, and the supernatural.* New York, NY: Oxford University Press.

Clarke, E. (1999). *My mother who fathered me: A study of the families in three selected communities of Jamaica.* Kingston, Jamaica: University of

References

the West Indies.

Cohen, A. (1979). *Natural and the supernatural Jew: An historical and theological introduction* (2nd rev. ed.). New York, NY: Behrman House.

Cohen, J. (1999). *Of giants: Sex, monsters, and the Middle Ages.* Minneapolis: University of Minnesota Press.

Collins, K. (2000). *Exploring Christian spirituality: An ecumenical reader.* Grand Rapids, MI: Baker Books.

Collins, P. (1999). *Spirituality for the 21st century: Christian living in a secular age.* Dublin, Ireland: The Columba Press.

Colson, C., & Pearcey, N. (1999). *How now shall we live?* Wheaton, IL: Tyndale House.

Cooper, N. (1981). *The diversity of moral thinking.* Oxford, UK: Clarendon Press.

Cosette, K. (1987). *Supernatural fiction for teens: 500 good paperbacks to read for wonderment, fear, and fun.* Littleton, CO: Libraries Unlimited.

Covey, S. (2004). *The 8th habit: From effectiveness to greatness.* New York, NY: Simon & Schuster.

Craig, W. (2000). *The absurdity of life without God.* In E. Klemke (Ed.), **The meaning of life** (2nd ed., pp. 41-56). Oxford, UK: Oxford University Press.

Cunniff, T. (1985). *Supernatural in Yorkshire.* Clapham, Lancaster: Dalesman Books.

Damasio, A. (1999). *The feeling of what happens: Body and emotion in the making of consciousness.* San Diego, CA: Harcourt.

Das, S. (2001). *Awakening the Buddhist heart.* London, UK: Bantam Books.

Deane, P. (2003) *Sex and the paranormal: Human sexual encounters with the supernatural.* London. Vega Books.

de Los Santos, O. (2004). *Spirits of Texas and New England: Over 100 true encounters with the supernatural.* Waterbury, CT: Fine Tooth Press.

de Lisser, H. (2007). *The white witch of Rosehall.* Oxford, UK: MacMillan Publishers Limited.

Delbanco, T. (1991). *Enriching the doctor-patient relationship by inviting the patient's perspective.* Annals of Internal Medicine. 116. New Orleans, LA: The American College of Physicians.

Delvin, B. (1997). *Intelligence, genes, and success: Scientists respond to the bell curve.* New York, NY: Copernicus.

Derezotes, D. (2006). *Spiritually oriented social work practice.* New York, NY: Pearson.

Dickinson, S. (1920). *True tales of the weird: A record of personal experiences of the supernatural.* New York, NY: Duffield.

Dreiser, T. (2009). *Plays of the natural and supernatural.* Charleston, SC.: BiblioLife.

Dubensky, J. (2012). *4 Medical Miracles that Harness the Power of Sound.* [Online article] http://www.cracked.com/quick-fixes/4-medical-miracles-that-harness-power-sound/

Durkheim, E. (1972). *Selected writings.* New York, NY; Melbourne; Cambridge: Cambridge University Press.

Dutt, S. (1977). *The supernatural in English romantic poetry, 1780-1830.* Philadelphia, PA: R. West.

Edwards, T. (1980). *Spiritual friend: Reclaiming the gift of spiritual direction.* Broadway, NY: Paulist Press.

Einstein, A. (2005). *Relativity: The special and general theory.* Saddle River, NJ: Pearson Education. (Original book published 1916).

Emery, N., Clayton, N., & Frith, C. (2008). *Social intelligence: From brain to culture.* Oxford, UK: Oxford University Press.

Emmons, R. (2000). *Is spirituality an intelligence? Motivation, cognition, and the psychology of ultimate concern.* Internal Journal for the Psychology of Religion, 10 (1), 3-26.

Ewin, R. (1981). *Co-operation and human values: A study of moral reasoning.* Brighton, Sussex: The Harvester Press.

Fallot, R. (2007). *Spirituality and religion in recovery: Some current issues.* Psychiatric Rehabilitation Journal. 30 (4). Boston: Boston University.

References

Foster, R. (1978). *Celebration of discipline: The path to spiritual growth.* London, UK: Hodder & Stoughton.

Fowler, J. (1981). *Stages of faith: The psychology of human development and the quest for meaning.* San Francisco: Harper & Row.

Fowler, R. (2001). *Spiritual but not religious.* New York: Oxford University Press.

Fox, M. (1991). *Creation spirituality: Liberating gifts for the peoples of the earth.* New York, NY: Putman.

Fox, M. (2000). *Creation spirituality: Original blessing: A primer in creation spirituality.* New York, NY: Putman.

Freeman, T. (2010). *Scientist and mystic.* Retrieved from http://www.chabad.org/library/article_cdo/aid/148389/jewish/Scientist-Mystic.htm

Fraser, D. (1962). *Primitive art.* Garden City, NY: Doubleday.

Fukuyama, M., & Sevig, T. (1999). *Integrating spirituality into multicultural counseling.* Thousand Oaks, CA: Sage.

Fuller, R. (2001). *Spiritual but not religious: Understanding unchurched America.* New York: Oxford University Press.

Gallup, G., Jr., & Proctor, W. (1982). *Adventures in immortality.* New York, NY: McGraw-Hill.

Gardner, H. (1983). *Frames of mind: The theory of multiple intelligences.* New York, NY: Basic Books.

Gardner, H. (1993). *Multiple intelligences: The theory in practice.* New York, NY: Basic Books.

Gardner, H. (1999). *Intelligence reframed: Multiple intelligences for the 21st century.* New York, NY: Basic Books.

Gasparin, A. (1857). *Science vs. modern spiritualism.* New York, NY: Kiggins & Kellog.

Gay, V. (1989). *Understanding the occult: Fragmentation and repair of the self.* Philadelphia, PA: Fortress Press.

Geisler, N. (1976). *Christian apologetics.* Grand Rapids, MI: Baker Book House.

George, D. (2001). *The supernatural in short fiction of the Americas: The other world in the New World.* Westport, CT: Greenwood Press.

Ghezzi, B. (1996). *Miracles of the saints: A book of reflections: True stories of lives touched by the supernatural.* Grand Rapids, MI: Zondervan.

Gilmore, M. (1998). *Differences in the dark: American movies and English theatre.* New York, NY: Columbia University Press.

Ginsberg, H. (1979). *Supernatural in the prophets: With special reference to Isaiah.* Cincinnati, OH: Hebrew Union College Press.

Goleman, D. (1995). *Emotional intelligence: Why it can matter more than IQ.* New York, NY: Bantam Books.

Goleman, D. (2007). *Social Intelligence: The new science of human relationships.* New York, NY: Bantam Books.

Graham, B. (2006). *The journey: How to live by faith in an uncertain world.* Nashville, TN: W. Publishing House.

Greene, B. (2010). *The elegant universe: Superstrings, hidden dimensions, and the quest for the ultimate theory.* New York: W.W. Norton & Company, Inc.

Greyson (2014). *Consciousness independent of the brain.* (https://www.youtube.com/watch?v=en-3Bz1RMig)

Guinness, O. (1973). *The dust of death: A critique of the establishment and the counter culture – and a proposal for a third way.* Downers Grove, IL: InterVarsity Press.

Gurveich, S. (2011). *The self-hypnosis home study course: A complete course in mind-body healing.* New York, NY: Sterling Publishing Co.

Habib, N. (2019). *Activate your Vagas Nerve: Unleash Your Body's Natural Ability to Heal.* Berkley, CA: Ulysses Press.

Haisch, B. (2006). *The God theory: Universes, zero-point fields, and what's behind it all.* San Francisco, CA: Red Wheeel/Weiser.

Hamer, D. (2004). *The God gene: How faith is hardwired into our genes.* New York, NY: Doubleday Publishers.

Hamilton, A. (2008). *Scalpel and the soul.* New York, NY: Jeremy P. Tarcher/Putman.

References

Hardin, T. (1995). *Supernatural tales from around the world.* New York, NY: Barnes & Noble.

Hark, L., & Morrison, G. (2009). *Medical nutrition and disease: A case based approach.* Hobroken, NJ: Wiley-Blackwell.

Harline, C. (2003). *Miracles at the Jesus oak: Histories of the supernatural in Reformation Europe.* East Otto, NY: Doubleday.

Harris, G. (2003). *Corruption: How to deal with its impact on business and society.* Los Angeles, CA: The Americas Group.

Harris, S. (2010). *The moral landscape: How science can determine human values.* New York, NY: The Free Press.

Hart, T. (1998). *Inspiration.* Journal of Humanistic Psychology, 38(3). Thousand Oaks, CA: Sage.

Hauerwas, S. (1983). *The peaceable kingdom.* Notre Dame, IN: University of Notre Dame Press.

Hay, J. (2007). *Interventions: The mediating work of art.* The Art Bulletin, 1989, 71(2). New York, NY: The College Art Association.

Hodge, C. (1982). *Systematic Theology* (Vol. 1, part 1). Grand Rapids, MI: Eerdsman.

Hodges, D. (1992). *Sandino's communism: Spiritual politics for the twenty-first century.* Austin, TX: University of Texas Press.

Holroyd, S. (1976). *Minds without boundaries.* London, UK: Aldus Books.

Hood, B. (2008). *Supernatural sense: A scientist explains why he believes in intuition, superstitions, and God.* New York, NY: HarperOne.

Horton, M. (1994). *Beyond culture wars.* Chicago: Moody Press.

Houston, P., & Sokolow, S. (2006). *The spiritual dimension of leadership: 8 key principles to leading more effectively.* Thousand Oaks, CA: Corwin Press.

Houston, P., Blankstein, A., & Cole, R. (2007). *Spirituality in educational leadership.* Thousand Oaks, CA: Corwin Press.

Huff, M., & Wetherilt, A. (2005). *Religion: A search for meaning.* New York, NY: McGraw-Hill.

Hugel, F. (1974). *Essays and addresses on the philosophy of religion.* Westport, CN: Greenwood Press.

Hughes, P. (1989). *The true image: The origin and destiny of man in Christ.* Grand Rapids, MI: William B. Eerdsman.

Jacobi, J. (1973). *The psychology of C. J. Jung.* New Haven, CT: Yale University Press.

Jacobs, C. (2005). *The supernatural life.* Ventura, CA: Regal Books.

Jennings, R. (2005). *Supernatural occurrences of John Wesley.* Oklahoma City, OK: Sean Multimedia.

Johnson, B. (2005). *The supernatural power of a transformed mind: Access to a life of miracles.* Shippensburg, PA: Destiny Image.

Jones, A. (1998). *Soul making: The desert way of spirituality.* New York, NY: Harper & Row.

Jones, L. (1963). *Blues people: Negro music in White America.* New York, NY: William Morrow.

Jorgensen, O. (1994). *Supernatural: The life of William Branham: The man and his commission* (Book 3, 1946-1950). Tucson, AZ: Tucson Tabernacle.

Jung, C. (1969). *The archetypes and the collective unconscious* (2nd ed.). Princeton, NJ: Princeton University Press.

Kainz, H. (2006). *Five metaphysical paradoxes.* Milwaukee, WI: Marquette University Press.

Kaku, M. (2014). *The future of the mind.* New York: Anchor Books

Kan, P. (1996). *In search of the supernatural: The written record.* Stanford, CA: Standford University.

Kaye, M. (1990). *13 plays of ghosts and the supernatural.* New York, NY: Doubleday.

Keesing, R. (1981). *Cultural anthropology.* New York, NY: Holt, Rinehart & Winston.

Kemp, J. (1964). *Reason, action and morality.* London, UK: Routledge & Kegan Paul.

References

Khavari, K. (2000). *Spiritual intelligence: A practical guide to personal happiness.* New Liskeard, ON: White Mountain.

Kim, J. (1998). *Philosophy of mind.* Oxford: Westview Press.

Kimbrough, S. T., Jr. (2002). *Orthodox and Wesleyan spirituality.* Crestwood, NY: St. Vladimer Seminary Press.

Klotsche, E. (2003). *The supernatural in the tragedies of Euripides as illustrated in prayers, curses, oaths, oracles, prophecies, dreams and visions.* Whitefish, MT: Kessinger.

Koch, K. (1972). *Christian counselling and occultism.* Grand Rapids, MI: Kregel Resources.

Koenig, H. (2004). *Religion, spirituality, and medicine: Research findings and implications for clinical practice.* Southern Medical Journal. 97 (12). Williamsburg, VA: Southern Medical Association.

Korem, D. (1988). *Powers: Testing the psychic and supernatural.* Downers Grove, IL: InterVarsity Press.

Kosslyn, S., & Rosenberg, R. (2004). *Psychology: The brain, the person, the world* (2nd ed.). New York, NY: Pearson Education.

Kraft, C. (2008). *Worldview for Christian witness.* Pasadena, CA: William Carey Library.

Lampe, G. (1977). *God as spirit: The Bampton lectures, 1976.* Oxford, UK: Clarendon Press.

Langer, E. (1997). *Mindfulness.* Reading, PA: Addison-Wesley.

Larson, B. (1978). *The day music died.* Denver, CO: Bob Larson Ministries.

Lazear, D. (2004). *Higher-Order thinking: The multiple intelligence way.* Brookline, MA: Zephyr Press.

Lehman, A., & Myers, J. (Eds.). (1997). *Magic, witchcraft, and religion: An anthropological study of the supernatural* (7th ed.). Boston, MA: McGraw Hill.

Leslie, J. (2001). *Infinite minds: A philosophical cosmology.* Oxford, UK: Oxford University Press.

Leslie, R. (1965). *Jesus and logotheraphy: The ministry of Jesus as in-*

terpreted through the psychotheraphy of Victor Frankyl. Nashville, TN: Abingdon Press.

Lewis, C. (2001). Miracles. New York, NY: Harper Collins.

Livermore, D. (2009). Cultural intelligence: Improving your CQ to engage our multicultural world (youth, family, and vulture). Wheaton, IL: Baker Academic.

Lloyd-Jones, D. (1971). *Supernatural in medicine.* London, UK: Christian Medical Fellowship.

Losier, M. (2010). *Law of attraction: The science of attracting more of what you want and less of what you don't.* Victoria, BC, Canada: Michael J Losier.

Lucy, M. (1972). *Superstition and witchcraft, in Macbeth, Midsummer Night's Dream, and The Tempest.* San Luis Obispo, CA: Shakespeare Press.

Malarkey, K. (2012). *The boy who came back from heaven.* Carol Stream, IL: Tyndale House Publishers.

Marrs, T. (1996). *New age cults and religions.* Austin, TX: Living Truth.

Maslow, A. (1954). *Motivation and personality.* New York, NY: Harper & Row.

Maslow, A. (1964). *Religion, values and peak-experiences.* New York, NY: Viking Press.

Maslow, A. (1976). *The farther reaches of human nature.* New York, NY: Penguin Books.

Maupassant, G. (1997). *Dark side: Tales of terror and the supernatural.* New York, NY: Carroll & Graf.

Maxwell, J. (1993). *Developing the leader within you.* Nashville, TN: Thomas Nelson.

Maxwell-Stuart, P. (Ed.), (1998). *The occult in early modern Europe: A documentary history.* New York, NY: St. Martin's Press.

May, R. (1969). *Love and will.* New York, NY: W. W. Norton.

McGrath, A. (1999). *Christian spirituality.* Oxford, UK: Blackwell.

References

McIntosh, K. (2006). *Touching the supernatural world: Angels, miracles, and demons.* Philadelphia, PA: Mason Crest.

McKissack, P. (1992). *Dark-thirty: Southern tales of the supernatural.* New York, NY: Knopf.

McLaughlin, C. (1994). *Spiritual politics: Changing the world from the inside out.* Peaboy, MA: Ballantine Books.

McTaggart, L. (2008). *The intention experiment: Using your thoughts to change your life and the world.* New York: Harper Collins

McTaggart, L. (2008). *The field: The quest for the secret force of the universe.* New York: Harper Collins.

Miller, E. (1933). *Occult theocracy* (Vol. 1). Los Angeles, CA: The Christian Book Club of America.

Miller, G. (2002). *Incorporating spirituality in counseling and psychotherapy: Theory and technique.* Somerset, NJ: Wiley.

Miller, J., Karsten, S., & Denton, D. (Eds.). (2005). *Holistic learning and spirituality in education: Breaking new ground.* New York State University.

Minsky, M. (2006). *The emotion machine: Commonsense thinking, artificial intelligence, and the future of the human mind.* New York, NY: Simon & Schuster.

Moodley, R., & West, W. (2005). *Integrating traditional healing practices into counseling and psychotherapy.* Thousand Oaks, CA: Sage.

Moody, R., Jr. (2001). *Life after life: The investigation of a phenomenon – survival of bodily death.* New York, NY: Harper Collins.

Moore, T. (2007). *Culture matters: A call for consensus on Christian cultural engagement.* Grand Rapids, MI: Brazos Press.

Morris, C., & Maisto, A. (2005). *Psychology: An introduction* (12th ed.). Saddle River, NJ: Pearson.

Morris, J. (2005). *The reflective heart: Discovering spiritual intelligence.* In Ibn Arabi's **Meccan illuminations.** Louisville, KY: Fons Vitae.

Moyers, B. (1993). *Healing and the mind.* New York, NY: Doubleday.

Mower, O. (1961). *The crisis in psychiatry and religion.* New York,

NY: D. Van Nostrand.

Munhall, P. (2001). *Nursing research: A qualitative perspective.* Boston, MA; Jones & Bartlet.

Myers, B. (2008). *Side of the supernatural: What is of God and what isn't.* Grand Rapids, MI: Zondervan.

Nardi, D. (2001). *Multiple intelligences and personality type: Tools and strategies for developing human potential.* San Marcos, TX: Telos Publication.

Neal, M. (2011). *To heaven and back: The true story of a doctor's extraordinary walk with God.* Dix Hills, NY: Circle 6 Publishing.

Nee, W. (1968). *The spiritual man* (Vol. 1). New York, NY: Christian Fellowship.

Nezu, A., Nezu, C., & Diwakar, J. (2005). *The emotional wellness way to cardiac health: How letting go of depression, anxiety and anger can heal your heart.* Oakland, CA: New Harbinger.

Nicholas, M. (1986). *The world's greatest psychics and mystics.* London, UK: Octopus Books.

Noble, D. (2001). *Riding the windhorse: Spiritual intelligence and the growth of the self.* New Jersey: Hampton Press.

Oden, T. (2001). *Life in the Spirit: Systematic theology* (Vol. 3). Peabody, ME: Prince Press.

Painton, M. (2007). *Encouraging your child's spiritual intelligence.* New York, NY: Atria Books.

Pargament, K. (2006). *The meaning of spiritual transformation.* In J. Koss-Chioino & P. Hefner (Eds.), **Spiritual transformation and healing: Anthropological, theological, neurosci-entific, and clinical perspectives.** London, UK: Altamira Press.

Pascual-Leone, J. (1990). *An essay on wisdom: Toward organismic processes that make it possible.* In Robert J. Sternberg (Ed.), **Wisdom: Its nature, origins, and development** (pp. 244-278). Cambridge University Press.

References

Peale. (2003). *The power of positive thinking.* New York, N.Y.: Fireside.

Peck, M. (1978). *The road less travelled: A new psychology of love, traditional values and spiritual growth* (25th anniv. ed.). New York, NY: Simon & Schuster.

Peck, M. (1983). *People of the lie: The hope for healing human evil.* New York, NY: Simon & Schuster.

Peck, M. (1993). *Further along the road less travelled: The unending journey toward spiritual growth.* New York, NY: Simon & Schuster.

Perkins, J. (2004). *Confessions of an economic hit man.* New York, NY: Penguin Group.

Peppergurg, I. (2008). *Alex and Me.* New York, NY: Harper Collins Publishers.

Peterson, B. (2004). *Cultural intelligence: A guide to working with people from other cultures.* Yarmouth, ME: Intercultural Press.

Pfeiffer, W. (2002). *Forming of a pearl: A story of love embracing the power of God and the supernatural.* Enumclaw, WA: WinePress.

Phillips, M. (1972). *Bible, the supernatural, and the Jews.* Camp Hill, PA: Horizon Books.

Pinker, S. (2002). *The blank slate: The modern denial of human nature.* New York, NY: Penguin Group.

Prather, P. (1996). *Modern-day miracles: How ordinary people experience supernatural acts of God.* Kansas: Andrews McMeel.

Prayer and faith healing: Proof that prayer works. [Online article.] Retrieved from www.1stholistic.com/prayer/holistic _prayer_proof.htm.

Promey, S. (2003). *The "return" of religion in the scholarship of American art.* The Art Bulletin, 1985, 67(2). New York, NY: The College Art Association.

Radin, D. (2006). *Entangled minds: Extrasensory experiences in a quantum reality.* New York: Harper Collins.

Rauschenbusch, W. (1912). *Christianity and the social crisis.* London, UK: McMillan.

Rodney, W. (1976). *How Europe underdeveloped Africa.* New York, NY: Cornell University.

Rollins, L. (2004). *The treasure within: A study of the divine nature.* Cleveland, TN: Frontline World Ministries.

Rossiter, A. (2006). *Developing spiritual intelligence: The power of you.* Park Lane, UK: O Books.

Roth, S., & Joseph, L. (2009). *Supernatural healing.* Shippensburg, PA: Destiny Image.

Rowlands, M. (2001). *The nature of consciousness.* Cambridge: Cambridge University Press.

Russel, S., & Norvig, P. (2002). *Artificial Intelligence: A modern approach* (2nd ed.). Saddle River, NJ: Prentice Hall.

Ruth, M. (1999). *Shadow work: A new guide to spiritual and psychological growth.* Knoxville, TN: Growth Solutions.

Sager, A. (1990). *Gospel-centered spirituality: An introduction to our spiritual journey.* Minneapolis, MN: Augusburg Fortress.

Sanders, O. (1986). *Spiritual leadership.* Chicago: Moody Press.

Sanford, J., & Sanford, P. (1982). *The transformation of the inner man.* Plainfield, NJ: Bridge.

Schaeffer, F., & Koop, C. (1979). *Whatever happened to the human race?* Grand Rapids, MI: Fleming H. Revell.

Schmeling, G. (2009). *Your God spot: How the brain makes and the mind shapes all forms of faith.* Bloomington, IN: Author Solutions.

Schreurs, A. (2002). *Psychotherapy and spirituality: Integra-ting the spiritual dimension into therapeutic practice.* London, UK: Jessica Kingsley.

Schwartz, G. (2011). *The sacred promise: How science is discovering Spirit's collaboration with us in our daily lives.* New York, NY: Atria Books.

Schwartz, G., Simon, W., & Russek, L. (2002). *The afterlife experiments: Breakthrough scientific evidence of life after death.* New York, NY: Atria Books.

Sessa, A., Conte, F., & Meroni, M. (2000). *Cigarette smoking and the*

References

kidney: Seminar on cigarette smoking and kidney involvement. Basel, Switzerland: S. Karger AG.

Sha, Z. (2008). *Soul wisdom: Practical soul treasures to transform your life.* New York, NY: Atria Books.

Sheiman, B. (2009). *An atheist defends religion: Why humanity is better off with religion than without it.* Hudson Street, NY: Penguin Group.

Sherman, H. (1972). *Your power to heal.* New York, NY: Fawcettt.

Shields, C., Edwards, M., & Sayani, A. (2005). *Inspiring practice: Spirituality and educational leadership.* Lancaster, PA: Proactive.

Siegel, B. (1986). *Love, medicine, and miracles.* New York, NY: Harper Perrenial.

Silk, M. (1989). *Spiritual politics: Religion and America since World War II.* New York, NY: Touchstone Books.

Sinetar, M. (2002). *Spiritual intelligence: What we can learn from the early awakening child.* New York, NY: Orbis.

Sinner, S. (2003). *Twelve German tales from Russia: Twelve tales of fantasy and the supernatural.* Fargo: North Dakota State University Libraries.

Sisk, D., & Torrance, E. (2001). *Spiritual intelligence: Developing higher consciousness.* New York, NY: Creative Education Foundation Press.

Sitze, B., & Sylwester, R. (2005). *Your brain goes to church: Neuroscience and congregational life.* Herndon, VA: The Alban Institute.

Sowell, T. (1999). *The quest for justice.* New York, NY: The Free Press.

Spencer, H. (2010). *The indestructible of matter.* Kessinger Publishing.

Sperry, L. (2001). *Spirituality in clinical practice: Incorporating the spiritual dimension in psychotherapy and counseling.* New York, NY: Routledge.

Spretnak, C. (1986). *The spiritual dimension of green politics.* Rochester, VT: Bear.

Stevens, C. (2002). *Supernatural side of Maine.* Phillips, ME: John Wade.

Stone, S., & Marszalek, T. (2003). *Miracles still happen: Inspiring real-life stories of supernatural intervention*. Tulsa, OK: Harrison House.

Tarnas, R. (1991). *The passion of the Western mind: Understanding the ideas that have shaped our worldview*. New York: Ballantine Books.

Tart, C. (Ed.). (1976). *Transpersonal psychologies*. New York, NY: Harper & Row.

Tavris, C., & Wade, C. (2001). *Psychology in perspective* (3rd ed.). Saddle River, NJ: Prentice Hall.

Teilhard de Chardin, P. (1959). *The phenomenon of man*. New York, NY: Harper & Row.

Teilhard de Chardin, P. (2001). *The divine milieu*. New York, NY: Harper & Row.

Thomas, D., & Inkson, K. (2004). *Cultural intelligence: People skills for global business*. San Francisco, CA: Berrett-Koehler.

Thurston, B. (2005). *The New Testament in Christian spirituality*. In A. Holder (Ed.), **Blackwell Companion to Christian Spirituality**. Oxford, UK: Blackwell.

Tippet, A. (1987). *Introduction to missiology*. Pasadena, CA: William Carey Library.

Tipping, C. (2005). *Spiritual intelligence at work: A radical approach to increasing productivity, raising morale and preventing conflict in the workplace*. Marietta, GA: Global 13.

United Nations Department of Economic and Social Affairs, Division for Sustainable Development. (Agenda 21). New York, NY.

Vader, J-P. (2006). *Spiritual Health: The next frontier*. European Journal of Public Health. 16(5). (Editorial). Oxford, UK: Oxford University Press.

Vance, C. (Ed.). (1993). *Pleasure and danger: Exploring female sexuality*. Kitchener, ON: Pandora Press.

Vaughn, F. (2002). *What is spiritual intelligence?* Journal of Humanistic Psychology, 42(2). Thousand Oaks, CA: Sage.

Visona, M. (2005). *Redefining twentieth century African art: The view*

References

from the lagoons of Cote d'Ivoire. Farmington Hills, MI: Thomson Gayle.

Wakefield, G. (1983). *Spirituality*. In A. Richardson & J. Bowden (Eds.), **A new dictionary of Christian theology**. London, UK: SCM Press.

Walker, B. (1970). *Sex and the supernatural: Sexuality in religion and magic*. London, UK: Macdonald.

Warfield, B. (1968). *Biblical and theological studies*. Philadelphia PA: The Presbyterian and Reformed Publishing Company.

Warren, R. (2002). *The purpose driven life*. Grand Rapids, MI: Zondervan.

Watts, F. (2006). *Personal transformation: Perspectives from psychology and Christianity*. In J. Koss-Chioino & P. Hefner (Eds.), **Spiritual transformation and healing: Anthropological, theological, neuroscientific, and clinical perspectives**. London, UK: Altamira Press.

Webber, R. (1999). *Ancient-future faith*. Grand Rapids, MI: Baker Books.

Weber, M. (1963). *The sociology of religion*. Boston, MA: Beacon Press.

Wentroble, B. (2009). *Removing the veil of deception*. Grand Rapids, MI: Chosen Books.

Werning, W. (1975). *Radical nature of Christianity*. South Pasadena, CA: Mandate Press.

Whale, J. (2008). *Naked spirit* (2nd ed.). Long Beach, CA: Clear Lotus.

White, J. (1987). *The shattered mirror: Reflections on being human*. Leicester, UK: Inter-Varsity Press.

Whitmore, C. (1971). *The supernatural in tragedy*. Mamaroneck, NY: Paul P. Appel.

Wickett, R. (2007). *The spiritual and human learning*. In P. Jarvis & S. Parker (Eds.). **Human learning: An holistic approach**. New York, NY: Routledge.

Wieman, H., & Westcott-Wieman, R. (1935). *Normative psychology of religion*. New York, NY: Thomas Y. Crowell.

Wilber, K. (2000). *Integral psychology: Consciousness, spirit, psychol-*

ogy, therapy. Boston, MA: Shambhala.

Williams, M. (2005). *Beyond words: Talking with animals and nature*. Novato, California: New World Library.

Wilson, C. (1975). *They had strange powers*. Garden City, NY: Doubleday.

Woolman, R. (2001). *Thinking with your soul: Spiritual intelligence and why it matters*. New York, NY: Random House.

World Health Organization. (2005). *Bangkok Charter for Health Promotion in a Globalized World*. Geneva.

World Health Organization. (1946). *Constitution of the World Health Organization*. (Article 80). Geneva.

Worman, H. (2006). *The liver disorders and hepatitis sourcebook*. Columbus, OH: McGraw Hill.

Wright, A. (2001). *Spirituality and education*. New York, NY: RoutledgeFalmer.

Wright, S. & Sayre-Adams, J. (2000). *Sacred space: Right relationship and spirituality in healthcare*. Edinburgh, London, etc.: Churchill Livingstone.

Yung, B., Watson E., & Rawski, R. (Eds.). (1996). *Harmony and counterpoint: Ritual music in Chinese context*. Stanford, CA: Stanford University.

Zohar, D. (1997). *ReWiring the corporate brain: Using the new science to rethink how we structure and lead organizations*. San Francisco, CA: Berrett-Koehler.

Zohar, D., & Marshall, I. (2000). *SQ: Connecting with our spiritual intelligence*. New York, NY: Bloomsbury.

Zohar, D., & Marshall, I. (2001). *SQ: Spiritual intelligence: The ultimate intelligence*. New York, NY: Bloomsbury.

Zohar, D., & Marshall, I. (2004). *Spiritual capital: Wealth we can live by*. San Francisco, CA: Berrett-Koehler.

Zukav, G. (1989). *The seat of the soul*. New York, NY: Simon & Schuster.